The Little Summer of St. Luke

By

Doris Dix Caruso

Cover Art

By

Carolyn Teague

Also by Doris Dix Caruso:

The Violet Shawl, a Novel
Serenity in Sandy Shoes, Poetry
Sleep Song, the Spell, a Novella

The Dreamin' Tree,
A Novel and
the Sequel to
this Novel

Dedication:

For all those who come after us, so that they might treasure and be delighted in this person known as Maggie

*"Paradise itself were dim
and joyless,
if not shared with Him"*

Thomas Moore 1779-1852

*A special thanks to my friends,
Sally, Brenda, Alicindra, Nancy and Liz
for their editing assistance.
Their kind support has made this novel
come into being.*

A Novel by Doris Dix Caruso

The Little Summer of St. Luke

A mild spell of weather which usually
arrives about the middle of October.
St. Luke's Day, on the 18th, gives
it this name.

"We are here but briefly:
Should the fates capture for each of us
a bit of warmth, exhilaration and
beauty in our
Little Summer of St. Luke, this time will
have been
fine, well spent, and most wholesome."

Maggie

Skye, Glasgow and Edinburgh

1885-1886

Maggie wrapped the great coat even more tightly about her slender young body as the sharp October winds blew down from the Black Cuillins above the rocky quay. The emerald green scarf, flying long in the stiff morning breeze, made her look like a storybook character as she stood alone on the dock. She stooped to adjust the large carpetbag resting against her high black boots, then straightening, protectively held up a slim gloved hand to peer out into the cold, rolling waters.

The ferry was late, but then the ferry was frequently late, most deservedly so today, she thought in her best Scots logic, what with the signs of winter coming early again this year to Skye. Snow already lay in heavy caps on the coarse gabbro hills behind her, stretching far past the town. These were the brooding, spectacular hills of coarse grained black rock that Maggie had prudently made her protectors and allies from that very first day of her arrival on Skye. She was then a wide eyed four year old, landing on this very quay only twelve years before, alone then as now, until her foster godparents, Laura and Bruce McGregor, met her. They were an unsure pair themselves, newly married and now taking on the responsibility of their godchild with her bouncy auburn curls and shy appearance, this child to keep as their own for an unspecified time, one who was destined to become a huge portion of their lives.

The distant horn of the ferry as it rounded the outer promontory of this "Kings Haven" brought Maggie out of her warming reverie. She turned full circle on the heel of her boot for one last look at Portree, the Black Cullins and this magical Isle of Skye.

"Dear God", she exclaimed under her breath "I have come to love all this with a passion. The morning mists began hugging the heights of the looming shapes far beyond the town. Maggie was certain these mystic castles of her just ended childhood still held the secrets of the "Daoine Sidhe", those fallen angels sent down to watch over the little ones like herself, and just there in the dark hollows hid "Crodh Mara," the speckled red and black cattle enticing crofters' straying herds to the fairy mounds, should they wander near. And maybe "Ca Sith," the dark green fairy dog was there, lurking, ready to trap the unwary traveler. Many were the nights when Maggie sat at Bruce and Laura's feet by the glowing fire in crofter's cottage to hear the ancient storytellers of this island weave their mythical tales for the true believers. Maggie's opinions had been carved as slowly as a wood cut, but were now so etched in her brain that she was to forever remember them. These were her safeguards against all personal unhappiness and were her haven from the strange world that waited for her beyond the sea. She understood the island people feeling suspicious of all life beyond this shore and of why they easily accepted shrill, wild winds sent from the Cullins as easily as springtime's wafting, gentle breezes, for every one of them believed in the fairies, beasties and ghosts of these Hebrides.

As she gazed at the hills, she knew these spirits were a part of her formative years, and no matter what she called them, saintly or logical, they could never leave her private being. Her attention was suddenly diverted and her gaze lowered as a youngster of eleven came running at breakneck speed, down the curving path of hill leading to the ten small shops skirting the harbor, running for Maggie, arms open and panting heavily, coming out to the end of the quay where the ferry docked. "Faith, whatever is the matter? Is something wrong at the cottage?"

The tawny, straight hair of the child was wet. She was tall for her age and with breath so short she could barely speak, but shook her head quickly in the negative to allay Maggie's fears. "No, no, nothing wrong," she said, breathing hard, "Oh, Maggie, I promised not to come here when we said our goodbyes last evening with the family, but I couldn't let you go without giving you something I made for you and . . . Oh, I may never see you again . . . I just had to bring it to you."

Wide eyed, the youngster stood self-effacing, chin lowered and arm outstretched. Maggie instantly opened her great coat, pressing Faith's cool, rosy cheeks to her own warm body.

"How I love you, my darling Faith. I am not angry, don't fret. Quick now, though, the ferry is docking and I must be off in a few minutes."

Faith clutched a small parcel wrapped in brown paper, and then impulsively thrust it into Maggie's hand. "Open it on the ferry and never, ever forget us."

Faith stretched to kiss Maggie's cheek and with tears streaming down her own, she was off, running up the hill and out of Maggie's sight.

"Oh, what a grand girl she is," Maggie breathed. She knew the three miles down from the crofter's cottage to the village was difficult enough for an adult in this cool air and early morning fog. Maggie had come down in Bruce's pony cart with strapped trunk bumping behind them in the early dawn before the household stirred, so she might avoid just such a tearful goodbye. She realized Faith had to hurriedly dress and without breakfast, slip out just after them to run the entire distance. Lucky for Faith, Maggie thought, that she had begged Bruce not to stay, but go on to fetch the week's groceries and supplies. Otherwise he might have soundly scolded his eldest daughter.

How many times had it been, she mused, that she made the six-mile round-trip to this quay, once each week, winter and summer since she was ten, to meet this ferry and receive the packet of letters that her own mother, Jane, sent faithfully from Glasgow. Each Saturday the letters would arrive and she in turn would give her own for her Mum Jane to Mr. McTeague, the ferry master. It had become so familiar, seeing Jane's fine hand on the crisp parchment that McTeague said he scarcely needed to read her name. Maggie was always there patiently awaiting him. Mum

Laura at the cottage had given her permission for these trips, sensing their importance, as the bond grew stronger year upon year, mother to daughter.

McTeague enjoyed seeing Meg, as he called her, grow from that sweet, slim child into lovely womanhood, her broad smile never failing to greet him and her cheerful voice calling out his name. It had become so much a part of his life too that he could scarcely believe that this day he would be carrying her off on this first portion of her journey to the mainland, never again to find her waiting for his call at Portree. He saw her from a distance now, standing straight and trim next to her steamer trunk and he felt a tightness pull at his throat.

The sun broke through the mist just as he handed a line to Andy, his deckhand, who in turn threw it to Charlie on shore, who now as usual, silently and sullenly appeared out of nowhere to secure the craft to cement pilings on the quay, the weekly ritual.

As Maggie watched, her heart beating so that she was sure it was perceptible, the only two passengers disembarked. Gingerly at first, then surely, old and fragile Mr. Booth and wife made their way ashore. Maggie remembered now, they had been over to the mainland to attend the funeral of Helen Booth's younger brother, Raymond, who died last week in Oban. Tired, but glad to be back on the island and safely home, they both greeted Maggie warmly and wished her well on her journey. Everyone on Skye keenly knew of the comings and goings of the other inhabitants on this island, as in a huge family.

McTeague lifted two crates of fruit above his head and then down to Charlie on the dock; finally came the mail sack in its official gray coat. Now all that remained, after they all secured her steamer trunk aboard, was for Maggie herself to place a foot on the gangplank and move from Skye for the first time since the age of four. She took an extraordinarily deep breath and was off.

Episode:

"So the day has finally come then." This was Mr. McTeague's welcome as he helped Maggie into a tiny covered cabin, seating her upon the padded wooden bench secured to the cabin floor. He gently tucked a lap robe about her against the chill of spray and they set out southward on the Sound of Raasay, out past the Eilean of Scalpay to meet another larger ferry at Kyleakin, then west to Armadale and the still larger ferry bound for Mallaig on the mainland of Scotland. There she would board the train for Glasgow. In all, this voyage would take fully a half-day by ferries alone.

"What will the wee ones do now, Miss, without their bonnie teacher? Who will take 'yer place and keep their minds to the page?" Harry McTeague tugged at his billed cap and looked full into Meg's hazel green eyes all the while keeping his hand on the tiller.

Maggie did not respond. She knew he really expected none. When a person left Skye, not knowing when they were to return, despite what the future might hold, it was with a heavy heart indeed, and each Scot could keenly sense the other's discontent. Why, one might as well have left an arm or foot there, it was that kind of painful loss.

Maggie's departure did not go unnoticed. It was viewed with sizable interest by two persons from behind the glass window of the small stone storefront on the quay, its sign creaking in the wind, proudly displaying: McNess and Company, Mercantile.

"An unusual one, that Maggie McBain" voiced James McNess aloud, "The likes of her, we'll not see soon again."

Janet and James McNess were storekeepers on this quay for over thirty years and it was here that Maggie made her weekly purchases of life's essentials, never failing to stop and chat with them for a time. Her writing paper, pencils, chalks and such had come from their supply, as well as the small gifts she purchased on the occasions of her McGreagor family birthdays.

"There is much more in that pretty, ginger head than one 'aboot' here knows." James had solemnly spoken this same line to his good wife more than once as he polished the single pane of window glass displaying his wares and in so doing, took note of the comings and goings of life in general within Portree as an unavoidable consequence.

"Aye, Maggie is the true Scots lass with her proud bearing, her good looks and her quick wit, yet there is a soft kindness that makes her so easy to know, but more than that, there is a cool, mysterious thinking lass inside of her that you canna' help but feel when you are close to her; truly a magnetism, eh, what say you, Mrs. McNess? "

James stood, squinting over his spectacles at Janet, just then dusting the tops of the cracker bins.

Janet, plain, neat, grayed and thin lipped was also keenly peering out at the familiar ferry, now all but lost in the swells of the sea. She turned to James, agreeing with his words.

"A possibility, Mr. McNess, a distinct possibility! You and I have lived to see a good number of these young folk come and go, but there seems a bit of a puzzle where this lass is concerned. There are a few who are born out of their true time and place, more profound and deep thinking, so to speak, different than others of their age and really unaware of the distinction at all. It seems to me, these appear to have traveled this road of life once before, and are viewing it all from afar. She has quite astonishing thoughts, unlike the typical child, don't you know? Just think of our Maggie, unconcerned with the gossip in the village, and never one for the candies and toys as the others: why, she always seemed more an adult than a bairn, and never a whine or harsh word . . . truly a near supernatural aura 'aboot' her."

And then leaning forward, her hand held to her mouth, whispering, lest even the walls might hear, or as though the thought had just occurred to her, "Perhaps she is truly one of the gentle Seal People, the Raoine, those maidens who are compelled to live for a time among mortals, but when their seal caps are stolen and they recover them, are allowed to go back to their own...to the sea!"

Somberly, peering hard out into the tossing waves and with a quick shake of her gray head, she said, "What think you, Mr. McNess?"

And the small ferry was completely lost from sight.

Episode:

Maggie could hardly believe the ferry ride had begun and it was time to move her things to another craft heading for Armadale. She could not resist placing a wee kiss on the rough cheek of Mr. McTeague as he helped her off his vessel. So many parts of her life at an end and now boundless new beginnings for his 'Meggie,' undeniably his moist eyes left her a bit shaken for just an instant.

The larger ferry from Armadale to Mallaig was busy with all types of cargo, crew and fellow travelers, including sheep, and the excitement left her little time to be reflective.

Invigorated by the deep, rolling waters and the smell of ocean air, she filled her nostrils as the ferry crossed the Sound of Sleat. Far off to the south, she fancied she might make out the islands of Eigg and Rhum with their running red deer, but of course these were many miles from her sight. Perhaps one day she would return to this splendid land and she might view all the islands, now valued only in her many books.

After an hour of pure enjoyment, she walked to the bow to see spread before her in full sunshine, the charming town of Mallaig, with its low white buildings scattered over the hillside, much like the snowy white sheep on this vessel, and all bordering the harbor, and much as it had appeared in Maggie's recurrent dreams. She blinked her eyes in disbelief. How could she have known? Suddenly, everyone was busily engaged in embarkation, and an urgency to set foot on the mainland of Scotland became the only concern in her mind.

Dockside now and the first person to speak to her was a small, swarthy man asking if he might help with her luggage. His worn suit coat seemed held together by only threads and Maggie marveled that it did so at all. He was the only porter nearby and plainly ready for business, pushing a low, rough handmade cart, propelled on coaster wheels.

Since it was clear that she had no way of managing the huge steamer trunk above her on deck, she pointed to it and thanked him. Springing eagerly to the task, she was aware of how important it seemed for him to complete his work and get back to another passenger for a gratuity. This, her first incident of paying for any service, made her acutely conscious of the man's need and she slipped a generous supply of coins into her pocket for his pay, all the while mindful of her own limited supply.

As she did so, there deep in her coat she felt the soothing comfort of another object. Maggie had opened Faith's parcel just as the smaller craft turned out of Portree harbor. Now her eyes were wet with more than mist as she fingered the painstakingly stitched, purple pincushion trimmed in white lace, and enclosing happy memories, for Faith had filled it with fragrant heather from their splendid hills of Skye.

Episode:

The train to Glasgow ran twice daily beginning in Malliag on the high bluff above the harbor. After only a brief wait, she heard its deep hum along the rails, as she stood, her mind soaring, next to the neat white wooden depot, her anticipation mounting with every instant.

"It is coming, it is coming." Maggie's breathing quickened as she could barely contain herself watching smoke rise from the narrows between the dark jagged face of stone cliffs. Now with one roar of engine, the mammoth black shape finally crept towards her. And she felt alternately giddy and jubilant standing so close to one more contributor to her dreams. Wildly superstitious, she suddenly turned her back with the last, long chug, for she felt that gazing on it now might break a spell. At last, when it was silent, she closed her eyes deliberately, her hand clutching the train ticket snugly folded into her pocket, and swiftly sharing her most charming Scottish grin, she opened her eyes, again turned upon her heel and boarded the train.

She chose a seat facing forward in the rear of the first car. Maggie was thinking happily that she certainly wished to see where life was headed, not being one to look back. Only a few persons boarded here in Malliag, but she guessed it might be full when it reached its destination of Glasgow. The journey was to take four hours. She presumed the train would be quite filled with people boarding from all across the Highlands.

Mum Laura had packed a large lunch, and Maggie now felt grateful. Her new carpetbag of green paisley rested on the adjoining seat. As Maggie felt into its depths for the lunch in a brown paper parcel, her hand felt a bound notebook that she knew was not her own. Panic seized her. Could she have mistakenly picked up another's handbag like her own? No, too much coincidence for that. Cautiously, she pulled a rust colored volume from the valise, and then more assured, found the string-tied lunch beneath it.

Opening the notebook's first page, she read in Laura's fine hand,

October 18, 1885.
For Maggie McBain on the occasion of her
Sixteenth birthday...
This is your travel companion:
I trust that you will record your
journey so that nothing will be
forgotten.

It is my hope that this volume will be but the first in a series of Journals which might bring comfort to you in your 'old age', and to

give recall to the pleasant events that will now become your wonder-filled life. God love and keep you, my sweet.

Mum Laura

Eyes tearing, she turned from this page to a blank one now representing all of her future and began to write. Her pencil worked quickly over the pages, eyes darting from scenery to book in a rhythmical pattern: so much to see, so much to record, so many feelings to put on paper. What a kindly, wholesome lady was her sweet Laura.

All sorts of travelers boarded at the numerous stations along the route, young and old, seemingly poor or well heeled, some quite cheery and others plainly dour. Her fellow passengers, seated in this warm, wood paneled coach, appeared unaware of her nervous anticipation, as she, feeling her cheeks flush in sultry sensation, wondered if any could guess that as a traveler, she was such a novice.

Carefully considering the solidly built, middle-aged woman, now sitting in the seat opposite, as she dozed and coughed alternately with a sound that rattled the close window of the car, Maggie surmised that she was a cottage worker from the large, woven basket of hand-made tatting in the seat alongside. Her strong, muscular hands told of an industrious woman taking the labors of past months into Glasgow to sell to the shops for holiday trade. How Maggie wished she might speak to her, to find out about her life and if these assumptions were true; however, she had been taught that the older person must be the first to speak, otherwise, the younger might be perceived impertinent, so she held her Gaelic tongue.

Soon, the printed name of Lockhart drew her attention to a scholarly looking gentleman just across the aisle, reading from the clearly visible title, *The Life of Sir Walter Scott*. Maggie had read this biography to her seven students only last spring and now her thoughts grew nostalgic. How she wished she might speak with him to know if his feelings on this stimulating book matched her own, but truly that too would be considered presumptuous.

Teaching her small group of seven was another thing she would sorely miss. Maggie was schoolmistress for the past two years in a tiny, old croft cottage converted to the schoolroom that held such happy memories. There she taught the delightful seven: her foster sisters, Faith, age nine when she began, Hope, seven and Charity a petite five. Then the twins, James and John Buchanan, age eleven, their father the town blacksmith, and Christopher Grant, the eldest of her pupils, who at twelve walked his way a mile down the burn, and trailing behind him his constant companion, wee Molly McDuff, just five, orphaned and taken in by the Grant family.

Those had been wonderful days for Maggie, for she thought often of how she learned more from these children than she could ever teach. She promised to write letters regularly to them for they seemed very sad at her departure.

Maggie was just fourteen when she passed the equivalency test for primary teaching. The test, given yearly in the town of Portree, honored her with the distinction of holding the highest score yet posted on the island of Skye for a beginning teacher. And it was all due to the painstaking lessons taught to her by Laura, starting when she was four. Suddenly there came to her mind a reflection, she must have traveled this identical route, but in reverse when age four, to be cared for by her godparents. Yes, she could faintly remember that journey for it had to be precisely so. How terrible it must have been for her mother, Jane, to have to leave her child, to place her safety in the hands of the ferry master that day and to travel back to Glasgow on these very rails and alone! How would she ever make up to her Mum Jane for all these lost years? She closed her eyes tightly with the promise of doing just that.

Recalling those early years with Laura, she remembered how she told her often of the days when Jane and Laura were then Maggie's age of sixteen, and of how the then Laura Stewart and Maggie's own mother, then Jane Fraser, were the closest of friends, attending the University of Edinburgh. Mum Laura told Maggie of how they spent long hours talking of the day when each would marry and teach their own children the lessons they so valued. Laura told her of how she had spent her early days in community school with all its harsh rules and customs, for *her* father was an impoverished candle-maker and her family lived above his shop. Maggie's mother, Jane, on the other hand, had only the best of tutors who called at her gracious home daily, for Maggie's grandparents owned the largest textile mill in Edinburgh, supplying woolens to gentry. Jane was their only child and her home was huge and elegant. The Frazer's hired teachers to guide Jane in rhetoric, literature, the sciences, mathematics and languages. Then twice weekly she studied elocution with Dr. Bell in his home just up the road, as was the custom for a girl of privileged circumstance.

What a pity, Laura had said, that both of Maggie's grandparents died in the cholera epidemic leaving Jane alone with nothing but her education, for the mill was held by creditors and the lovely home gone to the hammer at auction. Jane was forced then to make her residence with Aunt Tibbie, her father's sister, married to a professor of Botany at the university. In this manner, Jane continued her education, but only until she was eighteen when she and Laura were invited to journey with Aunt Tibbie to the Isle of Skye for an extensive summer holiday. What a merry holiday it had been as Laura met Bruce McGreagor and his cousin.

Robert McBain met Jane, all quite properly in a teashop, and the four young people hit it off immediately. Robert and Jane fell in love so swiftly, so completely, and so perfectly, it became apparent to everyone in only a matter of weeks that this blending was certainly heaven-sent. Yet in that time, Laura and Bruce only became great friends, taking a more cautious path to matrimony.

Maggie sat back in her seat, the train motion making her lethargic, with an overstuffed, firm cushion at her head; she relived and treasured the love story of her parents that Laura had told to her many times over. She begged for it regularly as her bedtime story soon after the first telling.

She never tired of hearing how the four young people spent their days together near Broadford, climbing the hills, having picnics on the ledges, endlessly laughing and easy with the others. The gaiety lasted many weeks as Aunt Tibbie merrily brought up the rear, becoming chaperone and vainly trying to keep up with the carefree foursome, "playing the gooseberry" so to speak, as was the Scottish expression for their overseer.

Bruce and Robert were on holiday as well, for in a matter of one month, Robert was to leave the croft life on Skye, exchanging it for the wild world of the sea. He had signed on a whaling ship out of Glasgow and would be a sailor for at least two years. He said that it was to be a great adventure, to be absent from the croft life of his parents, but by doing so, he might save enough money to buy a piece of land of his own, to farm as he wished, and not to be held in debt to any man as his parents were compelled to live out their days. He was a serious and thoughtful young man.

Jane and Robert were married at the end of that happy summer with Bruce and Laura as their witnesses. Then, unexpectedly, but fortunately, Robert's voyage was delayed because of repairs to the hull of the ship on which he was to sail. Thankfully, for the newlyweds, the next months were theirs alone in such sweet delirium of pleasure that Laura could barely express to little Maggie. Jane so beautiful, in her complete bliss, and Robert delirious in *his* happiness.

Robert remained on Skye for five months of total enchantment with his sweet Jane, until his vessel was ready in January. The four friends were then parted, little knowing what devastation the next three years would bring to them all as they bid sweet farewells to their smiling Robert headed to sea, never to be seen again.

Uncle Gordon and Aunt Tibbie had moved to Glasgow in that time period, when a Botany grant from his alma mater involved Gordon by using his expertise in the classification of varieties of the iris.

With Robert off to sea, Jane was glad to find employment with the University of Glasgow during that winter, and she willingly stayed on with them while patiently waiting for her sailor to return. Jane was ecstatic when in March, she found herself pregnant. She worked until June, residing with Tibbie and Gordon until the day when Maggie was born, October 18, 1869. Jane's gladness was lessened then despite the birth, for on that very day, a tragedy occurred when Gordon died as a result of a fall down a flight of stairs at the campus, and this was another man that Maggie was destined never to meet.

Jane declined living with Aunt Tibbie after Gordon's accident, for she thought a baby would be too disquieting in the home of a woman so distraught with grief. Her aunt had a companion who helped her with the housekeeping, and Jane felt her aunt was better cared for by Ella's capable hands. The aunt who Jane had come to know as that jolly, laughing lady was never the same, but became a recluse, keeping to herself in the upstairs sitting room, just sorting through the lovely flower prints her husband had so carefully collected all through their married life. Jane was saddened at this state of affairs. Even the visits she made to acquaint Aunt Tibbie with baby Maggie, did not brighten her aunt's days, no matter how often Jane tried.

When Maggie lived with her godparents in those twelve years on Skye, Jane's letters to her often described visits to see Aunt Tibbie in her comfortable home near Kelvingrove, where she was still cared for by Ella. Maggie could scarcely remember being in that home, yet she faintly recalled a woman with white hair sitting on the floor and rolling a large blue ball to her and of her returning it. It was one of her first memories. That woman must have been her mother's Aunt Tibbie!

Jane and Maggie lived in a two-room apartment within walking distance of the university and when Maggie was two, she was placed in the child care facility the school maintained for its employees. Not long after, when Jane heard of Robert's death at sea, Maggie was barely four and she realized that it would be impossible to manage raising her child alone, so she took Maggie to live with her best friends, Laura and Bruce who lived in crofter's cottage on the Isle of Skye. It seemed to be the only option for a woman with no family and who must work to support herself. The farm/croft life was the best way to bring up a child, she concluded, and Skye was where she would have raised Maggie, had her father lived.

As to employment, Jane had been fortunate. The university kept her on well over ten years, working in many departments, sometimes a record clerk, a substitute teacher, and finally, near her departure, secretary to the president of the University of Glasgow.

Jane wrote, in a letter to Maggie only two years past, of her then opportune meeting with Vincent Deal. He was a friend of the university president and he noting her skills with people there, offered her employment as manager of his bookshop on Ingram Street in Glasgow, and for a considerable increase in salary. It was so much of an increase that now she could plan to have Maggie travel to live with her. Jane, living so prudently had visited Skye only twice, once when Maggie was ten and again at thirteen. At that time she was able to stay for one full month of summertime, yet it was all too short to become truly reacquainted with her daughter.

"Loch Lomond on yer' right now, lads and lassies, you'll ner' see the likes of such again! Just aboot' the next bend. Look sharp in just a minute, and you'll view a proper treasure!"

It was the conductor, stridently calling out to the passengers as Maggie, swiftly roused from her 'wool gathering,' gazed out of the window at a site that would live in her memory for the remainder of her life: the huge valley below with its expanse of lake, miles across, glittering in the warm rays of an autumn afternoon sun like a dancing fairy in a children's school book. Its painted trees about the edge had turned every color from deep crimson to mustard yellow and the sparkle of the water gave a mirror image to the hugging shore. Oh, what a grand memory to store, thought Maggie. What a glorious country is this Scotland. I *will* come back to take this train again when I am older, wiser, and perchance share it with someone that I love. Yes, truly, one day *I shall* return to Scotland and to Skye!

Episode:

Maggie had read that the extreme, steep descent of the train coming into Glasgow station was unlike any on the continent. Not very long after viewing Loch Lomond, the train began the careful, braking process with a steady descent from the Highlands. At this slower pace she could recognize more beauty and color of the forest, so close she felt she could touch the foliage if she extended her hand out of the train window. These were not trees distinctive to Skye where pines and ash were prevalent, but here she also saw birch, maple, a larger ash and walnut, all rampant and stirring her senses.

Abruptly, the train entered a dark tunnel, so slowly, she felt sure they must be approaching the station. It had been nearly three years since she had held her darling mother in her arms and kissed her. 'What a joy it will be . . . only a few moments now . . .'

The locomotive emerged from the tunnel to a burst of dazzling sunlight and then began its grinding, screeching halt into the wide, dimly lit station. Passengers all about her were scurrying, reaching for coats, parcels and baskets, standing and stretching as the conductor filed through to help anyone needing assistance. Maggie's heart was beating wildly as she seized her carpetbag and moved forward with the crowd as in a dream.

The train finally came to a solid stop and she stepped lightly onto the graveled-bed adjoining the tracks. Promptly handing her trunk claim to a porter, she focused all attention on the lighted station a quarter-mile ahead, and with her boots feeling as though they were not touching ground, her arms open wide, she thought of just how she might ever express this pure feeling of rapture in her new journal.

Running so, Maggie felt as though she was soaring when she recognized, precisely beyond the gate, her mum racing to meet her.

Mum Jane looked the same as she always had to Maggie, perhaps only more lovely, for she was seeing her now as a grown daughter. The two were the same size, just about five foot, two inches, as Laura had proudly announced at Maggie's last measure on Skye. Jane's hair was done up in a knot of full curls tied with soft blue ribbon at the nape of her neck, a few light wisps worked into their auburn softness. Ringlets still fell about her ears in tiny tendrils in that carefree manner that Maggie remembered.

They could have been sisters, sitting there in the little teashop opposite the station. The petite, straight noses, the fair, wide-set hazel eyes and a radiance of being that glowed distinctively in both oval faces. Indeed, the woman at the counter from whom they ordered tea, had tried to guess for herself, sisters or mother and daughter? She could not make the choice, for Maggie looked well beyond her sixteen years and Jane certainly did not show her thirty-five.

The scones were sweet and fresh. The marmalade and clotted cream sent shivers up Maggie's spine. 'Oh', is the living off Skye to be all like this or have I been sent to heaven for a bit of a pilgrimage?' Maggie's head was racing with opulence and delight.

Mum could not take her eyes from her daughter's face. She wanted to ask so many questions and all at once: was the trip fine, did Maggie feel well, how were Laura, Bruce and the girls? And then their plans, Jane wanted to speak of their plans, but just now only to enjoy this meeting after these many years apart. It was like holding the grandest party in the entire world, only the two of them in this tiny shop, sipping tea, eating cakes and squeezing hands across the table. Suddenly they both cried out in their happiness. It was as though they had never been separated.

The rooms Jane had taken since managing the bookstore were more spacious than Maggie could have imagined. Her mum had arranged for a daybed to be situated in her own bedroom overlooking Ingram Street below. There was a neat, square parlor graced with an ornate, charcoal-fed stove set up on short legs, two floral decorative, upholstered chairs with a small round marble table between them for taking tea or supper, and all placed on a worn, but brightly patterned carpet. There was a writing desk in one corner and a small alcove off the parlor complete with a gas plate for cooking, and dishes orderly set on blue shelves. Only two other tenants shared the bath just down the hallway. The rooms were on the third floor and above the bookstore, making it most convenient for Jane to work her long hours unburdened with travel. "It truly saves on the shoe leather," she whispered playfully, with a shake of her auburn locks and that special signature wink that Maggie fondly remembered.

As Maggie wandered through the rooms, she noted impressively that her mother had spent a pretty penny fitting them for her arrival. She saw what looked like a colorful, charming new cover on her daybed, a nosegay of dainty pink rosebuds on the marble table, sweet chemist shop soaps on the nightstand arranged on lovely new pale green towels, her favorite color. There was even a small dish of peppermints on the desk. What paradise, to be with her mum, perhaps now for a full year before going off to her schooling, and amid such luxury! It was beyond any expectation.

Promptly at seven the next morning, Maggie stirred to the sharp sounds of china placed on the marble table, the aroma of the brose steaming on the hotplate and tea steeping beneath the quilted cozy. Mum had placed an orange next to her bowl, unheard of in their class, except possibly on Christmas Day, for citrus fruit was the treat of the entire year.

She was certainly going to speak of this extravagance for her sake, yet she hesitated to do so today, lest she take away Jane's generous and obvious pleasure in her deed.

"I'll be down to the shop now, Love. I must open before eight. Whenever you decide to come down, just come ahead. Get settled in here though, take your time dressing and do eat your breakfast. Become acquainted with the place." And with a kiss to Maggie's forehead, she was off, leaving the delicate scent of lavender behind in the warm, comfy room.

Maggie chose a plain white waist and her long tartan skirt for her first full day in Glasgow. She owned but three skirts, four waists, one traveling coat and one high neck, cream-colored woolen sweater made for her by Laura. She put on her everyday pair of stout climbing boots and set aside her prized, shiny new black ones.

Clothing was never abundant on Skye, and she had grown at such a rate in these past three years that it would have been foolish to own more. She was glad that they had been passed down to Faith, and because of this she was in the habit of keeping all her things in immaculate condition. Now, standing before the hanging mirror above the night stand, she decisively realized she was a full grown woman and if she secured satisfactory employment, could add to her wardrobe, a piece at a time. Then, after she finally accomplished her secret dream, she would have a wealth of suitable clothing as she traveled to the new world, across the sea.

She sipped her tea with a leisurely pleasure never before experienced. 'So this is what city life and relaxation is about,' she mused. 'What I have read of in the stories about fine gentlemen and ladies calmly sipping tea.' Yet almost immediately as she drained her cup, she was on her feet, washing the china, finished with daydreaming. Maggie brushed out her long "ginger" hair, as McNess always called it, and with vitality pinned it back so it fell softly on her shoulders. Then she tied a red, tartan ribbon to hold the soft curls and began placing the remainder of her belongings into bureau and wardrobe. Each container that she opened smelled so delightfully of Jane's lavender that she abruptly wanted to rush down to the shop to be sure this was not merely a dream and Mum was actually there.

As she closed the solid door to their rooms, another opened, just down the hall, and the kindly face of a woman in her declining years appeared.

"Oh then ye'll be Maggie," appraised this frail, wisp of a woman with delicate white hair, summarily moving her thin hands as a bird flutters his wings. "And we have all been waiting for thee,' aye, myself along with the others, soon for the darlin' to arrive. Heavens, your mither, must be in lofty spirits, for it has been all that she has talked of for weeks, and here ye be! Jane was fair out of her head, she was, with the worry of your train trip, and she was that uneasy, you know. So welcome then... I am Mrs. Burns and I have lived in this building over twenty years. I have known your mum for two of those and a sweeter soul, I have yet to meet on earth, a marvelous and generous neighbor, always looking in and fetching my small necessities."

Maggie moved from one foot to another as she spoke, and seeing her sway a bit, the woman said," Oh, my dear, you need to be off to the shop now to be with your mither." And so saying she half turned into her rooms but not without her last words, "Get on with you, darlin', know we're all glad ye are here and safe, Miss Maggie McBain. Just stop and visit with me anytime!" Maggie extended her hand to the tiny woman, while giving a huge smile to this Mrs. Burns; then she turned politely to hurry down to the bookshop.

As Maggie descended the varnished wooden stairs she noted this old building was well kept and had an artistic feeling about it with the small octagons of leaded colored glass lending a pleasing esthetic feel to the dark wood. These were fixed into each landing catching the morning sunlight in every tone. She guessed that someone of meticulous taste had built the building. And as she made her way to the ground floor with that thought, she found herself rounding the front entry to the street and into the tidy Deal Bookshop.

Ay, what a smell, och', what a spectacle! If cakes and tea were good, then this was truly grand. Books, so many beautiful, wonderful books with that smell of leather bindings mixed with the deeper, heavier aromas of printer's ink. This was an intermingling of the elixir of the gods and the culmination of another fantasy, that is, to be in the company of so many books.

Mum was nowhere to be seen and the shop stood empty, save for the fat, yellow-striped tabby curled on the wooden chair very near a charcoal stove in the middle of the room. The creature looked so much like a figurine that Maggie was compelled to place her hand out to touch the fur to assure her that she was real. The melodious depth of the purr dispelled any doubts.

"Do you like cats? Could I interest you in a kitten of your own?" The man's deep voice came out of somewhere in a dimly lit corner of the shop from behind a great pile of volumes on a huge oak table and startled her. Maggie, trying to accustom her eyes to the soft light, peered deeply into it, as she took a timid step forward so that she might make out the shape attached to the voice.

"My name is Vincent Deal. I own this shop and I take it you are the much awaited Maggie McBain, for your countenance is a good deal as your mother's, no mistaking that."

The vague shape took on a tall, slim silhouette, as he rose and took steps toward her, his hand extended. A fine-featured gentleman with sandy color hair and the fashionable pince-nez eye glasses clipped to the ridge of his bony nose asserted a scholarly air. He appeared to be in his late forties. Maggie guessed him a man of means judging from the cut of his gray frock coat and doublet with gold watch chain glittering across his broad expanse of chest.

"Yes, I'm Maggie and I am pleased to meet you" she said as she shook the offered hand of Mr. Deal. "Mother has mentioned you often in her letters."

Then somewhat shyly, sweeping her hands so as to include the entire shop, "The books here are so many, and so glorious to see and to smell. I never tire of reading. I wish that I might possess every one of these."

As she spoke, her fingers caressed the leather binding of *Oliver Twist* on the closest shelf at elbow's height. Mr. Deal observed all this with tender interest, confirming his judgment. Of course, being Jane's daughter, she held an absolute passion for the written page.

"You are certainly welcome to take any book from the shelves here to read of an evening, as long as it is in place in the morning, Maggie. Is it to be one year that you plan to stay with your mother here in Glasgow? Do you think that you shall read all of these?" And he too, swept his arm to encompass the large square room, smiling broadly in a teasing manner, exposing a handsome set of gold teeth matching his gold chain.

"Is mother here?" Maggie asked timidly, not knowing where else this conversation might go, for while she was accustomed to speaking easily to adults in pleasant conversation, she was slightly more reserved here with her mother's employer.

"Jane has taken some parcels of books to the post for me. You see, we do a good deal of mail order business with customers all about Scotland and especially in the villages, concentrating in service to schoolmasters and private tutors in the Highlands. I come here each morning to review our records and find if I must obtain additional books from the printers to supply our orders. I also make sure that your mother has all under control, but that has never been a problem. Jane has worked here for over two years, and I would not like to think of the shop without her. Our customers have become dependent upon her excellent judgment and pleasant manner."

Maggie smiled, it was good to hear another voice those qualities she knew in her dear mum.

"Well, I must be off as soon as Jane returns." Mr. Deal beamed as he turned to the small corner desk with its green shaded oil lamp as he said, "You see I own a publishing business in addition to this shop. It is on the other side of the city and there I spend the greater portion of my day. We are issuing a series of the classics at present. This Scottish populace canna' seem to ever get enough of reading. Thanks be to God!"

He had just finished this sentence, turned down the lamp and faced the door, when Jane came bustling in, her cheeks aglow with the morning cool.

"They're sent then, Mr. Deal, and will catch the morning train, Mr. Crew assured me of that...Oh, Maggie, and you two have met then." Jane quickly noticed her out of the corner of her eye. "You are certainly down very early. I dinna' expect you so soon, come, let me show you the shop. Good morning, Mr. Deal."

He tipped his bowler hat to the ladies and for the first time, Maggie noted the merry sound of a bell as the door closed behind him. She had not noticed it before, but now she felt that the ring much matched her mood.

Jane took pleasure in showing Maggie the beautiful editions of each category in the shop, from poetry to science, economics to politics, history, fiction and school textbooks. The entire stock was meticulously arranged and spotless. The medical books, sold to university students, were housed and attained by a metal, circular staircase leading to a loft at the rear of the shop. Jane's desk stood just beneath the stairs and was merely a huge library table stacked neatly with folders, journals, stationery, pens and an inkwell. Maggie was impressed. Now she could imagine her mother each day in her workspace and the thought was comforting. It was curious, but by viewing her mum's desk, she realized what she had never been able to explain to anyone, least of all to herself, exactly why the orderly display of paper, envelopes, pencils and pens and all manner of writing materials gave her such a fine feeling. It sounded foolish even now as she thought of it.

The day passed so quickly, Maggie found it hard to believe that it was six o'clock and closing time. It had been a wonderful day; she had stayed, sitting at Jane's desk, reading and mainly observing Mum with the variety of customers, men, women and children. They had shared the luncheon that Jane had brought down that morning, and Maggie prepared tea for two in the cranny behind Mum's desk.

Jane locked the front door after pulling the dark green shade over the glass and they made their way to the rooms above. This would be their special evening to plan for Maggie's future, just where she might find work, and when she might begin to attend a university.

With their small supper complete, they sat before the warm stove and in this snug manner.

Jane began, "I have given your employment much thought in the many days while I waited for you, darlin', and I've come to some essential facts. First, I feel that you should not travel far from our rooms, for two reasons: first, for your safety in these dark hours as winter progresses, and also for the saving in any cost of a journey. That is, if you can walk to work, I think it best. There are many merchants here who are always looking for honest, reliable help. Nonetheless, and this is so fortunate, my acquaintance, Molly Grant, at the local teashop, just one street over and two streets north, has told me of her need for an excellent girl to help in her kitchen and mainly to serve the meals. I know the pay might not be the highest and it is not the teaching work that I know you love, yet it is honest labor and could be done until we find something else. What do you think? "

Then rapidly, without an answer, Jane went right on, so excited was she to tell of all her plans.

"Your teaching experience is of great value, but we would be hard pressed to find a position now in mid-term unless we are prepared to sign the two-year contract as is usual and that would delay the start of our goal of the university far too long. Then, there is another possibility; a tutoring position might be found. Persons of means about this city are in need of specialized education for their children. They have money here in Glasgow. I see wealthy customers who frequent the shop wanting only the best for their family. Why, even a number of shopkeepers are turning to the private teacher for their children. What do you say, dear?"

Wide, eyed and certainly stimulated, Maggie beamed at her vibrant, enthused, darling mother. Only now did she understand how these concerns weighed so heavily and plagued her mind. So that by placing her arm about Jane's slim shoulder in *her* best jovial, *mothering* manner, Maggie exclaimed to the impassioned Jane, most clearly, "Yes, Mum, of course, yes," and smiling all the while patting the arm of her very best friend, she agreed to all Jane had said with this loving affirmation.

Episode:

Mrs. Molly Grant took the sixth and last tray of oat scones from her huge, iron oven with a sigh of relief. It was nearing eleven-thirty on a Monday morning and her back was in a bad way. She often thought that Monday was the hardest of her six-day work week by breaking that steady routine with two church services and the pure leisure of her Sunday afternoons.

Her shop smelled delightful and looked the same, "as neat as a pin on a cushion," was Jane's description to Maggie of the tea room on Langley Street, only a three block walk from the bookshop. It opened under the Grant management after Molly was widowed. Formerly a scurrilous looking affair, prior to the Scot scrubbing hand of Molly, for two men had 'run it into the ground' as she always described their management with their dirty ways and poor cooking. They had lost it to the bank and moved out, yet this proved fortunate for Molly, for due to their 'muck,' as she spoke of it; she was able to buy it with the small amount of money left to her at Mr. Grant's untimely death. Now the shop displayed charming, ruffled, stylish white curtains on its glass front and it was immaculate. Molly had built an excellent trade with the working folks in this fine, retail shop-quarter of Glasgow. Genteel bankers often brought their clients here for luncheon, and because the largest engineering firm in the entire city, occupied the full two floors above the tearoom, her income was assured. For as long as she continued to produce the hearty, thick Cock-a-Leekie soups, Inverray Salmon tarts, Glasgow Cod, Leek pies, Forfar bridies, Clootie dumplings and her famous Oat Scones, Molly felt confident and secure. She did not even blush when some said she was most celebrated baker and cook in this town!

Molly Grant worked feverishly from sun up until the eleven-thirty deadlines, when she opened the shop with only herself and Mary Dee, her kitchen helper, turning out the luscious and varied menu. Her reputation was becoming legendary, even capturing the favor of university professors who traveled full across the city to partake of these culinary arts. High tea, the second meal, was also served each day, and during this fashionable repast, her acclaimed Fochaber Gingerbread and Dundee Cakes were lauded. These two desserts were portions of her own heritage, for as a bride Molly moved to "Glasgotown," as *she* called it, from the more rural town of Dundee.

At present her work was heavy indeed, for Molly had recently lost her only waitress when Jean suddenly moved to Newfoundland in search of 'adventure,' as Molly disclosed to Maggie with a somewhat dismissive tone. This left Molly to not only prepare the food, but following her morning labor, to serve it as well. She fancied that it would make her life easier in times like these, if one of her three shipbuilding sons had been born a girl, so as to help in the shop.

Maggie had never waited on the public, but now, here, in the center of this orderly dining room, with the starched white apron pulled smooth over her dark, long skirt and white waist, her hair gathered to the back of her head and tied securely in a black velvet bow, she hoped that no one would suspect that she was not the most competent of waitresses.

Molly Grant was precise in her instruction, arriving an hour early this morning, in order to make time for Maggie.

"Serve from the left, take away from the right. Be quick to take the order as our seating is limited, especially 'aboot' the noon hours when there will be persons waiting for a table. You must never give a hurried appearance, however. Memorize the specials of the day. They usually are the same each week: Tuesday, Salmon Tart, Thursday, Leek Pie and so forth, yet this is not always true; there are times I canna' find the right, fresh supplies at market and we have to change 'aboot', you see."

Molly Grant sighed, giving a quick glance at Mary Dee, stirring the Partan Bree, and then testing the Buttery Rowies.

"It is a quick mind and a sharp eye that you must keep, Maggie; the tea must always be hot. Watch for the silver to be bright and shiny, napkins pert. Never fail to ask the customer about a sweet after the main course, for it means precious extra pence, but then, most will ask anyway, for we are most proud of the fine desserts that we prepare.

Get to know yer customers by name if you have a good head for face; they like that . . . don't you know!"

Molly bubbled over in her exuberance to tell Maggie everything that she needed to know and all at once, or so it seemed.

"These little buds kept on each table for a bit of whimsy must be fresh. Our china is Staffordshire, so hoist the trays with care. We canna' spare a plate. And know we serve no whiskey or ale here as I am firm agin' it, but that proves no problem here, that is to say, our first rate cooking, is what they come for."

She gave her worldly wink of pride, and turning into her kitchen thoughtfully added, "Are those shoes comfortable? You will be on your legs, most assuredly, from eleven in the morn until eight at night. Of course, you know that we close on the Sabbath and that is your holiday. Near every shop closes and it is my family day. My boys are at home and spend *that* day with me," she confided proudly, now straying from her litany of rules. "Your pay will be half of my usual for the first two weeks, and then if we prove agreeable with the other, it will be the same as I paid to Jean, four pounds a week and your meals. Well, now we are nearly ready."

Molly keenly surveyed the oval dining room, designed to seat thirty-two persons, and swung through the two wooden half-doors into her hot kitchen. Maggie inhaled deeply, preparing for the challenge and strode to the leaded glass front door to open it for business.

Episode:

It was nearly three weeks later when Jane asked Maggie just how she was getting on at the tearoom, secretly fearing this work might be far too demanding, yet wishing to give it a fair trial before she inquired. She found, to her surprise, an enthusiastic girl, keenly awaiting the start of each day, uncomplaining of the nine-hour stretch on her legs, but only quick to share her endless stories of the fascinating persons met and the lovely foods prepared there by the delightful, indefatigable, Molly Grant.

It was a good match then, Maggie receiving a fair wage, enough to enable her to save for college, with Mrs. Grant obtaining the benefit of a totally dedicated and cheerful worker.

Maggie still lit the lamp in the cozy parlor when she returned from the teashop and mother and daughter chatted and read their books for several hours, content merely having the other close.

Over a month had happily come and gone since Maggie's arrival. The November winds were blowing cold down from the Kilpatrick Hills in the north of Glasgow. On this Sunday, Vincent Deal had invited Jane and Maggie to attend church services with he and his wife, Anne in the cathedral dedicated to St. Mungo, the patron saint of the city. Afterward, they were to take Sunday dinner at their home in the west end.

Maggie was in a merry mood. It would be good to see a bit more of Glasgow than in only the few streets between bookstore and tearoom. Sundays, thus far, had been devoted to sleeping an hour later than customary and attempting to wash and repair her clothing for the coming week, then reading or talking with Jane of her future. This morning was filled with a new promised pleasure.

Finally, it was evening and Maggie lay back on the soft pillow of her bed, this lovely day over, and with the steady stream of moonlight entering the near window, softening the furniture shapes close by, she could consider and appreciate this charming day, hour by hour. How grand it had been to be present in the immense and ancient cathedral. This was the largest building that she had ever entered. She sat in awe of the quiet worshippers amid the sounds of the choir raising their voices in praise, and that sound echoing, no, truly bouncing off of the stonewalls. For Maggie it was like pulling in a splendor never felt before. Life has so much to offer!

The elegant dinner shared with Anne and Vincent in the huge home near Kelvingrove Park, was another first, for hired servants served it. The Deals not only had a cook and butler, but a serving girl, as well. The food was delicious, beginning, with a fish soup, then a roast of lamb, glazed carrots, browned potatoes and a sweet raisin pie for dessert accompanied by a whipped cheese sauce, all utterly delectable. The Deals' table was graced with fine silver and stemware from France. The china was from the south of Ireland. Vincent spent considerable time abroad due to the publishing business, as he took great pride in bringing to his home the best of what he found there. Walls were hung in rich tapestries from Belgium and with large oil paintings from Holland. Jane happily remarked on each lovely piece, while Vincent seemed justly proud to show her his latest acquisitions.

For Maggie, it was an introduction to the finer possessions in life, and she questioned these, as she situated herself more snugly into her bedcovers. Would she ever have husband, child and be mistress of her own elegant home? As she hovered in that liquid state, somewhere between sleep and reality, she almost felt that this entire day had been a hallucination. For when Anne took Mum and her up to the nursery after their dinner to where the precious children were rousing from their naps, they were introduced to blonde Penelope, just three, and to Christopher, a darling boy of two. Anne dressed the children in warm clothing and carried both downstairs to bundle them into the horse drawn sleigh. Finally, together with Jane, Maggie, Anne and the proud father, Vincent, they were jubilant as he urged his handsome pair of sorrels over the newly fallen snow. They seemed to soar all about the roads of Kelvingrove to the shouts and the laughter of them all. To Maggie, it seemed a dream come true.

Episode:

Vincent Deal looked up from the long column of figures that he was adding as Jane came bustling into the shop.

"Ah, Jane, I dinna' expect you so soon. I'll be up and cutting your wages if you like this shop so well as to be here an hour early." Jane blushed as was her habit when teased.

"I promised old Mr. Caruthers, a list of books from which he might choose his grandson's birthday gift, and I know that he likes to come into the shop promptly at eight as we open, right after he makes the rounds on his daily constitutional. He's such a sweet old man, even though he tries to hide it. I dinna' want to disappoint him. I believe the youngster will be twelve on Monday."

"You've been a godsend to me, Jane McBain. I have often wished to tell you how reassured I am to leave this bookshop in your capable hands when I am far across town or off on a trip. Just before I found you at the university I had been through such a succession of lazy and unreliable persons, that I was just about to close the shop entirely, for to my mind, a poor run establishment is better with the door locked, and then I met you. I have kept the business these many years for chiefly nostalgic reasons, although now it is certainly turning a good profit."

He eyed his column of figures and continued, "As you know, this was my father's before me and the beginning of my interest in and my love of books. You have brought back our former customers with your patience and efficiency, as well as the great number of new individuals moving into our growing city.

I've not ventured to say these things to you before, as I was, and am now, wary of your leaving one day.

I do not know what I should do then? With your Maggie here, I feel things might be changing, since I sense that you will wish to be off with her to wherever she chooses to attend a university. Is there any chance that she might attend Glasgow University and permit things to remain just as they are?"

Jane was visibly touched by her employer's fine compliments. She had always believed that he was pleased with her work over these past years mainly by his silence. He had let her take free reign in running the shop, and she knew that his accounts were in much improved shape than in her beginnings. This speech was something very fine to hear out loud.

"I have not given much thought to *where* I shall be in one year. We canna' decide which school she is to attend until we see what we can readily afford and those which will offer the subjects that best suit the studies she wishes to pursue. I do hope that she will decide to stay close for a few years, at least now that we have finally come together. Maggie, you know, is *my* full reason for living!"

Jane's eyes felt moist in admitting this to her employer, so that she turned slightly, removing a volume from the shelf closest at hand, while using a handkerchief to dab at her eyes. Vincent pretended not to notice and kindly offered, "Anne and I so enjoyed your visit of last Sunday. Maggie really took Anne's heart. She remarked on that evening of how she could only hope that our Penelope will have half the grace and stature at the same age. You have done a remarkable job there, Jane."

"Nay, I've not done much. It is Laura and Bruce there on Skye we've to thank for her presence. I owe them a great deal, much more than can ever be repaid."

A sharp tapping on the glass of the shop door brought both of them to attention. There stood old Caruthers, his ivory cane handle firm against the glass. Jane glanced at the clock and stood aghast; it was already five minutes of eight. Time had slipped away during their lengthy discussion. She placed the book in her hand on the front counter and quickly opened the door, giving a strident hello to her persistent old gentleman.

Episode:

James, Mark and Matthew Grant were in the habit of taking their supper in their mother's establishment for at least four of the six nights of business. The three lads were a handsome assemblage as they sat at the round family table in the rear of the shop next to the kitchen, enjoying their late meal. They usually arrived together, before the tearoom closed at eight, and right after a busy high tea had been served, so as to not take away space from customers. All worked in the famous Glasgow shipyards on the waterfront of the River Clyde following the tradition of their father and grandfather before them. Glasgow had become the greatest shipbuilding city in the world in these past one hundred years, and these young men were the first to tell you all about it. They seemed consumed with pride, despite the sad fact that their father had died of a fateful heart attack at the works.

James, the eldest, now twenty-six, and just promoted to foreman in the foundry, was the tallest of the three and the most verbal and expressive. All of the boys shared their mother's good looks with sandy hair, fine straight features, ruddy skin tone and a general appearance of healthy enthusiasm.

James had a likeable, easy way about him and could judge exactly the right amount to tease Maggie and Mary Dee as they worked in the tearoom. He could easily get their dander up, yet keep his banter to a pleasant style. His teasing days were numbered, however, as Miss Elizabeth Consort of Tewkesbury Circle, Glasgow, had promised to become his bride in the coming spring.

Mark, twenty-two, was the quiet one. Despite his extraordinary good looks and open smile, he seemed the peacemaker for the brothers and spoke little. He worked in the engine plant on the docks as his father had before him. These young men had not been privileged to attend college, but had learned their trade on the job at the shipyards. It was Mark who Jane knew best from the hours he spent in the bookshop, reading and purchasing both technical and literary works, for he rarely was seen without a volume under his arm.

Matthew, the youngest at nineteen, seemed to mimic his eldest brother in so many ways. Maggie thought of him as a mirror image of James, for he hung on his oldest brother's every word. He was liked about the yards and was moving ahead rapidly as he worked for James in the foundry.

Molly Grant was especially proud of all of her 'boys' as she called them and did not hesitate to tell you so. They in turn were respectful of their mother. Maggie found this a credit to their caring upbringing.

On this day, in chilly mid-December, Maggie stood on a wooden chair at the far end of the teashop placing paper silver stars near the ceiling for holiday decoration with hammer and small nails. This was the job her employer requested she complete before opening this day. Now it was rapidly approaching eleven' o clock, with an anxious Maggie hastening to finish when Mark poked his head in through the kitchen doors.

"Wait, a bit now, Maggie," he called out across the room, "you'll be slipping off that wicker chair you are stretching so," and he rushed over to help her.

She seemed startled at the male voice and truly almost lost her balance.

"Mark, whatever are you doing here this morning, have you run out of jobs at the works?" She smiled broadly at his worried face as she teetered again at her station just as he reached to steady her.

"I've the morning off . . . once in a blue moon; actually you are right, we are waiting for a big engine that's been delayed by rail, so they have given us the day. No pay of course, but I thought I would stop in to find out what lunch tastes like. James is off to see Elizabeth and what has happened to Matthew, who can tell? Here, let me put up the rest of these, I'll make short work of it." And so he proceeded from the floor level to reach places she had been aiming for with the chair, so the stars were in place as he put his arm about her waist to help her down.

"I know you are in a rush now, Maggie, but I never get a chance to speak to you in the evening with the others about. Is there a possibility . . . do you think that next Sunday I might take you on a tour of the town? You mentioned, on the other evening, that you have seen Kelvingrove and St. Mungo's, but there is so much more of Glasgow that you must see!

I was born here and I know every street. I have a chance to hire a friend's carriage and even though it may be cold, I think we could see a great deal. What do you say? I could pick you up on Sunday morning?"

Maggie was surprised. This was the longest speech Mark had ever uttered in her presence during the seven weeks that she had seen him here in the tearoom and she was plainly flattered. She knew it might seem strange to this young man of twenty-two, who she secretly admired, if she confessed that in all her sixteen years, she had never been alone with a gentleman on any type of excursion. So smiling sweetly, she said, "I'll be asking Mum and tell you tomorrow evening, all right?"

Flushed and warm, not knowing if from the jumping off and on the chairs, or from the closeness of Mark, she gathered the remainder of the decorations and held them high, high enough to cover her rosy cheeks as she hurried across the room to put on her starched, white apron.

Episode:

Sunday seemed to take forever to come round. Pulling on her best black boots and lacing them up quickly she took pleasure that it had not been difficult to convince Mum of this sightseeing trip with Mark.

Jane was washing the breakfast things in the tiny alcove they called a kitchen, while feeling the sweet poignancy of her own memories at Maggie's age with a boy about to call. She wanted to say the right words just now and after drying the last dish, walked into their small bedroom.

Jane liked Mark Grant. He was an interesting, respectful young man, both in the bookshop and in the tearoom. She actually preferred his quiet nature to those more boisterous.

Maggie was at the mirror brushing wayward auburn curls that fell about her ears and asking her mother if she should wear a hat. Jane smiled, "Your choice darling, I do hate to see those pretty locks covered, but it is likely to be quite cold in the carriage and I believe it may snow before the day is over." Jane stepped to the window looking over the street. "Best, you take one of mine just in case." And she handed Maggie her lovely jade green, velvet cloche.

"Why, thank you, Mum, I'll be careful of it" beamed the delighted girl as a knock on the door removed any idea of those words of wisdom, mother to daughter that Jane had intended this morning. As she saw the pair off, laughing their way down the passage of stairway to the street, her thoughts were all of her sweet Robert, and that no advice was probably the best course, after all.

The day was somewhat dour, with a bleak gray sky overhead and a distinct raw chill in heavy air, but the young people did not let that spoil their gaiety. Mark had mapped a real tour, so eager was he that Maggie should see his city. They began at Mercat Cross on Saltmarket Street, viewed St. Andrew's Church, the Barras and Glasgow Green, where Mark proudly pointed out that the first golf game in the world had been played, centuries before. They saw Tolbooth Steeple and leaving the carriage parked, walked about the medieval building of Provand's Lordship built in 1471, opposite the Cathedral, just off High Street. This edifice, he said, had at various times housed James II, James IV and Mary, Queen of Scots.

This realization that Maggie stood in the same places where these famous persons had once stood, seemed all at once overwhelming. As they walked close to the Necropolis behind the Cathedral, where so many Glaswegians were buried in elaborate tombs, she was grateful that she and Mark were walking this portion of their tour during the short interval when the sun finally broke through the leaden skies. She, most certainly, would have been plagued by despairing spirits if she were in this hallowed place at dusk or in darkness. Maggie truly believed that sunlight dispelled hopeless spirits and she encouraged Mark away from these ancient ruins before the sun withdrew.

Mark then took her to George Street, to show her the handsome building newly built by merchant John Burnet, and on to the city's council chambers nearby. They saw the stylish, new Mitchell Library, for which all of Glasgow was justly proud and then to the ruins of Cathcart Castle. He drove out past the Music Hall, only opened in 1878 in the Gorbals, heart of the workingman's land. He voiced that although he had yet to attend a performance here himself, that perhaps one evening, Maggie's mum might allow her to see one of their offerings. Blushing, Maggie thrilled at the prospect and said yes, she would ask her.

The sun again appeared in the late afternoon and Mark suddenly remembered the grand luncheon that Molly had placed in the wicker hamper in the carriage. How could he have been so thoughtless, he said, to forget it for all these hours? Maggie declared she had thought little of food for she was so busy enjoying herself.

They ate, sitting on a bench set on the banks of the River Clyde, exactly where Mark had planned the completion of the excursion. Molly had painstakingly packed a grand assortment of little meat pies, some buttery shortbread and a flask of warm cocoa. On this grand setting, which served as a park in the summertime, and sharing tasty food with a thoughtful young man, Maggie's mind was overwhelmed with the thought that she would remember for all time, this first rendezvous with a true gentleman.

The dock was peaceful on this Sunday with no one about except the watchman who Mark knew well. Mark had saved his own workplace for the last and it was Maggie's initial experience in viewing a huge commercial enterprise. The mammoth vessels in all states of construction seemed complicated. The two young people hitched the horse to a post at the far end of the quay and walked the entire length of the docks and the shipbuilding area, seeing ships of every description in all stages of construction from keel laying to spar building.

At the end they came upon the large harbor, where lay at anchor seemingly every type of craft imaginable. Mark amazed her with his knowledge of brig and sloop, of clipper and schooner and of the iron hulled steamships about which his work revolved. Finally as they were near the completion of their long walk, just barely visible in the dusk and rolling mist heading in from the sea, Maggie made out the outline of a three-mast whaler moving laggardly with the wash of her berth. As Mark explained, she was awaiting her crew and soon would be heading for open sea in search of the mysterious whale.

Suddenly Maggie was caught with shortness of breath when she came in sight of the craft. Mark, not knowing of her deep feelings for the father she'd lost which this scene evoked, placed a firm, protective arm about her shoulders, for he felt involuntary shivers convulse her slim body as in the beginning of a chill. Worried, he turned her about, away from the sight to hurry both of them back along the path they had come, back to the carriage and on to Maggie's home.

Episode:

"Tell me all about your day." Jane was justly inquisitive, hoping that her daughter enjoyed seeing the city as well as the company of her first young man.

"I will, Mum, I promise, but first I want… I *have to know* more about my father. Mum, a strange thing happened on the docks just before we started home." And Maggie went on to tell of the queer reaction she had in seeing her first whaling vessel afloat.

"It was more than melancholy, Mother, since I never knew my father and it is not the real missing that I believe I'm feeling, but it is something much more than that. It is mystic, supernatural. Oh, I know you believe I have these strange feelings from living with the riddle of Skye. I do know I have a deep-rooted sense of the supernatural world from childhood, but when I viewed that ship today, I felt connected to it somehow, or to whalers or whale men. It is as though something is missing in this whole puzzle and I'm left searching; Oh, I wish I could express it better! Can you understand what I am trying to say?"

Maggie sat curled, like a tiny child on the warm carpet, her head on the arm of Jane's chair. It was nearly bedtime and Jane stroked the springy golden-brown curls while she voiced feelings that she herself had not dared to reflect on in these thirteen years since Robert's death.

"I know, I know, Maggie, my sweet. You see, many years ago when there was still the slight hope that your father's ship would be coming into Glasgow harbor, or that some whaling vessel might bring word of seeing it out in that cold, bleak sea, I would travel down to the docks whenever I could and occasionally you were in my arms or by my side. It made me feel closer to him in that I was doing something fine, something positive, just being there watching for him or hearing some word. At that time there was still the faintest flicker of hope. I have never told you more than that your father, Robert McBain, was lost at sea on a whaling vessel, but I believe now that you are grown, it is time that you hear the story told to me by the whaling captain when you were just three years old there on the quay as the two of us watched and waited."

"You understand, when a man signs on a whaler, he does so, not for a set length of time, but he is bound to that ship until they obtain the full cargo of oil and baleen which they set out for; otherwise the owners and the men themselves come back with nothing for one, two or even three years of their lives in grueling cold and miserable conditions.

"When he left, I knew that Robert could be gone for a year or perhaps even two and that wasn't so bad when I received his letters. You see, every ship headed out to the same fishing grounds carries letters for another ship and they exchange as they meet at sea. At times, I would receive ten or twelve letters at once when a ship docked in that first year, and beautiful letters they were. In fact, Maggie, I have every one of them and perhaps one day you will read them. Mostly, they speak of his everyday work aboard, the boredom of watching for sight of the whale's spout, and mainly of his homesickness for us.

"He knew by my letters, that we had a beautiful little girl named Maggie and you made him all the more anxious to be through with the sea. He vowed that when he returned home, we would take his share of the profit from the voyage and settle down on a farm on Skye. He longed so for his boyhood home in those letters, but he never once said that he was wrong going off to sea. Robert felt that it would give us the start we needed for a good life especially now with our little one. Oh, he was cheerful and hopeful, just so lonesome for us."

Jane shifted in her chair and swallowed visibly as she began again and Maggie realized that the missing part of the years that had been closed to her too was now about to be told.

"Mr. Drummond Evans was the name of the captain of the whaler Fortune that came into Glasgow Harbor that October of 1872. I was working at the university doing record keeping for Professor Spire in the English department and you were in the nursery there that was set up for children of the staff. News travels fast when you keep an ear for it and we arrived at the pier not three hours after the Fortune docked. The tall ship had been out for nearly two years and was heavy in the water with whale cargo.

"Her crew was briskly unloading in that mid-afternoon sunshine, all laughing and singing while I waited to ask anyone of them if they had seen your father's ship, Tempest. A weather-beaten sailor came down the plank, quite close to us, bearing a seamen's bag on his shoulder and I waved and stopped him to ask if he knew anything of the Tempest, had he seen her at sea? I will never forget his lined face as he looked from you in my arms and me waiting for his answer. It was as though all the blood drained from his dark face as he blurted out something inaudible then motioned and muttered words to Captain Evans just above him on the deck while pointing to us on the dock. I cannot tell you of the horrible empty feeling then in the pit of my stomach. I felt faint seeing the pallor on that seaman's face. So quickly that I cannot say how, but the captain had you and me aboard and into his cabin. He was wafting a sickly smelling salt under my nose. To this day, I cannot smell ammonia but I relive those terrible moments.

"He was a kindly man with bushy white hair, seemingly too old for such a vigorous life. His eyes were piercing black, I remember, and with his hair so light, it made an odd contrast. We sat on an overstuffed chair, strange I thought for a ship's cabin. He sat at a small neat desk, clamped to the wall, tight with journals and log books in rows behind him. A small coal stove sat near our feet, and I had a swift fear that it was hot and you might touch it, but I came to my senses, of course, we were at anchor and it was not lit.

"I try to tell you these details to make the picture clear to you as it always remains in my mind."

Jane rose then, and out of her desk drawer from under sheaves of papers, drew a small brown book and returned to her chair.

"These are some of the words from the log that Captain Evans gave to me on that cheerless day, my darling. I will read the words he put to paper."

'This is a bitter day in August, Tuesday, 12th 1872 Wave's dash higher than our decks...unusual storm for this time of year is upon us. Our hold is near full with casks of oil and blubber and we look for one last school of whale to finish off our sail and turn for home. Our course has taken us west of Greenland in Baffin Bay searching for the Right. Today we came in sight of the bark Tempest tossing wild in the waters, her name clear just above the waterline. She seems empty of crew and riding the waves like a ghost ship. Gale is blowing fierce and we cannot get a line to her for any help, for we are heavy with cargo. Alas, in the dark we lost sight of her.

'August 13 1872 ... Today the gale has abated and we come in sight of the Tempest once again, but now she lay on her

side, all masts in the sea and taking on water. We come alongside and send grappling hooks securing her. We find a lone sailor clinging to her boards, amid ships looking doomed to slide into the sea. I sent a crew out to get him and they managed it. He gave his name as Caleb Coffin, third mate on the Tempest, but his voice was raw and he barely spoke, parched and starved, he seemed.

'August 14.1872…Today Caleb Coffin, ill and weak is able to tell us his story and as best as I could understand his words, I enter them here:

What follows is Caleb Coffin's account:

"It was near end of July. *We be at sea for twenty–three months, suffered terrible bad luck, killing but few whales. In the first week of August we had good fortune in a fine catch taking seven Rights and a Sperm. We worked night and day, every man of us, putting all below. Early on the seventh day the men went wild and shouting, another school sighted and if caught, we could think of turning for home. When we came close, I saw the biggest Sperm ever, a monster he was, and I tell you true.*

Of thirty men sailed out of Glasgow town, twenty-seven were aboard, two deserted when we took supplies in Greenland and a second mate killed in a harpoon mishap early on at sea.

This day, Captain Door put all three whaleboats out in a wild sea with their eighteen men; he was that anxious we would have that Sperm. Nine men were left aboard, captain, helmsman, myself and six on deck to raise the boats. All went well, but as whaleboat number one drew close, and that Sperm's eye could be plainly seen, the mate's harpoon struck him broadside, yet it was not a killing blow. The wounded whale suddenly sounded and before they could slice the line, dived near a mile straight down swamping everyone. Men were flying in all directions. It was a sad sight to see, I tell you.

It seemed a moment more when the beast surfaced and came charging full force at the second boat, flipping it skyward with those gigantic flukes, breaking it all like matchsticks. The third boat made rapidly for our ship, but as it came alongside and we made ready to pull her in, the monster shot up so completely out of the water to spill the men being hauled, forcing them all into the sea. Now the whale turned its fury toward the Tempest and with one mighty crash, stove in our hull and we began taking on water.

As speedy as the beast had come, it was gone, but then the wind began to blow a gale and all I could do was to hold my arms about the grindstone amidships and hang on for dear life. With that wind a blowing and us taking on water, I never saw another human soul. I have no idea how many hours I held that way, maybe for a day, maybe more. I remember nothing else until you found me frozen to that stone and so cold...I've never been so cold.

What I do know is that I saw three whaleboats total ripped, sunken with their men swept to the ocean. I do not believe any man could live in the storm and cold of that sea."

Jane, tears in her eyes, placed a marker in the book and laid it in her lap; the reading was difficult for her. Maggie too, was visibly shaken and distressed, but after a few moments, Jane straightened, wiped her eyes and continued.

"Captain Evans read all this to me there in his cabin, while I sat with you on my lap, and as he did so, he placed some fingers to his temple, as though these words were too sorrowful to imagine. Then he looked directly at the two of us and held out his arms, asking if he might hold you for a bit. He seemed a lovely man and I know his heart was very heavy telling the tale, yet he knew it must be told. He went rocking you on his knee, touching your ruby ringlets and in that manner finished his description:

"We, on the Fortune spent all of the next few days circling the waters for miles about the wreck of the Tempest. She finally sunk completely an hour of our taking Coffin from her. We did find a few scraps of debris: some splintered boards, two steering oars, a bailing bucket and a marking flag, but never a man. It was a terrible time for the crew and myself, I will tell you, as we were so saddened for those men and their families. With Coffin in such a bad way, we started for home, forgetting any more whales. We

encountered one more storm around the tip of Greenland and on that rough and stormy night, Caleb Coffin died of pneumonia. He must have been but twenty-five. We buried him at sea the next day and with him said our goodbyes to all of the men on the Tempest. I knew Captain Door well and a fine man he was, as was your husband, Robert, little lady, I am sure. I am so very sorry to have to tell you this account."

"He looked directly into my eyes at that moment and I will always remember his kind yet piercing black eyes "Jane stopped then in the telling, sitting up very tall in her chair, looking afar off into a dark corner of the room saying firmly, "I have never told this to anyone else, I shall never tell it again, but now you know exactly what happened to my Robert, your sweet, sweet, father. Oh, Maggie, I loved him, no, *I do love him still.*

My darling, hold me very close."

Episode:

For some days following the revelation of her father's death at sea, Maggie went about her time at Grant's Tearoom and at her home in a silent mood of sadness. The mourning that *she* felt, Jane had already experienced, and she knew it would have a sobering effect on her daughter, yet seeing the complete lethargy it caused, she questioned herself even revealing it, so great was the change in the light-hearted Maggie that everyone knew.

"Will you be off to the tree trimming party at the Grant's home tonight?" called Jane as she crossed the doorsill after her trip up the back stairs from the outside coal-bin, bucket and scuttle in her hands.

Maggie sat curled up on the window seat of their bedroom, silently looking out on the quiet wintry scene below on this Sunday afternoon, counting only a few carriages making their way through the bitter cold winds. It was now a full week since their talk and she was the same dispirited girl.

"It's warm here and I have no desire to go, Mum" Maggie did not turn to her mother's question but continued holding her face in her hands, gazing out into the dusk.

"Shall I tell Mark that you are not feeling well then, when he comes to call for us in an hour's time?"

Jane knew that it would be good for her daughter just now to mingle with other young people, especially in this holiday season.

"I have been invited too you know, Maggie, and I really want to visit Molly's home and be there with her lively boys. I will not go without you. I do know that Elizabeth is to be there and a new friend of Matthew's, Sybil Grey, the young girl who works for the chemist. You know her, ay? Now, that will leave only Mark without a lady friend at the party. Molly and he will be *so* disappointed."

Finally with this last speech, Jane saw that she was breaking through the melancholy, for Maggie turned purposely to set her feet firmly on the floor.

"Oh, will you look at me, I have been so selfish, feeling sorry for me and what I've lost and look at you and what you have suffered these lonely years. You have been so very good to me and here I sit brooding. You keep a cheery face always; Mum...I *am* a wicked girl!"

Maggie was on her feet and pulling out dresser drawers "What does one wear to a tree trim; I've never been to one?"

Jane came up behind her, placing her arms about Maggie's shoulders and turning her about to see a shiny, smiling face once more. "There's my girl. Your father would be the first to shout, *'take hold, live and experience the joy of life.'* Nothing stopped him, Maggie. When Robert set out for a purpose, he lived every minute of his short life with joyfulness and he would want you to do the same. I don't care what the others may wear! We will wear our finest, with tartan McBain ribbons in our hair to show just who we are! Hurry now; Mark will be here shortly...we must be ready for the merrymaking!"

Episode:

Mark sat at the upright piano for nearly all of the evening with Maggie by his side, while the others trimmed the tree. He played brilliantly. She had no idea that he possessed this talent, and he seemed a different being as he took pleasure in the music, thus she saw an inspired young man, unlike the very quiet person when they toured the city. So there were two sides to *"her Mark,"* a phrase that Maggie said only and often to herself, and yet one that gave her shivers of delight when she thought of it.

He knew old quaint ballads, many Maggie had never heard. Here, at the Grant home the entire family made the most of the holiday with gatherings and parties of all sorts. Jane observed that Christmas held a magical spell for her friend, Molly. She had never seen a grown woman become as excited by it. Molly had popped corn by the bushel, or so it seemed to the young people stringing long chains to circle the fat tree. She had fashioned hundreds of paper cutouts, lacy and gossamer, giving the tree a filmy appeal. Finally, as the merry group of young people added the last gilded ornament and velvet bow to its branches, the entire tree took on a vision of enchantment, and it made for immense joviality as the tree trimmers joined in singing the season's songs they all knew. Even, Jane and Molly were caught up in the lilt of the melodies while directing the distribution of the fragile glass ornaments that Molly had saved for last and had kept so carefully over all of her boys' growing years.

Although the strict, reformed church took no part in the "pagan" holiday, as they so bitterly called it, Molly had been raised in a family of more lenient persuasion in the countryside near Dundee.

Each of the participants voiced regret with a sigh when the last scrap of adornment was in place, but when James brought out a high stool to firmly attach the silver star to its top, as he had every Christmas since he was tall enough to do so, Mark burst into the strains of, Oh' *Christmas Tree,* and at that, everyone joined in the chorus, while they stood back to admire their handiwork.

Maggie was absolutely enjoying her first gathering with young persons of her age. Her face glowed warmly with the exhilaration of the evening, rather than from the roaring fire that the boys fed in the fireplace.

Molly Grant kept a fine house for herself and her sons. No wonder that she worked so hard in the shop to keep this style that she had accordingly perfected. It was an old, huge two-story home on Clifton Court, kept as neat as the teashop, and this evening with the tree in place, the roaring fire and the music, it gave Maggie a glorious feeling of family.

Suddenly the young people were aware of Molly trying her best to catch their attention as she, in a grand flourish, threw open the double pocket-doors separating parlor from dining room to display a feast of such abundance, it bewildered the eye. Where had she found the time? She must have worked late into every night and all of this morning to produce such lovely food. There in beautiful display was Loch Fyne kipper, Barley soup, Oatcakes, Bacon Stovies, Potted Hough, Kippered Salmon, Cullen Skink and Aberdeen Butteries, plus for dessert, her famous Dundee Cake served with hard sauce. It was a culinary miracle to think that one woman could produce such a display.

The boys lost no time in encouraging their girls to partake of the banquet, happily devouring enormous quantities themselves.

Thus, Maggie's first real party ended with Mark escorting Jane and herself back to their lodgings through a crisp, clear, starry night with snow falling lightly about them. Mark reached for her gloved hand, and with her cheeks warming; Maggie felt his action made this magic evening absolutely superior.

Episode:

"I do believe that you could do it, Maggie! I know it will mean getting up very early and a bit of a trip to Kellvingrove, however my friends, the Grahams, could have their carriage pick you up here at home and bring you back in time for your work at the tearoom at eleven."

It was a few days after the party and Vincent Deal seemed very intent as he searched Maggie's face for an answer. He had come to their apartment late on this evening, through a winter storm, to plead this case for his friends. He explained that Henry Graham, a professor in the English Department at Glasgow University, and his wife, Cynthia, had come to him seeking his help early that same morning. Their young son, Peter, who just reached his seventh birthday, strangely and incomprehensibly had never spoken one word in all of his young life. Every physician in Glasgow, it seemed, had been consulted in search of a reason and a remedy, but all to no avail. It was becoming an obsession with both parents when all the doctors agreed that they could find no physical explanation for this malady, and had merely urged only patience and love. This, the Grahams gave generously, but now Cynthia's health was beginning to suffer, so great was her desire to have her child normal and happy. He, Vincent, as their friend, had been singled out in their desperation. There had been a series of teachers and tutors brought into the home since Peter was four, but none had benefited him.

Vincent explained that he had gone to visit Peter only that morning, on the urgent request of his parents. He found the youngster, introverted, pale and small for his age, glumly sailing a make-believe wooden toy boat about the floor of his mother's sitting room. It was this fact, that Peter could think of playing such a game, which had convinced Vincent he was in no way stupid, but only joyless and yet dogmatic in the manner in how he persisted in his effort. The visit had left Jane's employer sad and unsettled. He said that he had stayed a full half-hour trying to raise some response from the child with none accomplished; however when *his* wife, Anne, stopped in to leave three year-old Penelope with him on her way to a board meeting, he noted in only in the few moments as the children came together, that there was a distinct change in Peter's behavior. There at last seemed a spark of life and reason that was not detected formerly.

He had told nothing to the Grahams of the idea that occurred to him on his journey home, but the more he dwelled upon it, the more sense it made. He was hardly able to wait until Maggie arrived home from her work so that he could put his idea before Maggie and Jane.

"Here is what I propose, and the hope I have. Peter has not responded to all the teachers and the other adults who have tried so diligently to teach him to speak. As I see it, and clearly, a young person, who he might relate to as a playmate, might possibly evoke that hidden key to turn on his speech. Of course, children of his own age or even a bit older, could not understand what was asked of them to accomplish the task, but Maggie here, only sixteen, and already with some teaching experience, just might bridge that gap. I am sure it is worth a try, that is, if you, Maggie, could find the time? The Grahams can well afford excellent wages for your trouble. Eight until ten in the morning is a splendid time for teaching children. It would, most probably, only take the form of simple play at the beginning. We could try it on an experimental basis. Say, at the end of four weeks or so, if we see progress, we can continue, or if not, end the practice. I am so energized at the prospect; I could hardly wait to ask you what you thought of it?"

Flushed and realizing that he was repeating himself, he stopped now awaiting Maggie's answer. Jane and Maggie sat quietly, absorbed in all Mr. Deal said. It was plain by their facial expressions, that they were moved to hear of this child's sad plight . . . Jane spoke first.

"I, in no way wish to speak for my daughter. This undertaking should be entirely her decision; however, I only caution that a month's time should be the maximum for trial, as I feel that *her* health could suffer with such a rigorous schedule. I am convinced it is a most worthwhile endeavor, and I might say that she could leave the Grant Tearoom to take it on, for the need seems that great, but Molly is dependent upon her, and it would not be fair to her if Maggie should leave her employ."

Maggie waited, tolerantly, to speak and then unruffled, and as fresh as she always appeared at six on every morning, answered him firmly: "Oh, Mr. Deal, what a great challenge! If you think there is a chance that I could help Peter, I should love to try. My experience in teaching seems very limited as compared to the specialists that have seen him, but then you know this. I am certain, even if there were no wages; it is exactly the sort of test that appeals to me. Of course I will do it. When can we begin?"

Vincent beamed. He honestly believed that Maggie would be game to try. "As soon as I work it out with Cynthia, I will let you know. Let us see, today is Wednesday and Christmas falls on next Monday. I intend to close the bookshop that day and give your mother the day off. I do believe Mrs. Grant will be closing too. Perhaps we could begin on that very next day, Tuesday morning. I feel there is no time to be lost, for this child's sake."

"Fine," said Maggie gleaming, "Just fine."

Episode:

"We celebrate the Christmas Day in so many varied ways right now in Scotland," voiced Molly Grant aloud over the stirring of her Cock-a Leekie soup of Thursday. "I canna' decide what to do. Since the Reformation time, when that holy day was suppressed and labeled only Catholic rite, most shops stay open for business as usual on the twenty-fifth, and there is no real policy in the entire town. Some shops are open and others shut tight, all at the owner's whim." Her voice began to trail off again with, "I canna' decide."

Close by, Mary Dee was peeling a tub of 'taters and keeping her ears open wide to Molly's ramblings. It was near nine in the morning and all jobs were progressing well. She had only to finish the 'tater tots, fill the bridies with meats, roll the scones, cut them, and place them on the baking sheets, then set the dining room for luncheon, filling jam pots as she went. Feeling for another large potato, she thought that she could use the day, sure enough, even if it meant no pay for the leisure. She had not had a day off but her Sundays for almost a year now, and one day was not enough time to take the coach to Inveraray to visit her parents, family and possibly see old friends. If she had two days in a row, she could spend the night and return the following afternoon. She didn't mind the five-hour coach ride, each way. It would be worth that, but Mary could in no way enter into her employer's decision, in any case. Molly Grant was good to her. She had a steady job and some independence here in Glasgow, and though she had little free time, she was far better off than at home with her seven brothers and sisters and with not a poke of work in town. There she would be compelled to do 'cottage trade,' with only pennies for her keep. The food here was elegant by comparison, and although little Mary Dee did not look as though she could put away huge quantities of food, she dearly loved her victuals!

"If I knew that the engineers were going to close for the holy day, I'd have a better idea of just who I'd be hurting by the closing," Molly deliberated, as she turned to Mary, caught with her paring knife in mid-air in a small daydream about returning home.

"Take a moment now, Mary dear, and run up the back stairs to Mr. McCrimmons's office. Please, to ask him if they will be closing for Christmas Day, but be quick, so the tots will be done on time."

McCrimmons was a youngish man for the responsible position of chief engineer for Jessup and Jessup, the firm above the tearoom. He was accountable for seventeen engineers, three apprentices and four office clerks. Mary rapped sharply on the diffused glass pane of his lettered-name door. She did not read well, having only finished fourth grade, but she knew which door was his office.

"Well now, Mary Dee, what brings ye up the stair? Have ye' brought me a warm bannock or bap? I am that hungry for Molly's luncheon today."

Mary shook her head side to side and obediently voiced the query about the holiday, open or closed? She was, all the while, keyed up, holding her breath with her fingers crossed double behind her back for the right answer.

"Well, now Miss", McCrimmons, said, as he tugged at his side-whiskers and then his reddish beard, "I have just spoken to Mr. Jessup exactly on that matter and he has decided to declare a holiday for one and all. It's time enough for a spot of merry making, I say, religious or not at the end of this profitable year. Aye', there Mary, you look as though I've given you a gift."

The child was beaming from ear to ear at his pronouncement, as she quickly curtsied and turned to run downstairs. McCrimmons called out loudly after her,

"See now, that I get an extra serving of that Dundee Cake at luncheon today, my little, happy one!"

Episode:

Depending on their religious persuasion, an individual might attend some sort of service in Kirk on Christmas Eve in Glasgow, should they desire to do so. Since Maggie was completely open-minded about sects or denominations, she asked Mark if he were going to any service, and if so, she would really like to go along.

Maggie truly believed in the universal god of all mankind, as Laura had taught her very early in her early years of virtually all religions and had not restricted it to the Christian faith.

Mark was delighted that she wished to be with him again and so soon. He suffered some small frustration, when after their tour of the city, she had become ill, and that it might be his fault in some manner, though they had been so compatible earlier that day. True, she seemed very happy at the tree trim, but that was with a group and he was still unsure of her feelings for him. Now, he had the chance to escort her again, and on such a sacred day, he felt honored beyond doubt. He *was* a spiritual being, yet it mattered little which church *he* attended. He explained to Maggie that only this morning, his friend and fellow-fitter, Paul, had mentioned that he would be taking his little family to the midnight mass at St. Mary's Church in the city.

Paul was a married young man, who had worked side by side with Mark for over two years, and in this time wed his sweet Glasgow lass named Sally. They were now blest with twin baby girls. This sometimes made Mark feel as though he was 'dragging his feet,' with the two of them the same age, and Paul so well into a life pattern. Mark had never been seriously interested in any girl until Maggie McBain entered his life.

"The service at St. Mary's begins at ten-thirty on tomorrow evening, Christmas Eve, Maggie. Could we go there?" asked Mark. "I have never attended a Catholic service, but we could sit near Paul and Sally and follow whatever they do, so as not to be incorrect in the church. And it wouldn't do for you to be out alone anyway, so late in the evening. It would be grand to be together," he further pleaded his case.

Maggie just replied sweetly, "I would love to have your company at the service, Mark. It will make the holiday just about perfect."

She smiled into his eyes, and her steady gaze with its candor took him into a matchless place. He flushed while moving the pastry about on the plate before him. Could he be reading this feeling right? He had to admit that he was experiencing a definite attachment, a very high regard indeed for this lovely girl. Was he just 'eating air' as one of his mother's favorite expressions often noted, or could he believe that Maggie really cared for him as he did for her?

Her presence at the candlelit service resulted in Maggie holding one of the seven-month old twins for the entire two hours in the Kirk of St. Mary's on Christmas Eve. This act made the homily even more significant as she cuddled the sweet child sleeping peacefully in her arms. While Maggie pulled in the beauty of these mystical surroundings, Mark glanced at her from time to time, still keeping up with the ritual of kneeling and standing in proper measure. How very beautiful she seemed, the soft candle glow edged her warm auburn curls and her serene face glowed with tender expression as she held the sleeping child.

Mark was absolutely sure in that instant . . . He *was in love!*

Episode:

Only a short time had passed since that wonderful night, and on this day Maggie was weeping, crying large, salty tears that poured from her in convulsing streams. Completely alone in their rooms, she was finally permitted to lose all the pent up emotion of the last days and hours. "God, good God, why, why?" she sobbed with fists clenched in white knots as she longed to beat on something hard, anything to release this intensity of horrific hurt surging within her. She sat in the armchair, her slim body held in this rigid state for what must have been several hours, since now the rooms were in total darkness, and then she rose to feel her way to the oil lamp to light it, casting her own long shadow on the vacant wall before her.

Why, why, when *he* had so much life to live, so much to give and to share? That silent loneliness she had felt so often as a child, without either mother or father close to her, returned with engulfing waves washing over her body, as she alternately cried and sat stiff and silent in the dim room. Finally, she rose again to wrap a wool shawl about her and curled up again on the chair, her feet beneath her to sleeplessly wait out this heartbreaking night.

Mark was buried in the same plot in which his father rested. The chill January winds whipped all about the small assembly of mourners in the gray of early afternoon in Forest Haven Cemetery. Maggie stood next to Molly, tightly gripping her hand. The previously jolly, bouncy woman seemed unresponsive, stone faced, not shedding a tear. She appeared to hear no one.

As the clergyman spoke over the bronze casket, Maggie's thoughts were all on the scene in the tearoom on the first Wednesday of the New Year, only two days before. The busy luncheon crowd was just leaving when James strode through the room and stood before his mother who was taking cash from a customer. He swiftly took her into his strong arms and led her to the family table at the rear of the shop. Seeing him there in the middle of the day, Maggie knew, instinctively, that something terrible had happened, but never with a hint that it had to do with Mark. She passed the two on her way into the kitchen with a heavy tray and could not help but overhear James's deep voice calmly, yet haltingly, telling his mother of an accident at the shipyards, of a chain breaking that held a great engine, just as it was being lowered into a hull, of Mark and Paul being in place to receive it and as the faulty chain began to snap, of how Mark had lurched forward and forcefully pushed Paul out of harm's way, only to have the engine catch his body, pinning him beneath the giant, metal brute. It had crushed the chest of his handsome, likeable brother and killed him instantly.

Maggie stood beside the casket, remembering, again hearing James's words, and how she had all she could do to catch herself from dropping the heavy tray, and of how she stumbled into the kitchen with the shock screaming inside of her. Now that long day was but a blur of misery.

Feeling for the arms of the chair, she roused herself from a nightmarish sleep that must have finally overtaken her. For a few hours she was released from the despair of the finality of death and the agony of burial. She woke to hear the sound of a key in the door-lock; it was morning. Jane had been away. She had accompanied Cynthia Graham, Anne Deal and young Peter to Edinburgh for a three day stay, while they saw yet another specialist about the child's condition. Yes, now Maggie remembered, this was the day of Jane's return. All of Maggie's grief had occurred in these few days, days that now seemed an eternity. Unexpectedly, her face burned with shame; how could she be feeling so sorry for herself when poor Molly must be suffering such emptiness at this moment? She jumped to her feet, tripping over the small carpet, as her body was cold and stiff from sleeping upright in the chair. Jane, tired from the train trip, was startled to find her daughter at home. It was after eleven and she should be at the tearoom.

"Are you ill, darling?" Jane stood in the doorway, alarmed, as she gazed on the disheveled clothing and the tearstained face of her daughter, then Maggie rushed to her side with open arms.

"Oh, no Mum, no" and then, unable to hold back tears, fell into her mother's arms. "Sit...sit down, Mum, I have something to tell you, and then we must be up and quickly go right over to Molly Grant's... Mum, oh' Mum... *Mark... my Mark is gone!*"

Episode:

Slipping out of the rooms very early on the third morning following Mark's burial, Maggie felt the need for time to herself. She wanted to walk and think and to sort out her feelings in all that had happened. She wrote a note for her mother saying that she would return in time to have lunch with her at the bookshop.

The Grant Tearoom was closed for some days so that Molly could do her grieving within her own walls, as she put it. She had no wish to take her burden to the persons who frequented her shop. Maggie was thankful to have this time alone, and after she wandered through countless cold, slippery streets, she surprised herself to find that she had walked far out to the edge of town and to the cemetery that stood on a narrow hillside. She reasoned that she had traveled this far-off distance in well over an hour's time and her hands were raw with cold on this gray, bitter day. Now, getting her bearings, she made her way to the brown, newly mounded grave, where she found a curious thing. For huddling in a corner of wood crating, meant to be hauled off by the groundskeepers, was a small young cat. The tiny creature, knotted into a tight golden ball, meowed weakly as she neared the head of the grave.

"Why are you here, little one?" Maggie reached with her hand and lifted it to feel its warm fur comforting her icy fingers. "Where is your mother?" You canna' stay on this cold hill or you will freeze," and so saying she scooped the kitten even closer, tucking the fur ball into her greatcoat. Now, she felt its rapid heartbeat as she stood silently looking down at Mark's grave. This must be some sort of omen was her thought, for clearly, the McBain crest, as she had ever been taught, was the 'wild little cat.' Swiftly, she knelt down, and there, alone, save for the kitten and in a reverent manner with this wild warm comfort pressed close to her heart, she was able to speak aloud her quiet farewell to this beloved comrade, *her* Mark.

When Maggie returned to the bookshop, she placed the kitten on the wooden chair very near the old tabby still enthroned there by the potbellied fire. The wee thing moved easily to curl itself up and partially under the huge old cat and promptly went to sleep. Viewing all this, Maggie was sure she had found a warm, welcome place for this sign, this divination, the "wild little cat" that she named Golden Hope.

Episode:

"Maggie, dear, I know this is a difficult time to think of anything else but Mark and his family, yet I do want to tell you of the wonderful possibilities that we found in Edinburgh for little Peter."

Jane had laid out a wholesome, simple luncheon on the small counter near her desk in the rear of the shop, hoping Maggie would try to eat. The tearoom was still closed and she had noticed her daughter skipping most meals. Jane was justifiably worried. Now she tried to shift aiming to ease this heartache, if she could. Maggie's present sorrow to other thoughts,

"So, I'll tell you then. We arrived late in the evening and Cynthia, Peter, Anne and I stayed in a fine hotel on Princess Street. Then, early in the morning after a small breakfast of scones and tea, we were off by carriage, keeping the appointment made earlier in the week with Dr. Bell. He resides for a short time in Edinburgh at his residence there, but for only a few months visiting with old friends, for, as you know, he now lives full time in

Brantford, Ontario, in Canada. He answered the door himself to greet us, making Peter feel immediately at ease by lifting the boy up onto his great knee, all the while conversing warmly with us ladies. His gentle wife, Eliza, was there, but kept to the background until the great Dr. Bell rose with Peter, ever so confidently, to say they were going to have a private play time in his study and left us all abruptly. We sat with Mrs. Bell, who you may know is deaf, yet manages wonderfully well by signing.

In half an hour's time, the two returned hand in hand, all to the delight of Cynthia. I will say that her face took on more color that day than I had ever seen before: I knew that her glow was a result of the possibility that something affirmative was being done for her Peter. Dr. Bell made no promises then, but said, within one week, he would be in communication with the Grahams to give his assessment on Peter's case; and now our week of waiting is almost at an end. Somehow, it was with nearly girlish gaiety that the three of us and a smiling child departed from the good Dr. Bell.

I should say here, that I never thought he would recognize me. For that reason, I wished to take nothing from the serious mission we were about. Though, just as we were at the door, he put his huge hand on my head and said, "And now Jane Fraser," for he knew me only by my unwed name, "are you not going to acknowledge your old elocution teacher? Why, it must be twenty years since you graced this house with your presence. I have not forgotten you, really you look the same as that bonny lass who stood right here to recite for me . . . 'Come again and visit with us, would you? *We* would like that very much.'" And he smiled after those words at Mrs. Bell.

"What a wonderful man he is, Maggie. I do hope you will meet him one day and soon. He told us of his son, Alexander, who is now in America as a lecturer to teachers of the deaf. What a talented family . . ." Jane's voice trailed off as she gazed out into space and Maggie thought that she was reminiscing on those sweet days when she was a girl in Edinburgh and of good times past.

Episode:

The tearoom opened a week later, but nothing was the same. All the customers were kind and tried to keep Molly in good spirits, but a heavy sadness hovered over everything, and nothing could break it. Maggie, once untiring, now arrived home with no energy or desire to do anything but work and sleep. Her mornings with Peter, nonetheless, were the only bright spot in her day. It seemed that when she was with him and the two were alone, she could lose herself, oblivious to all else. They would play as two small children, and it became evident that this was the best part of Peter's day too.

It was for this reason, that when Vincent Deal again came to see Jane, to ask the favor for his friends, the Grahams, that she was not as hesitant as she once would have been. The consultation findings from Edinburgh were received and the recommendation clear; Dr. Bell would accept the boy for special treatment, but only if the entire family would take up residence in Edinburgh for a period of six months. After that time period, Dr. Bell must return to Canada. Vincent said that the Graham family was determined to set out, but could not hear of the sojourn without Peter's new found friend.

"So, you are saying that it will mean Maggie must live with the Grahams in Edinburgh from February through July?" voiced Jane, as much in recitation for her own logic, as to confirm it with Vincent, for she most certainly understood him.

"Yes, Jane, but really it will not be too difficult for you, as Maggie will assuredly have the weekends off, when she can travel home, and the salary will be most generous for her trouble. You, who understand Peter's situation so well, can appreciate what this may mean for his future and for his family's. Do say yes, Jane, and I will tell the Grahams."

And so it was arranged, Maggie would finish the month of January with Molly at the tearoom, while she found someone to take her place, and then in February would travel with the

Grahams to take up residence in Edinburgh. It was agreed with Glasgow University, that Henry could teach one semester at Edinburgh University as guest professor, while his young family attained the needed help for silent Peter.

The remainder of January was as heavy for Maggie and for all of the Grants as the leaden, Glasgow skies above. Maggie was a conscientious worker, trying to take as much pressure off Molly's shoulders as she possibly could. In fact, it was she who managed to find a good replacement for herself in Margie Staunton, a girl who had just moved into the lodgings above the bookshop. Margie seemed a capable, sweet girl, qualified as a teacher too, but finding no work this semester was happy to take Maggie's place, even if it might be only until the fall.

The Grant home was where you could find Maggie on those last Sundays in Glasgow. She and Jane stopped by early in the afternoons, bringing with them scones and jam. Elizabeth, James and Matt were there as well, to keep Molly from being alone.

"It will seem strange here without you, my dear," said Jane, as they walked slowly home in the dusk on their last Sunday visit to the Grants. "I'm so accustomed to you being in the rooms with me, I know I shall be lonesome, but then, not to dwell on negative thoughts, what you are to do in Edinburgh is important to the entire life of one little boy, to his parents, and really to you, as well. This can be one more positive experience in your process of maturity. I do believe that a force we cannot comprehend leads us in many paths only clear in later years. I have always hoped that you would one day live in Edinburgh for a time. Growing up there holds so many happy memories for me. I trust that you will find time to see all of the places that I will list for you, and you will visit some of my dear friends."

"Just, don't worry about me, Mum, I'll be just fine," smiled Maggie, and for the first time since the terrible accident, Jane saw a small brightening in her child's face and in her mind-set. She would miss her, but yes, this was without doubt, the right thing to do.

Episode:

Everything had been made ready, and on the first day of February, the entourage met in Glasgow station to embark on the train trip to Edinburgh. Cynthia Graham, looking even paler under her beige bonnet, held tightly to Peter's hand, as the child appeared excited about boarding the train. Henry was concerned, counting each piece of luggage and trunk, so that it was placed properly aboard. Sarah, their maid, bustled about, collecting baskets and boxes from the carriage that would accompany all of them in their compartment.

All the while, Maggie stood somewhat apart with Vincent and Jane, watching this scene as though it were a play and she a part of the audience. Her life was taking yet another turn, and it did seem trains were a component. Jane hugged her tightly. Mr. Deal courteously took her hand in goodbye and thanks. Maggie patted her coat pocket to be sure her journal was waiting there. Then, the little group was off, leaving the heavy smoke of Glasgow behind them.

Maggie was enchanted with the grand city of Edinburgh. Each day brought new delights. Yet she was not without the pangs of homesickness, and an hour did not go by without that sudden squeezing empty feeling in her recollection that Mark was gone forever, but these new beginnings permitted her invulnerable spirit to rise and meet the challenge of each fresh day.

Her new little family had been in their lodgings for over a month, with the worst of the winter behind them. In the bustle of this city, none seemed mindful of anything as inconsequential as weather. Dr. Bell had been a miracle for all in the family. Although Peter was not yet able to communicate by voice, between the daily sessions with Bell, and the longer hours that Maggie spent with Peter, all following Dr. Bell's plans as to materials and games, the lad was a different little person than he had been in Glasgow.

His shyness was barely apparent and a stranger might observe him as a most normal child.

The home, that had to be quickly chosen by Henry Graham, was one of the loveliest that Maggie had ever entered, except perhaps for the Deal's. Her own large room opened upon a small courtyard, where she envisioned flowers and birds abounding in the spring and summertime. The professor who owned this ancestral home was away on sabbatical, and Henry not only took his teaching job, but the rental of this home, as well. Cynthia seemed to bloom here at the sudden prospect of a well child. In fact, she began taking in the sights of Edinburgh for herself, once her household and Peter's care were running smoothly.

And after one month, Maggie too, found a much-desired indulgence, for after attending to Peter for six hours of the day, she had ample time for sightseeing. Subsequently, in these outings, there came a thorny decision, for she broke down, taking her first weeks of payment, to purchase a charming dress and bonnet in the latest style, after which, she felt grand and wicked, all at the same time.

One morning over breakfast, Maggie made bold to ask Mr. Graham if there might be any classes that she could sit in on at the university, but without changing her schedule with Peter. He was pleased to place her in these, and so by mid-March, Maggie found herself in late afternoon courses of English Literature, Logic and Rhetoric and one in Moral Philosophy. These offered interesting diversity from her daily routine, and since she had missed but three weeks of the term, Henry obtained the beginnings of each course for her, should she care to study and try for credit in these classes. For her It all seemed a dream come true.

Maggie thrived on all of it: the stimulation, to finally be able to attend a university, and such a prestigious one, the company of friendly young people, and most of all, the structure of class work, something to put her energies to was for her like being given a wonderful gift. Each morning she arose, looking forward to her day with unbounded anticipation.

It was about this time that Maggie had her first long talk with the famous Dr. Bell. He had, during the month of February, merely outlined the course that he wished for her to use with Peter, and he did so in the Graham's living room. Now in mid-March, he requested her presence at a formal dinner party in his home on a Wednesday evening, honoring his son, Alexander, who, along with his wife, had only recently arrived from America for a brief vacation. The guests included a portion of Edinburgh society, university professors and prominent business people. This was to be just the first of many hours that Maggie would spend in his 'aura.' She was to learn a great deal from this man who made such an enormous contribution for his fellow humans.

This evening, settled into a huge wing chair, and before a roaring fire, Maggie felt a luxury, not only in the fine surroundings, but also in the intellectual richness that thrilled her very soul. The company at the sumptuous dinner had been delightful and the evening sped by. A musical hour was shared in the drawing room, immediately following dinner, consisting of cello, flute and violin. What a gracious mode of living, thought Maggie, this enjoyment of music professionally performed, and in one's own home, truly an extravagance that she would not soon forget.

Now, in the last hour of the evening, Dr. Bell sat in the duplicate chair to hers before the hearth, while Mrs. Bell, Alexander, his wife, and Edward Ferguson, publisher of the Edinburgh Gazette, the leading newspaper of the day, all relaxed on various couches and chairs about the warm room.

All other guests had departed, leaving only this small circle to enjoy the stimulation of serious conversation in the relaxed atmosphere. This was the end of a perfect day, thought Maggie.

She spoke little, only when spoken to, but pulled in and remembered every sentence. These learned persons talked of world conditions, their concern for the poor, and most especially of the city's lunatic asylum, now a major sadness for one and all.

They talked of the countless persons living in miserable conditions, without means of support, those who were being placed in this institution unjustly, only to live out their lives in wretched, filthy surroundings. The group felt that they must play a part in righting this wrong. The editor-owner, Mr. Ferguson told of a campaign that his newspaper was about to begin in defense of the poor. Finally, the evening ended with Maggie, settled back into the soft cushions of the carriage dispatched to take her home, reflecting and savoring each portion of her first truly adult gathering.

By May, her life in Edinburgh took on a satisfactory pattern. She was able to make two trips to Glasgow to see Jane and Molly, and on this coming weekend, plus one added day, Jane would travel to Edinburgh as a guest of the Grahams. Mr. Deal agreed to care for the bookshop in order that she might visit her hometown.

Maggie was elated. She had saved her visits of entire sections of the city, those that were most memorable to Jane, so they might share them.

Peter was growing more confident with each sunrise, and the Grahams insisted Maggie should be free to accompany Jane, and with no concern for her lessons with their son during her visit.

Her class work was nearly at an end. She was regretful for this; it had become invigorating, and she pondered what might fill her excess time in June and July, but that answer was not long in coming.

This was the Thursday before her mother would arrive, and just after a spirited game of "Goose" with Peter and putting him down for his nap, the sharp rap on the doorknocker brought to the doorstep a caller in one Edward Ferguson, editor of the Edinburgh Gazette. This dapper gentleman, in his mid-forties, hat in hand, stood now in the foyer. This was announced to Maggie by maid Sarah, "a gentleman to see Miss Maggie McBain." Then Sarah curtsied, her face in a most perplexed manner.

"Mr. Ferguson, how good to see you," said Maggie, extending her hand. Edward was now a familiar friend, for

Wednesday evenings had become a regular occurrence at the home of Dr. Bell, as he had exclaimed, "he so enjoyed the company of young persons with their fresh ideas." And so he had made these evenings a weekly leisure pursuit, just after his son returned to America. Maggie, never excluded from the guest list, was embarrassed one evening, when Dr. Bell said aloud, that he so prized her company that he would maintain it for as long as he might do so!

The varied assemblage on these evenings consisted of musicians, writers, the scholastic world, trades persons and scientists, all interesting, and the gathering always included Edward Ferguson, the good friend of Dr. Bell. These evenings held an endless wealth of resource for Maggie, for this exchange of countless opinions soon became the highlight of her week. After each one, her pen was busy on the pages of her journal, capturing all that was believed and revealed. It gave her purpose, in that she found a way of life that was fresh and stimulating as well as her new sense of maturity.

"I know this may seem impertinent, Miss McBain, and I should have sent my card ahead to ask if I might call, but I was just passing Moray Place on business, and remembering that you lived here with the Grahams, I . . . I," he stammered here slightly, "I hoped that I might see you and perhaps converse with you for a while . . . that is, are you busy right now? Could it, would it be, ah, convenient for you to come for a drive? My carriage is just at the curb and the lovely flowers are beginning to bloom all about Castle Gardens. I would so enjoy showing them to you."

Edward Ferguson was a widower. Dr. Bell had told Maggie all about him one evening when she had lingered and was last to leave their little fellowship. Edward had lost his wife in their first year of marriage when she was only eighteen, a lovely girl, Dr. Bell explained, who simply took a cold, and within a week's time was dead, unable to counter its effects on her slight body. He told of how Edward then plunged into his work, exhausting himself for years afterward, trying to overcome his great loss. Dr. Bell spoke of his own affection for the serious young man of his son's age, who tried to use the power of the press to make the people of Edinburgh see injustice in their society and take a firm stand against all wrongs. "A great leader he will become, one day, this I predict," Dr. Bell had said with satisfaction.

Episode:

From the very beginning, after being introduced to Edward, Maggie felt some sort of kinship. He was a brilliant man who she looked forward to seeing on their Wednesday gatherings; however, she respected him as a man old enough, she judged, to be her father, as there were at least twenty-four years between them. She had listened attentively when he espoused lengthy treatises that were very wise, to be sure, yet as he stood before her now, she was taken aback. He appeared nervous. She had no idea that he might call, and less that he would ask her to join him for a carriage ride. She thought quickly, she must not hurt his feelings by a curt answer, but if this was a courting sort of ride, as she observed, what must she reply? Should she seek out Cynthia's help and ask permission? What was correct and proper? He certainly would not have proposed such an excursion if it were not innocent. She felt the unmannered mores of a highland girl in this precise, ceremonious society made her particularly wanting. Yet, she answered in her calmest, adult voice, reasoning it through hastily.

"Of course, Mr. Ferguson, I would love to see the gardens. Just let me go to tell the Grahams where I will be and when I'll return. How long shall we be away?"

Edward, as flushed as any schoolboy, answered quickly, "Oh, surely two hours will be time enough. Thank you, Maggie, thank you."

That lovely trip through Castle gardens was one that would come back to Maggie's memory many times in later years as a sweet, healing journey. To be sure, the gardens were a beautiful sight, but on this particular day with all of springtime bursting forth: green buds swollen, hyacinths heavy with perfume at every turn of the carriage, the sweeping vistas of tulip, iris and daffodil, all made this trip much like a fairytale pilgrimage for an incredibly grown-up girl.

Edward knew every small, charming area of the extensive flower trail, calling out each variety by name. Maggie, who had never studied botany, sat utterly captivated. For during this concise time, her face aglow in the cool twilight, she lost the somber burden, carried so heavily since January, to finally find a peace within. Edward caught sidelong glances at her face, as he reigned in the mare, turning this way and that on the multifarious pathways, and it was with a peculiar sense of happiness that *he* found himself, precisely as he had hoped it might be.

No thoughts now of those labored moments, earlier this day, when he felt anxious in asking her on this excursion. For the first time in these many long years, since his wife's death, he had finally ventured out with a lady, and he was enjoying it very much, indeed.

The days were growing longer, and with the extended light, Maggie's eagerness to cram every moment with intense pursuits like this now seemed urgent to the determined girl. Life had once again taken on meaning!

The following day Maggie and her charge, Peter, sat on the huge oriental carpet which all but filled the library floor. The two were at play in this sunny month of May. And it seemed unusually lovely with its geometric patterns of dark red crossed by sunbeams at right angles as they filled the room with brilliance. Peter loved to use its wide borders as his pretend roads for the wooden carriages, horses and trains. It was in this make believe occupation that Maggie found herself, she becoming the great trestle as she hunched over to permit the train to climb over her back. There was easiness about their play now, for after these many months, she felt much as an older sister to a prized little brother. She never pressured him to any lessons, but rather found this unhurried, imaginary world permitted him to release the silent child who was imprisoned inward, giving *him* a sense of freedom.

Peter was on the far border of the carpet while Maggie sat with her back to him, now reaching to choose a story from the low bookshelf, while awaiting his make-believe, four o'clock mail train from Perth. She talked to him incessantly of just such things. Her theory: the more words he heard, the more he understood, accordingly, the more he might say one day. As the child came to the corner of the carpet with his toy train, he suddenly turned his wrist sharply, it hurt and he was upset. In his urgent need of her attention, he uttered loudly, "Mah-gee, Mah-gee." She spun around in the most astonished manner, hardly believing her ears. The lack of her quick response for insistent aid made him only repeat, "Mah-gee."

"What did you say, Peter Graham, what did you say?" By this time she was on the floor beside him, making sure his wrist was merely strained, but Peter, so self-important, would not stop hearing the sound of his own voice. Smiling from ear to ear, and gazing proudly up at her, he kept repeating her name, quite forgetting the smarting wrist.

The slight, seven year old, looked surprised when Maggie swept him into her arms and literally burst into the drawing room where Cynthia and Henry sat reading. Cynthia's first impulse was terror. She lived with the constant fear that some dreadful thing might befall her son, but when she saw two beaming faces, her heart calmed.

"What has happened?" were Henry's words when Maggie let the child fall into the soft cushions of the couch.

"Here is what has happened," smiled Maggie broadly. She looked expectantly at Peter, who with no additional prompting, opened his mouth, very conscious of their happiness, as his parents gasped, for much like a year old baby, he repeated over and over again for their delight, "Mah-gee, Mah-gee, Mah-gee," pointing his finger at her, while he beamed incessantly.

Episode:

Dr. Bell greeted his visitors with all the savor of a man in his sixties when two lovely ladies come to call. Jane wished to make his home the first stop on the long planned outing with her daughter in exploring Edinburgh once again. She was still feeling some guilt in her last visit to this home, when she had not reintroduced herself to the dear man who played such a part in her growing up years, but she found that little explanation was needed. He was a very astute, understanding intellectual, and not much escaped his perception. He spoke of how he felt that he knew Maggie now as well as he knew Jane, mainly because of their Wednesday evening gatherings. Then he spoke to Jane of when *she* was a lass of sixteen, with Maggie relishing every moment of their conversation.

By this day, he had heard the news of little Peter and they talked of it. The Grahams had lost no time in bringing the boy to him and thanking him for the miracle of speech, which Maggie and he had worked for their son. True, he told them, now would only start the education process, as Peter learned to shape his words and make them sound like our own. It would be just the same as any child learning to speak, but with Peter the development would move ahead rather speedily. However he urged the Grahams to be patient in the progression.

Mrs. Bell sat in the corner of the room smiling, thoroughly enjoying the pleased satisfaction of her famous husband. He had a habit of pantomiming the stories that he told, for the two had developed this form of language between them: nothing was missed, she understood completely. Tea was served, and as the delightful afternoon came to an end, Dr. Bell asked a most reasonable and pertinent question.

"And where will you be attending university, Maggie, right here in Edinburgh, I presume, for there is no finer?"

The girl smiled, and responded quickly:

"No, Dr. Bell, I have a genuine desire to see the new lands over the sea; my senses seem to be pulling me there. I have been reading of the schools in Nova Scotia, and since Dalhousie University in Halifax has just opened its doors to women, I believe this is my *absolute* choice.

"Well, then, you must *have* heard of the test and the scholarship and are trying for it. " He expounded, "it is a truly great opportunity for any student. Why, I received those papers on the scholarship about one month ago." he said, with his hand stroking the long white beard. "I had no idea you had thoughts of Dalhousie, Maggie." As he saw her shake her head in wonder, he said, "Goodness, I should have called it to your attention much sooner."

He crossed the room and began rummaging in the huge pile of documents that covered his desk. "It should be here, dear, I know I read it." And after a few suspenseful moments for Maggie..."Um, yes, here it is, why the date for the examinations is June 2, that's next Friday, by Jove . . . what a coincidence!"

Thus, Maggie found herself, on Tuesday morning, engrossed in all manner of textbooks, spread out on the floor of her sunny room at the Graham's. Her weekend had flown by with Mum, for they toured Edinburgh Castle, the Camera Obscura, Grassmarket with all its old shops, Cannongate Kirk, then, the high Kirk of the city, St. Giles, and finally the palace of Holyroodhouse. Both mother and daughter had strained legs and sore feet, but the pleasure of seeing all of these sights and together would never be replaced in their memories.

Before Jane caught her late train back to Glasgow, the Grahams entertained with a grand dinner party. There, in conversation of Dalhousie and the scholarship, Cynthia and Henry insisted Maggie hold off any effort with Peter, but to study for her tests on Friday. Jane was thankful for the encouragement these new friends gave, while they expressed their enduring gratitude for the girl who had given them the voice of their son.

With no idea of what the examination might contain, her studies seemed fruitless. Her inadequacy in so many subjects became more and more apparent as she tried in picking up one volume and then another, finally to become totally dismayed. Her weakness seemed greatest in mathematics and the sciences, so she vowed, rather than even trying to learn more of these in the few days, she would study only the subjects that she knew reasonably well.

The test was to be given at Edinburgh University. Maggie chose to walk the many blocks over brown cobblestone to the far side of the city in the early morning damp to clear her mind. How many good people she had met in this past year! Now walking through the streets of 'old reeky,' she was overcome with a sense of new beginnings, for her life seemed open to a bright future. While she had come to love these two old cities, and her beautiful Skye, she felt the heady pull to her uncharted destiny in the new world ever stronger.

She had first heard of Dalhousie from a fellow student. He told her of its founding in 1820 by George Ramsay as a model in the Scottish system, founded to instruct the youth of New Scotland in the classics and philosophical studies, primarily. These were the classes that precisely interested Maggie. It was founded with religious toleration for all persons and this she also greatly admired. It had seemed almost fate, when the young man, Samuel McLeod, told her of the sizable grant that his uncle had made to this university in 1882 for its expansion. He said his parents were considering sending him to it for his next term. When he spoke of it then, it all seemed beyond her wildest dreams, yet, she had saved most of the generous salary that the Grahams provided and this could see her through one year of a university. There was, of course, the passage to Nova Scotia to be considered too. A scholarship could mean all the difference. It would allow her to not have to work while attending, but devoting all of her energies to studies.

By the time these thoughts had run around her head, she found herself standing with some thirty other students at the doors of the science lecture hall on the university grounds. The broad, gray stone steps were lined with quiet, intense young people, mainly male.

The test began sharply at eight o'clock and lasted four full hours. Given by a serious science professor and his assistant, it was the first examination Maggie had taken since she qualified to teach the little ones their fundamentals on Skye. As the sheets of paper were handed out, she felt strangely calm and even grateful. Her fear of failure vanished and in its place the challenge of the task took over.

The administrator instructed at the outset that three prizes were to be awarded if *any* of the students qualified; otherwise, none would be given. One was the Waverly prize, strictly in the sciences. The second was for literature, The James DeMille prize. The third was in languages.

DeMille had been a prestigious teacher at Dalhousie and until his death in 1880. He had inspired such authors as Wallace for his *Ben Hur*, and Sienkiewicz's for his *Quo Vadis*. The prize was to be presented in the name of DeMille. The third prize was to go to the student best versed in classical language. Maggie's heart nearly sank when that prize criteria was read. She quickly decided to omit the language area entirely, to make a good attempt at the sciences, but to expend most effort in the literature category. Once begun, her answers came to her swiftly, as though some unknown person had taken over her pen. She could not believe the amount of information she had stored with her pouring over books. Entire pages, seemed to stand out before her, and she was able to recall countless passages of text, word for word. Finally when the test was over, she fairly flew along through the sunny, warm streets, humming old highland tunes and smiling broadly at each passerby. It was a lovely, lovely feeling.

Episode:

Edward Ferguson sat comfortably in the green velvet armchair in the Bell living room on this last Wednesday of July. His anticipation to see Maggie again was great. For this was to be a small, closer group when she arrived in this gathering of friends, for most of their discussion assembly was out of the city, off to the Highlands or the vacation spots on the North Sea.

The Bells had not yet come down from their rooms upstairs, and Edward realized, his own eagerness caused him to be very early this evening. It was this change in his usual precise habits that now troubled him. He was acutely conscious that his affection for Maggie was definitely shaping and changing his exceedingly set ways.

The two had seen each other frequently over the springtime and early summer, ever since that first carriage ride through the gardens, and he now considered them good friends. As he sat there so early, he felt a bit foolish in his impatient desire to see her again, to feel the closeness of her presence, for he had to confess to himself, that this woman was in his waking thoughts much more than he could ever admit to others, or to her.

And so, he was quite unprepared for the news that burst forth into this quiet room with the arrival of a jubilant young woman. Maggie fairly flew into the parlor, her hair falling in those bronze tendrils about her ears in that most disconcerting way, thought Edward, her face glowing with much more than the warm July day, as she spoke hurriedly upon seeing him sitting there.

"Oh, sweet Edward, I am so happy. I must tell you my news right away. It has just come by post," and she waved a letter-size sheet in her right hand. "I still cannot believe it, but I have won the DeMille Prize to Dalhousie, and I will be off to Nova Scotia to attend college in September. Oh, dear Edward, dear friend, can you believe how pleased I am?"

Edward wished, with all of his heart, to share the joy of this exuberant woman, for she no longer seemed a girl, but a full grown being that *he* seemed destined to lose before she was won. His faint, but real hope was now shattered, and by one piece of paper. But, not to show his true feelings seemed his only saving grace. Thus, he stood and turned to her gaiety, "How wonderful for you, my dear Maggie McBain, you certainly deserve this and every good thing that life has to offer you." He touched her shoulder gently and then quickly looked away.

Episode:

Two large trunks and a valise stood open on the floor of the untidy apartment, so unlike their normally neat home. Maggie stood in the midst of it all, in a flurry of excitement, trying on skirt and vest to see what might need mending, what she would take, and what to leave behind. Her books, alone, half filled the steamer trunk.

"I have a question for you, Darling. Would it take any happiness from your journey, that is, would it make it less satisfying, if you were to be accompanied by an ever watchful, doting mother?" Jane had phrased her question in her sly Scot manner, as she was so often inclined to do. She sat, skillfully repairing the edging of a hem and dared not look up to meet her daughter's eyes, as she voiced her query.

"Mum, what, you mean, you could possibly leave Scotland to come with me?" Maggie's eyes were wide and incredulous. The thought had never entered her mind. With a gasp, she whirled about and clasped her mother's hands in hers, forcing Jane to look into her face.

"You *could* come along? We *might* afford it? Oh, Mum, there is nothing in this world that I should like better. I didn't know...I dared not hope..."

Once Jane saw the true pleasure that this idea had upon her only child, she grinned.

"We have come into a bit of money, Maggie, in fact, a generous amount of money. The Grahams have set up a trust fund for you in appreciation of your work with Peter. They did not wish to tell you of it until the time of your departure, but with it and the sum that I have set aside for your college from my work at the bookshop, and because of the scholarship, I do think we could manage nicely. We can, in all probability travel to Nova Scotia together. Certainly, I will have to find some sort of employment there to cover our living costs, but yes, I do believe it can work!"

It was determined then, and on the 20th day of August of 1886, Maggie and Jane McBain, early on a misty morn, left the port of Glasgow for the new world.

A small group of well-wishers were on hand at dockside to bid a fair voyage and happiness to two women who had permanently touched their lives. The Vincent Deals were there, the Henry Grahams with Peter, Molly, James and Matthew Grant, but it was Edward Ferguson, who had journeyed from Edinburgh to accompany the ladies aboard the vessel and to see them to their stateroom. Edward held extremely tight to Maggie's hand until the ships bell rang for the last call for visitors to take their leave. As the ship at last slipped into the seaway, with these two women standing on deck, waving to their friends, each wondered if they should ever meet such wonderful comrades in their new home, if they might see these cheering, loving persons ever again...and most of all, what did their future have in store?

Episode:

Nova Scotia 1886-1887

Unlike many of their fellow passengers, neither Maggie nor Jane, felt the least bit queasy or in any discomfort on one single day of their passage. To the contrary, they were the first to rise from a dreamless sleep to take their oatcakes and tea in the dining room, always reveling in even the smallest curiosity of the venture. When the dolphins played in the waves off the bow, when a passing ship was sighted, with the leaden feel of the ship in the cool of night or the constant roll as she surged through the late summer seas, all of these were pure joy to the inseparable pair.

The passage was over all too soon for both of them, yet it had given them time to write copiously in their journals, to pen letters back to Scotland, to have long talks in their turns about the deck, while getting to know themselves and each other all the better. It felt as though the open sea was conducive to sharing innermost thoughts, and they took pleasure from what they found in each other.

Fellow travelers speculated that these were sisters, off on some quest, much as the teashop owner had discerned when they were reunited. For both of them, radiant in the brisk ocean air, gained new assurance and beauty in their decision for this journey of fresh beginnings, with every new dawn.

Jane wrote a very important letter to her friend, Laura McGreagor, on Skye, thanking her for the raising of her extraordinary child, while Maggie penned a sensitive letter to Edward Ferguson. Somehow, only in the moments of good-bye, did she come to realize his deep feelings for her. In her letter to him, she tried, with all the logic she could gather, to make him know that she would probably not be returning to Scotland or perhaps not for a very long time, if ever at all. It was her dearest hope, that he might find a lovely Edinburgh woman to share his civility, his knowledge and most of all his warmth. She sent her sincere feelings for him as a true comrade, and to know that he would never be forgotten. Then, early one bright morning, the port city of Halifax was shining in colors of soft pinks and lavenders, with sea maws circling in ponderous arcs above, making their presence known by the incessant clamor these conveyed.

All at once they were docking, and hurriedly aware of a budding continent beneath their feet. The customs procedures took most of the afternoon on this bright September day, but by early evening Maggie and Jane were settled into the new Hotel Royal Thistle, just a few blocks into this charming city. Maggie was very eager to walk out to see the university and all the sights of town before darkness settled in; however, in order to curb her daughter's explorations, Jane feigned exhaustion and asked if they might begin early on the next morning after a good sleep on land. They ate a modest dinner in the hotel dining room and retired early.

Maggie lay awake, for what seemed to her hours, in the cool, immaculate room, next to her mother while all the thoughts of new beginnings raced through her brain. However, one small poignant sight kept occurring to her, despite her concerted effort to block it in these hours before dawn. Had Mum noticed, or had she merely tried to keep her daughter's attention diverted from the sight? For just as their ship entered the picturesque harbor, with all of its welcoming, pleasant appearance, there, far to the left, in separate berths, a small fleet of sailing ships stood anchored, rocking and creaking to a tune all their own. Maggie saw not a soul about them, but their masts waved like dark sentinels, keeping her melancholy memories alive. Maggie was sure; these were whaling ships making ready to set to sea.

Days seemed to fly that autumn. The settling in fell amazingly into place, like the pieces in a jigsaw puzzle. On the morning after their arrival, the hotel-keeper gave them the name of Mrs. Wallace, who kept an orderly lodging house, only four blocks up and across the business district, Quite surprisingly, it was just one street from Dalhousie University, situated on the Grand Parade.

Mrs. Wallace showed Jane and Maggie a lovely room on the second floor of her home, overlooking the park. Petite, friendly, Agnes Wallace, a widow, made them feel immediately welcome, plus there was a distinct bonus, she turned out to be a remarkable cook.

Next, Jane found a position as assistant librarian at the university, thanks again, to Mrs. Wallace, who knew the post was open, as it was previously held by her friend's daughter who had just married and stopped working. The pay was modest, but enough to meet their practical needs, for surprisingly, living costs in Halifax were low, by comparison with Edinburgh or Glasgow. Again, all their travel could easily be reached on foot. Even the harbor, with all its bustle and attraction, was only an eight-block walk, and chiefly downhill. This feature drew the pair to its spectacle nearly every weekend.

Maggie's classes were well balanced in Literature and Rhetoric, Mathematics, Modern Language, and Philosophy, leaving her ample time to join both the weekly debating society and the student newspaper, the Dalhousie Gazette. This university was growing rapidly; she discovered medical courses had begun in 1870 and the law school was instituted in 1883. This was a dream fulfilled, for studying full time was as exhilarating as anything previous in her lifetime, with each professor and fellow student a stimulus. Maggie prized learning and wished to show interest in each person she met. Women had been admitted only five years before in 1881 and were much in the minority. Professors here, recruited from all about Europe, held excellent credentials. True, her personal goal in education was not yet clear, however, the pursuit of knowledge certainly was. Maggie's wish to excel in everything she tried was obvious to all.

The days now took on a predictable flow. Jane and Maggie rising early each morn, as was always their custom, taking a small breakfast with Mrs. Wallace in her cheery oblong dining room, and each new day busy with bright beginnings.

By the middle of October, Jane began to speculate just how they might celebrate Maggie's eighteenth birthday. It seemed to Jane that it would be presumptuous to try to include new school friends, and besides, she really had no extra funds for such a gathering. When she broached the subject with Maggie, her concerns were over, for her daughter had definite plans for her special day.

"Mum, since my birthday falls on a Sunday this year, I would like nothing better than to pack a picnic basket with lunch and go into the countryside to see the sights that are about us. It would be a grand adventure, just we two. If the weather cooperates we could rent a rig and horse from Mr. Campbell, the blacksmith on Cooley Street and spend the entire day out in the open air. What do you say?"

So it was agreed, Sunday, October 1887, found one pleased mother beside a buoyant Maggie, sitting high on the buckboard of the phaeton-style carriage behind a gentle bay, picnic basket securely stowed between them and a passionately motivated eighteen year old at the reins.

The weather had been seasonably cool in the beginning of October; in fact, frost had formed in the early mornings, but in the past days they were resplendent with dazzling sunshine, making temperatures rise to the mid-sixties. "The Little Summer of St. Luke" did not disappoint. As it repeated itself once more in Maggie's lifetime, exactly as it had on so many birthdays in the past, it added a special joy to her spirits.

Once, out of sight of the town at the first crossroads, Maggie turned the horse southward, hoping to explore the road that generally followed the shoreline. This high stretch of land, offered a magnificent view of the ocean's surf with multitudes of shorebirds hovering over the gray slabs of rocks below. They marveled to one another of this similarity to their own beautiful Skye. Having traveled in this manner for over an hour, they agreed to rest at a jutting shelf of huge slabs of stones that seemed to stretch as far as eyes could see. Tying the bay to a lone tree, just off the dirt road, and giving him a drink from the water they brought along for this purpose, the two ventured forth to spread their cloth and to place their picnic basket on the rocks in full view of the Atlantic Ocean.

Maggie guessed that it must be very near noon, by the sun high overhead and the rumblings in her own empty stomach. As they ate the delicious sandwiches that Agnes Wallace had prepared, they were ecstatic to share this gorgeous new land on such a beautiful day. Leaving the basket on the broad plateau of stone, the two carefully made their way over each new boulder in exploration, holding their long skirts high with each new discovery, yet fearful they might catch a foot between the slabs. The crevices were, at times several feet across, demanding an actual leap to the next flat rock.

Here, no human could be seen, only the gulls to watch the laughing, exuberant pair, acting more like school girls, than mother and daughter. Below them roared the pounding surf, above, incredible blue sky. The entire scene seemed a spellbinding cameo in time.

The hours slipped by swiftly and Maggie realized that her mum must be near collapse, for her own young legs were starting to feel extreme strain on the unyielding stone. They had come full circle and could see the carriage with horse standing patiently in the shade of the tree ahead, when, with a sudden shriek, Jane, just behind Maggie, was suddenly on her knees, her hands on her leg, twisting and turning this way and that, for her foot had lodged between two stones and caught firmly.

The small leather boot was hidden from sight, with only her ankle to be grasped as she moved about, so as to try to free her foot.

"Oh, darling, what have I done to us? I was looking ahead at the road and the horse and missed my footing." Jane wailed as she continued to tug and pull at the ankle.

"Stop, now, a minute, Mum, and let us see what we can do. You will be hurting your leg if you continue like that." Maggie leapt cautiously around her annoyed mother to peer on the other side of the stone and see how seriously Jane fared. She knelt down peering into the chasm to see the foot clearly, but wedged so tightly it appeared intractable.

"I believe the weight of your body, forced your foot in, and at the same time you lost your balance, but we cannot exert that much power in pulling on it to force your leg up and out without injuring you. Do you think that you may have sprained your ankle? Are you in pain? Do stay calm now, Mum," Maggie said soothingly, touching her mother's hair. "We'll get you out somehow . . . I'll just go to the wagon and see if there might be some tool that may help . . . I'll be right back."

She hurried off to the carriage in search of what, she could not imagine, but this might give Jane time to calm herself and Maggie to think. As she scurried over the last of the huge stones, and onto firm ground, she began to realize the real crisis in this drama, for not only were they two females in this deserted stretch of granite, but the afternoon was nearing its end and a moderate breeze had picked up. Branches of the tree above the horse's head were moving briskly. They should be on their way back to Halifax very soon for in the October darkness they would certainly not find their way.

The few metal tools in the box were disappointing. Only the crowbar might be of some help.

She grasped it firmly and began to set off, but as she looked up the road, she made out a shape coming towards her. As it took silhouette it appeared to be a man on horseback. Leisurely but surely he made his way up the road. Her first instinct was relief, for perhaps it could mean help, but then a sudden panic seized her what if it was someone who might rob or harm them? She stood there wavering, first looking back at her helpless mother, and then to the form coming on, now clearly defined as a large man on a chestnut horse.

When he saw her slim figure, the carriage, a woman in apparent distress and Maggie standing there straight and resolute, waiting for him to approach, a crowbar in her hand, the man urged his horse onward rapidly. In just seconds he was beside Maggie. As he peered down from what seemed to her, an enormous height with a questioning look on a face so open, so kindly, all fears vanished. She stood gazing up into a gentle face, and immediate trust and calm invaded her fear, with a pleased modesty taking its place.

"My mum has caught her foot between the stones" Maggie spoke up now loud and clear, "We have not been able to free her. I was about to try again and came back here to see what I could find." So saying, she held up the heavy crowbar with both of her small hands.

The large man did not utter a word but dismounted hurriedly to stand a full foot above her. He seemed not young nor old, only solid and amiable. Maggie quickly gestured to Jane sitting on the huge stone.

"Let me see if I can be of help, if you will allow me?" The man's voice was deep and sympathetic and he stood aside to allow Maggie to precede him on their way to Jane.

"Of course, do see if you can help us, I am so glad that you came by just now." she answered. She moved the short distance toward the man, passing the crowbar to him as she did so. As they walked on over the rocks, Maggie offered, "She is not in pain, although I fear if we pull on the leg, we could injure her." Now they stood above the self-conscious Jane, still pulling and straining to be free.

"Good afternoon, madam." He doffed his cap, "Sorry for your accident. Please allow me to see if I can be of assistance." Jane merely nodded and blushed.

The man was on his knees now, swiftly taking stock of the incident. Assessing the seemingly impossible situation, he peered, as Maggie had, into the deep opening and saw the boot held fast. He laid the bar down on the stone and attempted to put his large hand in beside the boot, to no avail. Finally laying his full form flat on the rock, he managed to forcefully wedge his hand into another opening, beside her foot, and with strong fingers, pulled at each of the tiny buttons, removing them from the black leather boot, straining and scraping his fist on sharp edges as he did so. At last, after the sixth and final button was removed, he told Jane to try and lift her foot once again, while he held tightly to the boot. With a sudden pop, Jane fell backward, and her small, bootless foot was free from its prison.

Startled and embarrassed, Jane began to laugh, more out of relief than humor. She started to stand up with Maggie's help, and began to hobble toward the road, when so quickly, neither of the women realized what was happening, the broad-shouldered stranger sprang to his feet and with the ease of a woodsman lifting a twig, swept her into his arms, saying as he moved, "Hold on now, this will never do, I will just transport you to your carriage, my lady." He was off with mammoth strides, while Maggie grabbed the picnic basket and the boot, to move over those same cracks, careful not to repeat the mishap.

This threesome made their way into town, all riding in the carriage, the chestnut tied behind them. They arrived at Agnes Wallace's boarding house just as darkness set in with a soft rain falling on the city. Once again, Jane was picked up and carried into the parlor, for by this time, her ankle had swollen to double its size, red and sore. She evidently had a sprain and a doctor was called to tend to it. After Jane was snugly settled in her bed and finally asleep, Maggie lingered on the front porch determined to see their defender to his horse. She then thanked him profusely for his kindness to both of them. He protested that it was nothing that any fellow traveler would not have done, and gladly. He politely said it was a *true pleasure.* This made Maggie blush freely and she was quite unable to account for this new phenomenon at all.

She asked if he must ride back on the road they had come to reach his home, supposing he lived in that area of the gray stones, but he said, no, he must return the horse to the livery near the harbor where they too had rented the carriage, as it was not his, but only a hire and he also said he would be happy to return their coach and horse, as well, saving them that trouble.

Maggie looked up into his broad, tanned pleasant face and said shyly," Of course, you can, that would be very kind. Do you know I, that is, *we* don't even know your name?"

Leaning forward, towards her from his height, he exclaimed, "Why, that's right, I'm sorry that I haven't introduced myself. My name is John, John Dix . . . Captain John Dix, that is, miss, miss..."

"Maggie, Maggie McBain . . . Captain Dix, and please come back whenever you like . . . and thank you once again." Upon which she turned her slight form and quickly disappeared into the house, auburn hair flying, and her face feeling that strangely uncontrollable blushing sensation once more. She felt grateful for the darkness, hiding this warm, new, strange occurrence.

Captain Dix's appearance at the Wallace boarding house became a daily state of affairs as the sprain slowly healed. Agnes

Wallace took pleasure in asking this kind benefactor to take tea with the ladies when he arrived each afternoon. His visits conveniently coincided with Maggie's return from classes at the university, every day at about four o'clock.

John was a reserved, almost shy guest in the company of the ladies, especially for someone his size, but possibly, since he admitted that he was not versed in the proper etiquette of taking tea, he did seem eager to learn. It was evident to all that he had his own secret reason for his concern of Jane's mishap. *He* might not realize it; however, his daily visits were fooling no one. He listened politely to the conversations, yet offered nothing of himself, only asking about Maggie's studies. He also was very interested in Scotland and their voyage to Nova Scotia. Jane offered most of the answers to satisfy his questions. She spoke of using this healing time to catch up on her reading. She asked Maggie to bring her the latest books from the school library to become familiar with them for her student's sake. The current novel that she was reading, and discussed at this teatime, was by Robert Louis Stevenson, and she made it very plain of her pride of the fellow Scot. She reviewed this book for their guest, John, saying he might like to read it at his leisure.

Now it was again a Sunday morning. A week had passed since that fateful day on the gray stones and Jane was up and about once again. John had no excuse to come to call in the afternoon as he had done every day for the past week. This he realized as he strode briskly up the path to the white clapboard house on this cool, bright morning. He viewed the ladies, assembled in the parlor, through the double-hung window of the porch. They sat, lingering over their morning tea when he tapped on the front door. Mrs. Wallace greeted him, and as he stepped in, cap in hand, he uneasily asked Jane if Maggie might be allowed to walk with him down to the harbor. She gladly agreed, and it was Maggie who now suffered unease for some moments, as she felt likened to a child, having her mother queried if she might come out to play!

But then, quickly realizing that John was trying to be proper and ceremonial about his words, she felt warm and flattered, all at once.

This week of seeing him daily had been wonderful. She hardy could keep her mind on her studies as she so looked forward to his call of each afternoon. She dared not, and really had not, thought that it could come to an end, but of course, it would when he had no excuse to call. At this moment, as she was running up to her room, to pull her coat from the wardrobe and meet John in the hall for their stroll, she could not explain just why her heart was beating wild in her chest.

The days had turned much cooler as it neared November and Maggie wrapped the coat snug about her slender body. She went off hatless, the ringlets of hair falling about her temples as she moved sprightly, walking just in front of John on the path to the road, wondering if she would now hear more about this man, away from Jane's and Agnes' ears. What seemed so curious to her was that he appeared so free, no work to attend to as he visited them daily, while other men worked at trades. It was a true mystery. He did not dress as one well-to do, although he was neat in the extreme. He wore the warm, dark clothes of a seaman, yet here he was on land and riding a horse when they met, curious, so curious.

They walked about two city blocks, before either spoke, heading in the general direction of the water, a familiar path that Maggie took on most Sundays with Jane, since arriving in Halifax. The tall masts waved in the distance, and the beginnings of a winter chill coursed through Maggie, as she was obliged to take three steps for every one of her companion's, while he walked leisurely and she scurried along.

"I'm so pleased you could come for this walk with me, for I want to speak with you today, away from the others." John stammered a bit, as though uncomfortable with his words, as he gazed out over the water and down the incline of the street.

"I have known you only a week, Maggie, and I realize that is precious little time to truly get to know someone...for you to know *me* that is . . . " His speech trailed off and he cleared his throat to begin again.

"This would be easier if I could go on seeing you next week, and the one after that, to take you to a dance and to do the proper sort of courting...but, but, you see." He stopped there in the middle of the street, looking down at her from that enormous height which she had noted on their first meeting. They had come to a full halt when he blurted out, "You see, Maggie, my ship sails with the tide tomorrow. She is full repaired today. We broke our mizzenmast at sea, nearly cracked through she was, and we limped into Halifax to have her replaced. That was two weeks ago. Oh, how I wish it could have taken longer . . . " He trailed off once again, looking apologetic and hopeful all at the same time wishing she would speak now and make this easier for him.

She was aware of his brown eyes and of the lock of dark hair falling on his forehead as he flashed a shy smile, making an almost boyish grin come over the face of a full-grown man all the more engaging, as he went on: "I have come to enjoy your company so very much. In fact, I have found that I really need it. I will be at sea for, who knows for how long, probably all winter, and possibly on into spring. I may never see this port again with my vessel, but do you think that if *I was* to return alone, if I could court you properly, you could find the time for me?"

John averted his eyes and began looking far off. "Perhaps there is someone at the university that you have a fancy for. Here now, I am being very bold in asking this, for I am so uncertain in these matters. You see, I have been at sea for most of my lifetime and have *never* had the chance to know a refined girl such as you, dear Maggie."

Finally as he finished the words that sounded prepared, John began to walk again, while Maggie felt true compassion for this tall, quiet man who she knew such a short time. She knew that he was having real difficulty trying to express his innermost feelings and at this moment she must reply. Racing to keep up with him, she boldly said, "But John, just where are you going on the sea? That is, I thought you lived here in Halifax. You've told me nothing of yourself. Without that information, how *can* I answer you?"

It was Maggie who stopped now. They had reached the harbor promontory, a large concrete circular bastion, railed in iron, overlooking the entire panorama of ships, wharves, docks and waterfront shops. "Tell me, John Dix, who are you, what are you, and where are you going?"

John's coloring took on an even warmer hue as he finally spoke decisively, gesturing out over the harbor, taking it all in with a sweep of the arm.

"I am an American, out of New Bedford, Massachusetts, as was my father before me. My grandfather, I have been told, came from St. John's Newfoundland. He was a whaler, my father a whaler, now dead, and John Dix, here before you, the first whaling captain in our family. You can just see my vessel far over to the right there," and he pointed his arm to a high riding ship with three masts. One mast plainly new, was not matching the others. He continued, "I am thirty-two years old, with a ship to sail and a sea to meet for the profit of my crew, the owner and for myself. I have thirty men to oversee and an owner who depends on me. I have *no* business *even talking* to a lovely young girl. For it is a seaman, that's who I am and proud to be" And now he took a huge breath and appeared defenseless. He shamefacedly sat down hard on the stone bench that formed the entire circular barricade. He could no longer look into Maggie's face, but instead turned his face to the sea.

Maggie knew instinctively that what she said now, and how she said it, was very important to the image this man had of himself. She sensed that he might easily be hurt by the wrong words. She quietly took her place beside him, to stare out at the same view. Slowly, cautiously, as if it were the only answer he might require, she slipped her small, eighteen year old hand over his wide, rough one there on the bench while a warm current of bonding flowed between them. No language need be spoken.

Episode:

All nights, from that sunny afternoon on the promontory, were very different for Maggie McBain. Each day, she carried on her studies at Dalhousie and the pattern there was the same. She excelled in her class work, receiving nearly perfect grades; she enjoyed debates and wrote valued articles for the Gazette. But when she was alone with her thoughts, late in each evening, especially as she lay in bed, all of her being was somewhere on the ocean's crest, riding the waves of a whaling vessel, just as had been her mother's fate before her. Continually, the mind questioned this strange, strange irony! God gave and took away and then gave again, and to me . . . why, Dear God, oh why?

She had given no promise to John as they spent some three hours on that late October day, sitting close together, talking earnestly. She learned so many things about him then. All his nervousness and shyness seemed to melt away. At last, with just the two of them, he became the confident whole, no longer self-conscious but in good accord, Maggie thought, as he must be with the men under his command.

He had talked of his boyhood in New Bedford, of how his father had died of blood poisoning, after being struck accidentally by a harpoon in 1865, when John was ten. Of how the weight of his mother's care had then fallen on him as soon as the share from his father's last voyage was paid out. He told her of how at twelve he had taken a full-time job, first in the rope maker's shop and then at thirteen, had signed on a whaler as a cook's apprentice.

He said that he was always large for his age, and therefore the owners signed him on easily, for he could do the work of any seventeen year-old, and effortlessly. He always lived near the ocean front and the sea was a part of his identity. His mother, who had never been well in John's lifetime, had died of an influenza epidemic while John was at sea when he was fifteen. He had one older sister, Anita, who married a law student, when she was just sixteen. She was three years older than John and had by then, moved to Philadelphia. Anita was now thirty-five. Her husband was a maritime lawyer and doing very well, for she wrote of a fine home and social connections in that city. Her husband came from a prominent Philadelphia family. They met when he vacationed at his parents' summer home, near New Bedford, on Martha's Vineyard. Although John longed to see Anita, his sea duty had kept him from that pleasure. He felt content that she was happy and well cared for.

John had made his way up steadily in the same whaling company that had employed his father. Only two years before this one, when he was thirty, he was made master of his vessel. His ship was named Gratitude, an old, but most maritime worthy craft, manned by a fine crew. They were eager to take to the sea again, for they knew little of how to behave on land in an unfamiliar port and for a two-week stay. He would be happy to return to the sea now himself, except for his meeting Maggie.

John explained that on the day he had come upon Jane and Maggie on the granite ledge, he had hired a horse from the blacksmith, when he found it impossible to have any work done that day on the Gratitude. It was the Sabbath in Halifax and all work was forbidden. The ship had limped into port on Saturday evening and he had finally arranged for the work to begin on Monday.

This was the second time he had been to Nova Scotia. Once before, he recalled, when he was a boy of eighteen, an epidemic befell the crew, and Halifax, being the closest port, had obliged them to come into harbor leaving two very ill crewmembers with a doctor here. That doctor gave medicine for the remainder of the crew, for they were quarantined on the vessel. His foot had not touched land on that occurrence. However, it was strange that even without those two crew members, and despite the sickness, the trip turned out to be one of his most successful. The ship returned to New Bedford, after only nine months at sea, with a cargo of whale oil, full to the rigging. It was with that share, that he bought a modest house on Union Street in New Bedford, where he could live for the short periods when he was home from the deep.

He had lived with his mother in rooms above the rope shop after his father's death, when they were forced to sell their fine home. He always had longed for a place of his own after that time, even though he had only a few weeks between voyages.

Maggie listened with pleasure, hearing of his life and his prospects. What a different man he was when speaking of his boyhood and of the sea. She could tell that this life meant much to him, but then, he truly knew none other. She could not see herself in his vision of the future, for these ideals held no hint of her own.

When he spoke of his mother, his eyes fairly shone.

"A truly lovely, proper English lady, she was, there at the seaside in New Bedford and married to a Yankee seaman, yet never once complaining. I suppose she loved him very much, though she never really said so to me. Yet, she taught me so much, Maggie, all about the beautiful Yorkshire Dales where she grew up, and she made me know there were vast, important places in the world away from the open sea. I missed her keenly after that trip when I found her gone and buried next to my father in the churchyard. I visit when I am in port for it gives me a safe feeling as I quietly sit there alone. The only other time I get that feeling is at sea, at night, when all are asleep, except the watch and me. I look up at the heavens on those quiet nights. Maggie, there is no sight on earth that can compare with that spectacle. Have you ever seen it? Do you know what I am talking about?"

Suddenly, he felt self-conscious again, as he paused in the long account. Maggie perceived that this might be the longest speech he had ever made to anyone, maybe since his mother's death. He had released a flood of feelings that must have been held in for many years. She totally knew that this was a caring, charming man, this Captain Dix, and she was flattered that he felt free to choose her to share his inner thoughts.

John had made no commitment to the writing of letters, so Maggie contented herself that there would be none. She could not hide the fact from herself, however, so that when any mail arrived which bore an unfamiliar hand, or from any distance, she secretly prayed it might be from Captain Dix.

Somewhere in that period of time, after four months or so, those brief eight days of his presence seemed more like a dream than reality. And she had to struggle to reconstruct each day in her memory, to be sure that they ever happened at all, but when Jane or Mrs. Wallace spoke of the tall, handsome seaman, who had been their brief companion, she knew it was all very real.

Episode:

Even with her concerns and longings, the winter passed quickly, and the Easter recess was upon her. Although April was cool in Nova Scotia, Maggie begged Jane to seriously think about the invitation they had received from the Alexander Bells, that is, to come to visit during this holiday. Since their arrival in September, both Jane and Maggie maintained a spirited correspondence with both the father in Brantford and the son in Boston. Now, the son, Alexander, was also building a home in Brantford, and it was his invitation to them that they considered. It was explained in the letter, that since their new living quarters were not quite complete, they had arranged for Maggie and Jane to stay with their good friends only a few miles distant. The daughter of this family, Marion Cameron, was the same age as Maggie, and they thought it might be a most enjoyable time for both girls.

Jane and Maggie sat in their sunny room in Halifax discussing the venture. The conversation was only about the lack of funds for such a trip that kept them from accepting, yet they reasoned it would only involve the train fare and perhaps a few incidentals, and so it was affirmed. This excursion through the bold and beautiful landscape of Nova Scotia would be a glorious experience.

Baddeck and its surroundings were gorgeous, the Bells, the same delightful family, and Marion Cameron, a charming girl, who would become a true friend to Maggie. Her days spent in the rambling Cameron home, with its twelve rooms was a new pleasure with all of its space and fine furnishings, yet it was not something that Maggie coveted. Small and neat, she decided, was to be the style of *her* life, everything in its place and not many frills. But it was grand to see how others lived and to become a part of it for a short time.

At eighteen, Marion was the youngest of the four Cameron daughters, and the only one living at home; however, she attended a boarding school for nine months of the year. She was a pretty, sturdy girl with long blonde hair and she stood a bit taller than Maggie. She seemed levelheaded, and Maggie found it definitely fun to be in her company.

Except for a few casual friends made at the university, Maggie had no close friend with whom she could share conversations of any personal matter.

Jane used the greater portion of her daytime hours visiting the Bells, leaving Maggie and Marion to their own activities. The two spent most mornings riding horses over the beautiful hills and then making their own luncheons in the huge kitchen. On nearly all afternoons they were up in Marion's bedroom, where they read, brushed their hair, tried on clothes, but, mainly just conversed about everything that eighteen year-olds are known to utter. Since neither had known the other before this week, they felt free to share aspirations, opinions, and use the other as a sounding board for their beliefs. In this manner, they both felt safe, swiftly sensing companionship with the other.

As Maggie looked back later at the words she had written in her journal for the time in Baddeck, she realized it was surely a joyous portion of her girlhood. This time being free of studies and exams and the pure independence of it, plus the friendship of Marion was perfect. Actually, just being able to express her thoughts to a person of her own age was a godsend. It was a relaxed slice of time when all her thoughts were directed inwardly examining her future life. Maggie felt that this week had a great influence on the remainder of her days.

"Tell me Marion, what were your feelings when your baby brother died?"

Marion and Maggie were interrupted during a very serious conversation on the day before, when Jane had returned from the Bell home and had called them downstairs to dinner. Now Maggie thought it important to have her new friend continue this sad story, for her own sake, as much as for Maggie's curiosity. At present, they had the time on this day, as they had just finished lunch, and the entire afternoon stretched out before them.

First of all, Marion felt she should explain the absence of her mother about the home during these days, except for her appearances at dinnertime. For the past two years, Mrs. Cameron had become a recluse, staying only in her rooms, venturing out just to Sunday church services, and an occasional trip with Marion to purchase school clothing.

"She, Mother, surprised us all when she announced that a baby was due; that happened over three years ago. She did not hide the fact that our doctor called it ill advised, but six months later, Mother gave birth to my brother in her forty-fourth year. He was a healthy, happy child and the joy that abounded in this house, between father, my sisters and me is memorable. My mother, however strangely enough, seemed detached, even indolent, letting others take care of little William all of the time. He was a darling baby, rarely crying, and always smiling up from his cradle. I hovered over him like a nanny, for he seemed to like my care most of all. My sisters, who have children of their own, would come by daily and fondle and pat him. Mother just remained in her room, rarely entering the nursery.

Father pressed the doctor for an answer as to why my mother was so distant and unconcerned, while he expected her to be beside herself with happiness, now having the son that she had always wished for. Dr. Laurence explained that sometimes this malady occurs, especially in a pregnancy of later life. He said it should disappear in some weeks, but, Maggie, it never did!"

Marion paused here, wiping her eyes, and Maggie felt sympathy for her story as she quietly went on.

"I had just returned to school that fall and mother had employed a good nurse to care for William, when I was suddenly called home in early December. William was taken ill and died within just twenty hours. He had developed a cold, had difficulty breathing, and then a fever set in and took him during that dull, gray afternoon, when no one or nothing could help him. He was gone so quickly that even Dr. Laurence had a difficult time with the reality. My father was in such denial that he would sit for hours in the corner of the nursery near the cradle during days following the funeral, while mother at last broke down completely, blaming herself for not taking care of little William. He always had the best of care, really Maggie, even the doctor said so. He took me aside and told me that everything was done to save him, but there are times, and he had seen this in his practice, that a perfectly healthy child has the onset of sudden illness and nothing can be done. He said it was God's will and there is no answer. I must accept what had happened."

Now Marion's eyes truly welled in tears and Maggie was aware that this girl had probably never really grieved nor told this story to anyone else. She put her arms about Marion. They sat on the window seat of her room, overlooking the cool, springtime garden. She stroked her back for some long moments, just as though Marion was a weeping child who needed soothing.

Now Maggie understood why Irene Cameron stayed in her rooms most of the day and why Marion's father, although very polite and gracious to his guests, excused himself from their company, to be off to his business in town for most hours of the days. How sad for Marion to be at home here with all of this gloom. It was best that she was off to boarding school for most of the year. She had not only lost her brother, but her father and her mother as well. It made Maggie all the more grateful to have Mum Jane as her joyful, constant companion, even though she had been denied a father, sisters or brothers.

Gazing now at Marion, she thought of how life was an unrelenting struggle, for one had to battle every step of the way in this world and keep their wits about them or life could overcome, and swallow you whole.

She vowed that she would stay in touch with Marion, for she might be someone who had need of her contact and who might wish to share more thoughts later on.

Additionally, she understood how wise the Bells had been in planning that Maggie stay here in the home to become Marion's comrade and confidant precisely at this time. The fates, oh, the fates, mused Maggie.

On the final evening of their stay, the girls asked if they might be allowed a last ride on the horses they both wholly enjoyed. It had finally turned sunny and warm, and the girls, as well as the animals, seemed to feel the surge of springtime all about them. With consent, the two were swiftly out of view of house and barns, exploring the magnificent hillsides. Occasionally, they came upon a clump of daffodils or small purple crocus that had not been there on the day before, and they shrieked in wild delight at each new patch of color.

After a vigorous spurt down the steep embankment bordering the small stream, which separated the Cameron property from its neighbor, the girls alighted and sat breathless on the new grassy bank.

The exhilaration of the ride brought color to their cheeks and again a need to talk. Marion began, "In all these days, Maggie, you have listened to all my uncertainties, my thoughts, but I still don't know exactly how *you* feel about life, or what you plan to do with yours?"

Maggie stretched her legs out before her on the moist ground and with a shake of her curls, leaned back on her elbows.

"Well, I do believe that I have a vision of what *might* be ahead. No one can see into the future, but I do know that fate plays a great part in most lives, that is, if we permit it to lead us. I know my early life was all led by fate, and I believe that I must follow that destiny wherever it might take me. I have told you about my growing up on the island of Skye and the joys I knew as a child, of the affection I hold for Laura, Bruce and their girls, who *are like* sisters to me. I felt loved in every precious moment of my days there, even though my own mum and I could not be together. I do know of her sacrifice for me so that we feel as one person now. I am all the more loved because of that. I was raised in a place where one believes in the Doonie Sidne, those fallen angels who did not descend into hell, but remain here on earth to watch over all we say and do. They are our protectors in this world. This is the part of the fate that I speak of. I trust too, in the Water Horse and the Seal People. All of these beliefs make me know that there are forces watching out for us at every moment, and we must be receptive to our fate, and not place ourselves in any way to block our own intuition.

"Fate played some part of my father's death, my teaching on Skye, on meeting the quiet beauty that was my Mark Grant, the work in the tearoom, and fate certainly enabled me to help little Peter to speak. It is that same power that led me to the scholarship at Dalhousie from a chance comment by Dr. Bell and see now, here I am in New Scotland, in the company of a wonderful new friend. Oh, Marion, you too, must let this fate or providence, or whatever one may call it lead you, for I know that it is real and I must absolutely follow it always, I must!"

Maggie looked into Marion's face and saw her rapt attention so she went on.

"I lie in bed just thinking about such things, for I deem we all are led to choices, and while there may be the easier course to follow, which probably means to stay just as we are and not to venture forth, this is where my life tends to differ with others. It is not merely adventure that I seek, but an inquisitive questioning of life. I need to know what lies beyond this safe, peaceful behavior; I know that my life holds many new, exciting possibilities, and my tomorrow will bring something incredibly special directly to me. Can you understand what I am trying to say, Marion?"

Maggie's face was a-glow in her exhilaration and zeal in attempting to explain her deepest beliefs. All the while, Marion kept her large blue eyes glued to her friend's vibrant face, amazed at her candor and her maturity, and only nodded.

"Before we part tomorrow, dear Marion, I must tell you a special secret that *only* you will know."

The sun was about to set just beyond the nearest hill and the spring mauve and pinks of a paintbrush sky made a dramatic setting for Maggie's mysterious confession. Marion listened intently, knowing something profound was near release.

"There is a person out there in the Atlantic Ocean, who at this moment may be gazing at this same beautiful sunset and he is perhaps thinking *only of me*!"

The manner in which Maggie chose her words was captivating and dramatic meant only for innocent Marion. This did not escape Maggie's notice as she continued,

"Destiny is once more about to play an important part in my life. I feel John's presence in all I say and do, in every part of me. I will not go into all the facts that led me to meet this man in Halifax last October. We were with each other for only eight, glorious days. Now he is gone to sea, possibly never to meet me again, yet I feel . . ."

Maggie knew her dramatic powers were having a substantial effect on her friend, so she could not resist keeping her voice low and guarded. Marion waited for more, feeling her own naïveté, as opposed to Maggie's sophistication, however she felt there was no embellishment here, and she listened intently.

"John is thirty-two years old, and so perfectly good looking. He stands about six feet, four inches tall and he has the thickest, dark brown hair that falls on his forehead when he stoops to speak to me. He has soft, brown-greenish eyes which turn very dark when he is excited or provoked, but he remains tolerant and controlled in tense situations and is the *most* reasonable man that I have ever met."

The effect here was to Marion, that Maggie had known several men in her short lifetime, furthering the air of mystery.

"John is the captain of a whaling vessel out of New Bedford, Massachusetts, and one of the youngest. He embodies all of the finest qualities that I can imagine in one human: tenderness and moral virtue."

By now, Marion, being no fool, was convinced that Maggie was much smitten with this person that she extolled, for even one as inexperienced in the ways of men and of passion as herself, could easily sense her friend's lofty spirit. She finally broke into this long litany with a question.

"But, how can you get to know so much about a person in just eight days?" Marion was peering earnestly, directly into Maggie's face.

"I should think it would take months, even years, to find all of these qualities. Perhaps this is merely a passing emotion. How does one ever know when they are in love?"

Marion had spoken the word aloud, the word that Maggie had held quietly inside of herself for these long months since John left her. The word was *love.*

Maggie sat sharply upright, yet still quite in control of her speech. The answer came out of some remembered passage, and it was to impress Marion, possibly more than anything Maggie had said until this time.

> "Quote, Christopher Marlowe, 1598,
> *'Who ever loved, that loved not at first sight.'*"

"Marion, this is my fate... I tell you...I know... I purely know!"

Episode:

Once back at school, Maggie found that May turned the entire town into a kind of festival. Everywhere, people went about scrubbing doorsills, raking mulch from flowerbeds and planting seed. Children appeared simply everywhere, skipping, laughing, and running. It seemed all the earth had renewed itself as suddenly as the snow had fallen in November.

Maggie gloried in every part of this activity, along with her fellow townspeople. Springtime had always given her a special exhilaration, but now in this silken spring of her eighteenth year, her senses heightened so keenly, that she wished she might reach out and embrace the entire world.

This expansive lightheartedness was apparent to those about her. Agnes Wallace had threatened in mid-May to 'sit upon her, lest she fly away over the tree tops and disappear, she seemed that light.'

This day, Maggie dashed down the rise from Dalhousie, auburn hair flying in the strong, warm breeze, confident that she had done very well on her final exams. Nothing had been difficult. Finding it impossible to leave the sun's warmth, she threw her heavy stack of books into the wicker porch chair, to sit on the top step of the lodging house, soaking in the comfortable sun of the late afternoon. Looking about her, she hailed this lovely part of her life, the charming old gray building with its sheltering porch, the fine friends made here in Halifax, and most of all, the uninterrupted year of companionship she shared with her mother in this peaceful town. She was relieved that the school year was at an end, for it was delicious to believe she could put aside all thought of studies for the entire coming summer. Jane and she must make plans. Too, she had to find some employment to save funds for next year's schooling, but all that seemed remote, only a momentary distraction. Her glory was in this amazing power of bountiful springtime.

The fat, old house cat, Pricilla, jumped from her sunny spot on the wide porch sill and plumped herself on Maggie's feet, curling her large body in a furry circle. 'Oh how free I am with no studies tonight, I must really celebrate,' went her thoughts, 'I wonder what I could' . . . and suddenly a queer feeling sent a chill up her back, it was an emotion too strong to deny. As she sat stroking the cat, facing west toward the university, idly watching her fellow students cavort in playful antics due to their liberation, she felt intensely drawn, as from a magnet's pull, with an irresistible urge to turn her body completely about. As she did so, in her sudden move, the cat leapt from her small hands, and when Maggie faced east, with the blue waters of the ocean as a backdrop, racing up the hill, coat open, heels flying, came John, *her* John, fervently waving, smiling broadly, as sure as all of the *fate* that she believed in.

Her John had truly returned to her from the sea.

Episode:

It proved to be a wonderful celebration dinner that Agnes happily prepared on short notice. There were six at the table. With candles lit, her best white linen tablecloth, and delicious food, it proved an exceptional dinner; John and Maggie sat side by side, Edna Dean, the science teacher sat next to a newly arrived boarder, Mr. A. T. Williams, a spirits salesman, direct from Aberdeen, Scotland. Jane sat on Maggie's right and Mrs. Wallace, at her customary head of the table. Sally, her sometimes kitchen helper, had been hurriedly pressed into serving the feast. It was Agnes' superb food that inspired all of the company to be energized and talkative.

The recently arrived Mr. Williams, opposite Jane, explained the reason for his mission in Nova Scotia. He proposed to bring the distilleries of his homeland to the attention of both the Canadians and the Americans by starting agencies in the large cities of Boston, New York, and Philadelphia with a central location of Chicago as his headquarters. He was a middle-aged, arresting widower, distinguished by his thick, lusty Scottish accent and his conspicuous grey mustache. Jane seemed to enjoy his apparent attentions, as they both took pleasure from Agnes' flaky beef pie.

John was busily explaining to Maggie of his hurried departure from New Bedford and separation from the Gratitude.

He gave the responsibility of the ship's fitting over to his first mate, for he had to move quickly when he found a ship bound for Halifax laden with a consignment of marine hardware, exactly on the next morning after the last cask of oil was set ashore. John felt so fortunate to hear of a ship embarking for his exact destination. He said that it was a one-in-a-hundred chance, and he guessed it must have been some sort of marvelous *'fate'* that arranged it so. Upon hearing that familiar word, Maggie could only look into her beef pie with a huge, knowing smile.

Such a degree of laughter, gaiety and happiness invaded the very walls on that evening that Maggie wished the dinner would never end. Captain Dix had returned, and it seemed to her a miracle. As the couple stood on the wide porch after the leisurely supper and while Jane, Mrs. Wallace and Mr. Williams conversed in the front parlor, in the dusky-light, Maggie looked thoughtfully up into John's face to remark: "It is difficult to believe that you have come this long way just to see me, John. I did keep hoping to see you again and soon, but such a long, tiring journey."

Maggie was 'fishing'; now, and she knew it. He must have certainly sensed it too. John beamed down at her small oval face, and taking her hand in his own, said: "It was all that I could think of at sea, Maggie. Every day, since I left here last fall, I have thought of nothing else. It was nearly impossible to carry on my duties. The only thing that spurred me on was the knowledge that the sooner we filled our hold, and could get back to port, the sooner I would be here beside you now. Oh, Maggie, what an absolute joy you are. I had terrible apparitions of you becoming engaged with another in these long months."

John squeezed her hand then, hard enough to hurt, yet she rather enjoyed the feeling, as he went on: "The ship had a truly successful run. It seemed pure fortune was riding the waves with us. Why, it wasn't two days out of Halifax that we caught the Gulf Stream, and not four days, when we came upon our first school of whales. I will have quite a grand share of money waiting for my return. This year, the Gratitude is to be fitted out with new sails, and more work done on that mizzenmast, so it will be at least several weeks until she is ready for her next voyage. This will give me the time . . . "

He stopped there and gave Maggie a huge grin.

"I have come to declare myself for that period of time to do the proper courting that I spoke of, Miss Maggie McBain. Hear me out now for you will have to help me. I have *never* courted a girl, that is, a woman, before this time, and I plan to *never* do so again!"

He grinned once more, wide and happy: "So then, you must instruct me in all the proper courting ways, so it is done just right. Will you?"

And before she could answer, he went on to place his two arms on the porch wall, leaning there, encircling her small body with his. "You are lovelier than even my memory held for these many months. Is that proper to tell a girl, in the courting way? It is God's truth, it is!"

Maggie smiled at his earnestness, his serious, open need to succeed on this course he had charted. "All right, Captain Dix," she boldly nodded, "We will see what we *both* can do about this courting business!"

Two weeks of pure enchantment slipped by easily. No matter what activity the two young people chose to do, it seemed glorious adventure for both of them. The increasing amount of time spent in each other's company was clear to everyone, but no one was more aware of this demand on her daughter's life, than Jane. Maggie was seeing John, morning, noon and evening, and Jane found small chance to see her alone for any length of time.

The courting pair was out riding, by carriage or horseback, from early in the morning, packing a lunch to accompany them, or walking down to the waterfront, to take their meal at the Sea Farer Inn, where the local shopkeepers and dock workers took their noon meals. Maggie found it instructive and exciting to be among the people who made the sea their lives, and those who cared for them. She readily saw that John was comfortable here with his own kind. He had taken a large, third floor room at this inn, and easily made friends with the owner and his wife.

On other days, they hiked up the hill to the campus, now empty of students, for John to see where Maggie attended classes and worked at the Gazette. John asked a great many questions. He was eager to enter into her world to understand it. Nevertheless she detected that university life was intimidating to him, but this was silently perceived. His comment of how confining it seemed, with its tight routine, concentrated in this small area, so unlike the open sea, gave Maggie a significant reaction. And it also gave her serious reason for some added questions later on. So they continued, he viewing her little universe, she seeing a piece of his, yet neither, so far, able to fit into the other.

On one particular evening, when John had returned to his room, while standing at his window overlooking the harbor and beyond to the open sea, he marveled that he was in this place at all; it began to seem that unnatural for he felt like the proverbial, 'fish out of water.' This girl, he sought to make his, was the only earthly reason he was in this place and it disturbed him, yet, perhaps illogically.

On the second Sunday of courting, after two weeks of nearly constant companionship, the two walked to their favorite spot, the promontory overlooking the harbor. It was nearing sunset by the time they arrived and again found it deserted just as it had been in October.

Maggie stood in her long dress of pale blue, a white yoke of pique round the neck and a cameo at her throat. She had fashioned her hair in a loose nape of curls, tied with a soft ribbon, but the warm evening breeze had tousled it sufficiently to make it dance about her face. She unquestionably was a portrait figure, thought John, as she stood a few feet apart from him, wistfully counting aloud the number of ships in their view. Composed, she turned to speak to him, only to find his face now turned downward to watch the unrelenting wave's dash upon the gray rocks below them.

It was he who finally spoke, not looking into her face, and sounding once more as though these words might have been rehearsed: "Would you say that I have done the proper amount of courting then, Maggie? I feel such a confounded beginner in these matters."

She moved to his side and placed her hand over his huge one, as he gripped the iron rail surrounding the bluff, sharing his stare out to sea.

"John, there is no exact courting time. It is just the interval when two people come to know the other and to see if they are suitable to become, well, good friends. Oh, I know that there are those in society who determine that one year is socially correct for such a period of courting, but neither of us are in that social circle, eh', Dear John?"

"What I am trying to say, I guess, Maggie, it is that I have this urge in me to be in motion and it is strong, near overpowering. Though I want to be with you more than anything on earth, it seems that somewhere inside of me there is this allegiance I *owe* to the sea. I wish I could speak all of this easily to make it clear to you.

I do not want to be parted from you for a moment, but this hold it has over me is powerful. I wish that I had been allowed to go to school and to know the proper, the responsible way to tell you this. I feel now like a prisoner here within myself, trying to break iron bands, defeated by my own ignorance. I dress myself down daily. Here, I have met the woman with whom I wish to spend the remainder of my life, and I am not equal to her . . . no, not one solitary particle."

Still not looking into her face, he sadly lowered his head even more.

Maggie's compassion for this man now nearly overwhelmed her. She rushed to renounce his words, causing her to speak before they were thought through. His frustration was painful, the savagery and torrent against himself enormous. She knew that she must say positive words right now, or lose him forever.

"You are wrong, John, so very wrong. I have not met any man in my lifetime that is so canny, so intelligent. You are faulting yourself needlessly."

Then, shyly at first, but finally, she forced him to look into her face.

"I will now tell you of all the qualities I see in you, one human to another and not as woman to man, for under those circumstances, truth is not always seen plainly for emotion gets in the way. First of all, your forthrightness is most admirable. I see no pretense in you. I have noted, in these past weeks that you are as compassionate as any person that I have ever known. You are appreciative and sometimes utterly charming! You have a careful, precise manner, your attitude is reasonable, besides that, your physical bearing is most agreeable."

Maggie stopped here a moment, as she felt herself blushing and hoped that he did not notice, but she went on: "You are expecting of yourself, evidence far above the normal, deriding yourself needlessly. In all, you are a *very* desirable man, who I must tell to put away this nonsense of low worth, and to believe that what I say is true."

Breathless, she stood directly in front of him, her face flushed and passionate.

His face softened into a smile, and slowly drawing himself up before her to his full height, seemingly gaining self-control as he rose, he suddenly beamed down on Maggie, benevolently.

"You certainly have a persuasive way with your words, then, miss. Your insight has surely convinced me. I am an able body, a fearless man, but only with you by my side to make me know that I am. Well, then, Maggie McBain, I see no argument as to why we should not face this world together as a pair. You will be my tutor in all that I am lacking, and I will forever be your scholar."

He reached for her small hand and finding no resistance, ended softly: "Any woman that I might ever meet, after this day, will be bloodless and pasty by comparison. You have roused true strength in me, my Maggie!"

This time, it was she who stood speechless. Who could have believed when she arose this morning, that on this promontory, late in May of her eighteenth year, she would be proposed to all future life with this handsome man standing before her? Fate, her inner voice shouted loudly. Maggie stood looking up into his face and curiously, words memorized in philosophy class kept turning in her mind.

Sophocles . . . "Dreadful is the mysterious power of fate; there is no escape from it by wealth or war, by walled city... or dark sea-beaten ships."

Episode:

The following week was the most arduous of Maggie's young life. She could not sort out the answers so quickly. She was conscious that she must think many matters through, before she gave her answer. Her first act was in asking John if they might see each other only once a day: at evening, say, to share high tea, for as much as it pained her to be without his company, this would give her time to resolve the future.

She spent most mornings rising very early, taking long walks alone into the late spring countryside. She spent her afternoons in the company of Jane or in long talks with Dr. Forrest, her literature teacher, a good friend and a man she respected. He was able to give her an unbiased perspective, without pressing his own opinions; in all, he was a fine sounding board for her inner thoughts.

However, no matter whom she went to for help, Maggie knew the decision was hers alone. All other words could but focus on the consequence of leaving this comfortable, chosen life in the sheltered cocoon that she found for herself in Halifax. The new life would be completely foreign to all she knew, but it would be with the one person in the world that she believed loved her above any other. The chance that she might lose him seemed dreadful, and then she had to consider the parting from her mother. She knew that it was out of the question that John might stay in her world here, for he plainly found no comfort in it and he would be miserable.

The fierce independence that was Maggie McBain ran warm through her veins on those long walks. As she pressed through the woods and over a meadow, a part of her was unyielding. She had worked so long for this education, and a future with John held little hope of continuing it. Had not her own mother done the same; married, leaving the security of familiar places and relative ease, to wed the unknown? Had not Molly Grant too, become uprooted from her cozy, rural upbringing, only to move to the large city, and to raise three boys, alone?

Yet, what was independence worth? She could keep true to her dreams, continue her own will, but at what price? Perhaps only to grieve and regret . . . and yes, even question her decision one day. Was she being too proud, could her fierce independence harm a marriage? As she tramped along today, one week after that day overlooking the harbor, she knew that the answer must be found now, and one she could never question, ever. 'Seize the moment' had been her advice to sweet Marion. Now, she was the uncertain one.

John took the path of patient endurance. He complied with Maggie's every wish, fearing pressure might ruin his dreams. A paragon of tolerance, he arrived each evening, promptly at six for their meal and rendezvous, leaving exactly at nine. The lack of his constant companionship, which Maggie had so enjoyed in the weeks earlier, only whetted her desire to see much more of him, and worked as a not so insignificant stratagem from John's point of view, that is, to play the game entirely to her desires.

On this evening, after their supper, as the little group finished the raspberry trifle that Mrs. Wallace had artfully prepared, Maggie asked John if he would come by at ten on the following morning. She asked if they might go off to those same granite slabs where they first met, if that was agreeable for him.

He looked anxious, not able to read this as a good or bad sign, but he agreed willingly. He would hire a carriage, she might pack a lunch, however for him, he reflected, this courting game is at least at an end, but to what end he was very uncertain.

Jane and Maggie still shared the lovely, airy room they rented nearly ten months before. It became as much a home for the two, as any they had known. The furnishings were refined and pleasant when they arrived, but at present they had put their own small touches about, to make it immensely inviting. Maggie always kept fresh flowers on their bureau, from whatever was blooming in the lush Wallace garden, and she had managed to keep sweet dried flowers all through the winter there. Books stood in abundant stacks about the room and the crisp, handmade doilies, brought in their luggage from Scotland, gave it a very cozy, personal appearance.

Jane was awake, awaiting Maggie's step on the stair, after she said her goodnight to John. It was precisely nine o'clock and late springtime warmth wafted through the open window, softly moving the lace curtains of their second floor haven, bringing with it the odors of the sweet garden below, mixed with the close salt smell of the sea.

"Sit down and talk with me, darling."

Jane waved Maggie to the one overstuffed chair, while she half-lounged on the end of their bed. Twilight was nearly gone as they sat in the half-darkness not lighting the lamp. Jane sensed Maggie's decision was very near.

Maggie, glowing from her run upstairs, seemed eager to engage in this conversation, one which she knew must occur. She began: "I told of my desire to meet John in the morning, before everyone tonight, for a good reason, Mum.

"I want you all to know that I am going to tell him tomorrow just what I intend to do with the rest of my life.

"If I do tell John that I will marry him, I will be making a commitment in my heart that can *never* be altered. I will never change my mind, once I make the promise, not for any reason. I know that you and I have had some long discussions about fate, or destiny, or whatever people call it, and you know it is my belief that our lives follow a certain pattern that is unalterable. If one takes the wrong path, that is, ignores what fate has in store, it can lead to a life of misery. This is why I am being so cautious. I must find the exact way, and when I am convinced it is right, I will never waver from it!"

Jane, whose head lay very close to the arm of Maggie's chair, merely affirmed her daughter's voice with her own: "I understand you darling, more than you'll ever know." And with that assertion, Maggie went on: "John and I have known each other for a very short time by any standards of most courtships; only those brief days, last fall, and now these weeks . . . I could never, in my wildest dreams, have believed that I should fall in love with a man of the sea, and a whaler, at that. Even as I say it now, it seems incredible and certainly the farthest thing ever from my mind. You were a young girl, living nowhere near the ocean, when you fell in love with my father. Now, by chance, I meet the same sort of man. I have given it a good deal of thought, Mum. Could it be that the secret lies in this, here is the type of man, each of us really needs, a bold, strong, self-reliant sort, unafraid to venture forward into the unknown? Yes, I think that is the key, we both have searched out this kind of person to love, whatever the personal cost."

Maggie paused to catch her breath and reflect on this last thought just occurring to her.

"Mum, if you knew, beforehand, that father would never come home from that first trip to sea, would you have married him, anyway?"

Her mother rolled her slim, still youthful frame over on the lavender coverlet to face Maggie, her head propped up in her palms. She knew this was a pivotal point, and much rested on her answer. She knew she must be absolutely honest. It would be possible here, by just bending the truth Maggie's resolve might be altered, but she had always been truthful with her child, and she would not change now.

"I had my doubts, too, dear, when I first met Robert. It was not the life that I had envisioned as a girl growing up. Then, I pictured myself a lady in a beautiful, large home, much as my parents had, on a quiet street in Edinburgh, where I would entertain prominent persons, do good works, probably married to a professor or business man with a safe, predictable life. Now, I know, these were all make-believe fancies to which little girls' imaginations lead them. In reality, I can think of no greater life with a man, than the short, beautiful one that I spent with your father. If I were only to have those few months again, no, I would *not change* those days with him for a lifetime of safe, comfortable years with another man, who I knew I could never truly love. So you see, I believe that deep down, I am a fatalist too. Your father and I were destined to be one, and you are the shining outcome of our love . . . No, I would not undo a thing. I would have married him, even if I *could* see into the future."

Jane reached for Maggie's hand, and squeezed it firmly. "You are the only one who can answer your heart, Maggie. I am sure this is probably the greatest decision of your life, for all consequent happenings will hinge upon it. Somewhere, deep inside, you know what is right for you . . . only follow your own heart, my sweet. "And so saying, Jane arose and soundly kissed her only daughter.

Episode:

One would think that the day of the telling, should be one of all sunshine and soft winds, but the day broke with thunderheads, gray skies, cool, even chilling blasts from the ocean, and with them, an occasional shower.

True to his word, John pulled up in front of the house promptly at ten, and seeing Maggie safely into the high seat beside him, was off to the craggy boulders of their first meeting.

John commented on the invigorating day. He seemed to take strength from the drastic changes in weather, it reminded him of the unpredictable sea and of how there, each day broke so opposite the one before it. He talked a great deal of the ocean and all of its beauty; of what it meant to him to be pitched against the savage elements, and the challenge it provoked within him, all this as they rode down the narrow road bordering that same sea.

Her heart and head were racing. She was glad that John was doing the talking, while the horse kept a steady trot, commanded by the reins of John's strong hands. At last they reached the exact spot where she stood when he approached her standing form in October. The sun was making a valiant attempt to break through somber clouds, as they stepped from the carriage, and she began to walk carefully over the boulders, taking special heed of the craggy stones. John, with picnic basket in one hand, held Maggie's hand tightly in his other, her slender fingers lost in his own.

Just after they spread their cloth on a flat, broad stone, the basket atop of it, John caught Maggie's shoulders and turned her to him, quite sharply.

"I cannot be strong enough now, dearest, to peacefully sit and eat our lunch, to speak of other things, when I must know and know *now* just how you feel about our future."

The veins were standing out boldly on the sides of his temples, Maggie observed this, and she felt suddenly ashamed that she was making this fine man suffer so. It was not in her character to tease or to trifle with affections; in fact, she abhorred those who 'played' at love. She knew the moment of truth had come. She began haltingly, gaining her voice as she spoke: "John, I have waited only these many days so to be positive of my feelings. I neither wished for you to be injured or for myself to make the wrong choice. It is as firm to me as these stones are beneath our feet that you are in love with me. I do not doubt that for a moment. My only concern is that I do not wish to become a wife who would ever look back and wonder if she had chosen right, for your sake, more than my own, I assure you.

"Our age difference is of consideration to others, but to me it matters, not at all. The difference in our lifestyles, you a whaler, I a student, makes others doubt our future happiness, but

I find that of no consequence. My faith in a higher power is what has guided my answer. I keep coming back to the invariable, inevitable fact that you came down this road and found *me*, as though some unseen hand had decreed it, perhaps, in some way, long before our births. I do believe this, but what is more, it is what *I want to believe*. Do you understand? My answer is *yes*."

John had not let go of Maggie's shoulders during her long speech. His face, through all of her words, alternately lit with her assent and frowned with her indecision, but finally, as she came to the end, he literally beamed when she proclaimed their future as being predetermined, and to her gasping surprise, he, with one huge sweep of his great arm beneath her, lifted the light, young body up into his arms, carrying her off with the ease of a small child.

His voice and words would be some Maggie would be able to invoke at will for the remainder of their days on earth. They filled her ears like a clap of thunder. As he strode about the giant stones, she in his arms, he announced, so all of the birds, the sea and the sky could hear:

"Our world will have no boundaries, my Maggie, my love. We will travel over the ocean and I will show you all the wonders that I have seen. Oh, we will be such a pair, my darling, our souls never apart, like no two people in this world. I promise my beloved, and you will know love as no woman has ever been loved!"

And now he whirled about in his rough way, dancing from stone to stone, his face to the sky of softly falling rain, completely oblivious to any of it. John, delirious, in his total happiness, twisted, turned and laughed ceaselessly, all the while, kissing and caressing *his* Maggie in his arms.

Episode:

John sat, ramrod straight, on a heavy oak chair in the sacristy of the Episcopal Church of Halifax. His palms were moist as they tightly gripped the wooden chair arms beneath them. The sharp tick of the clock on the bookshelf directly across the room seemed deafening. He found himself saying, silently or aloud, he was unsure of which: "Why, when I have brought a three-mast vessel through the wild sea, in a frenzy as high as this church's spire, and have an entire crew of men waiting on my every word for their lives, why then do I feel calm and in command, but now, waiting here for the signal to step into the church adjoining, do I feel weak as a newborn kitten and as warm as a boy on his first day of school? This question kept running in his mind, while somewhere softly, sounding over the pounding of his heart, came the sweet strains of the pipe organ, beginning the wedding march.

Maggie and he decided to marry on the 18th of June, a Sunday, and only one week following that glorious day on the granite stones. John sent word to the owners of the Gratitude that he would start for New Bedford on the 20th of June, on the ship offering the next passage from Halifax.

Thus, he would be ready to captain his next whaling voyage on July 1, just as they had wished.

Agnes Wallace, Jane and Maggie worked feverishly for the week to get everything prepared. When she returned from the memorable picnic, Jane did not even register surprise at the announcement of her decision. This only confirmed that she knew her daughter very well, indeed. The early date did catch her off balance, however. She did not realize that John must leave that soon for Massachusetts, and so they all immediately moved into action.

A lifetime member of the Grace Episcopal Church, Agnes Wallace, lost no time in meeting with her pastor to help with arrangements for the young couple. It would be a small, quiet ceremony, with close friends in attendance, at three on the next Sunday afternoon.

On Monday, Maggie chose an exquisite, refined gown of white linen at the Halifax Mercantile. Mr. Sneed had just received a shipment of gowns from London, and this one fit her perfectly.

The delicate bodice, bloused full as was the style of the day. It had long, fitted sleeves, a high neckline and a slim full length skirt that was daringly straight. It was absolutely plain of ornament, which suited Maggie totally. She loved simple lines and no ruffles. When she tried it on for Jane, however, in the privacy of their room, they both felt that one splash of color was needed.

Maggie had saved a tartan banner of the clan Bheann for years in the bottom of her trunk. She had purchased it while living on Skye for the pure pleasure of having a bit of her father's colors always with her. It measured some three inches in width and a length of some seven feet. Now the mother and daughter tried its plaid, diagonally across her torso from right shoulder to left waist, across her back, up to the left shoulder, permitting about one foot of it to fall softly down her back. They secured it with the Luckenbooth brooch that Robert had given to Jane on their wedding day.

Since there was no father to give the bride away, Maggie reasoned that she would proudly wear *his* colors on her most important day.

Bheann, MacBeans or McBain, as her father's name was derived, had come down from the ancient Scottish king, Donald Ban, and all those called Bain or Bayne had obtained their name from that "fair featured ancestor," or so her books had told her. Beann, also in Gaelic, meaning mountain, made Maggie feel even closer to her highland heritage.

The colors of her tartan were mainly red with charcoal black narrow bands and a fine white line throughout.

Maggie had always thought it to be the richest looking of all the tartans, but then perhaps, she mused, she was a bit prejudiced.

Lord Byron had written a poem about one of her grandest ancestors, a Gillies MacBain, who stood six feet, four inches, and who died *valiantly on the plains of Culloden in 1745. John had been born just one hundred and ten years after the famous Gillies.*

The clouds may pour down on Culloden's red plain,
But their waters shall flow o'er it crimson in vain,
For their drops shall seem few to the tears of the slain,
But mine are for thee, my brave Gillies MacBain.

Aye, it *was* a proud heritage, and Maggie determined to use her full name into whatever circumstance she might find herself in the future, for from this coming Sunday, and on to her end, she would keep the lofty, Maggie McBain Dix, as her legal signature.

Episode:

Father Sinclair met with John and Maggie in the study of the rectory on the Thursday night before the ceremony, as was his custom. He believed in a serious conversation with the betrothed couple before he bound them as one.

The two sat on the small couch before his desk, each clasping the other's hand tightly, as he spoke to them.

First, the regular forms had to be filled in with John's full name, which to Maggie's surprise turned out to be, John Foote Dix, including his grandfather's name. Then, his birth date, January 16, 1855. Place: New Bedford, Massachusetts. USA.

Maggie's full name: Maggie Fraser McBain. Birth date: October 18, 1869. Place: Glasgow, Scotland.

Father Sinclair asked then for the names of their witnesses. John chose Charles "Matey" Drummond, jolly innkeeper of the Safe Haven Inn, where John stayed these many weeks, for he was now as close to him, as to any man here in Nova Scotia, having spent many an hour in his company over a tankard of ale, swapping sea stories.

Although John had no wish to confuse that matter at hand, by telling the good father, all of these petty details.

Maggie had already spoken with the pastor about her choice of attendant. On Tuesday of this week, she had visited this same office to ask if it were permissible to have one's own mother as her witness, and finding that acceptable, had hurried home to tell Jane. On that morning, she found both her mother and Mrs. Wallace in the front parlor of the boarding home, knee deep in garlands of evergreens that they were interlacing with heather, or what they called *fraoch*, both of the purple and white variety. They were incorporating voluminous white ribbon bows into the greenery. With these, they planned to decorate the pews of the church immediately after services on Sunday morn. It was a very fragrant room that Maggie entered to kneel before the straight back chair on which Jane sat.

"Mum, will you be my witness on Sunday, as well as my attendant? Father Sinclair says 'tis fine, no rule against it, and I want it so, please . . . I've just come from speaking with him."

Then turning to Mrs. Wallace, she asked, "People won't think it peculiar, will they?"

Before Jane had time to answer, Agnes piped up.

"I think not Maggie, my love, but then, what do you mind if they do? You are the bride and can have it any way you care to, ay?" Agnes Wallace was easy . . . and so it was decided, Jane would walk before her daughter, to stand as witness when she became Maggie McBain Dix.

Episode:

After Pastor Sinclair had all of the legal documents taken care of, he settled back in his high-backed chair, to give the sage advice, he deemed necessary for matrimony.

"You are captain of a whaling ship, I understand, John" he began, peering over his small, round gold-rimmed spectacles.

"That I am, sir," replied the prospective groom with apparent uneasiness, not knowing if he was to be censured for his vocation.

"Well, I have known many a seaman in my years here, and a hardworking, cheery lot, they are. It is a hard life, of that I am sure and a lonely one for the wife on shore, as well as for the sailor. Have you both given these thoughts your attention?" He turned then slightly, and addressed his concern to Maggie: "There will be many a night of worry and desolation when John is out to sea. They tell me some of the whaling ships can be out for years without touching home port." He looked straight into Maggie's eyes as she sat composed and unmoved by his query. "I also note here that there is a fourteen year separation in your ages and I wonder if that could cause you two some problem in the future?"

Maggie sat demurely and yet was prepared for his questions. True thought the pastor, she seemed very adult for her age.

"May I quote one of my favorite passages of literature in answer, Pastor? It says everything that I wish to say." He nodded his consent and she began:

"And Ruth said, 'Entreat me not to leave thee, or to return from following thee: for wither thou goest, I will go; and where thou lodgest, I will lodge: thy people shall be my people and thy God my God:

Where thou diest, will I die and there will I be buried: The Lord do so to me, and more also, if ought but death part thee and me."

So saying, she turned her face to John, who stared overwhelmed by the long memorized passage of scripture. Then she faced Dr. Sinclair, smiling sweetly: "Sir, I have no formal religious training, but these verses were taught to me many years ago by my foster parents, and I consider them to be some of the most beautiful in all language. To answer your question, no, it does not worry me that John and I will be parted at times, for I will be with him in spirit wherever he goes. And as to the age difference, it is of no matter. Our love is strong enough to weather any storm the fates should care to send."

Then with a press to John's hand, she fell silent. The elderly priest sat looking into the serene faces of the two: "Well then, I feel there are no problems here that you will not solve, together. I do give one final word of advice to each couple that I see before this desk and it is merely this: Never let the sun set on angry words or any misunderstanding between you two, but settle it with a prayer and the new day will dawn as a happy fresh beginning. I must also give you one edict to remember during your lifetime together. It was St. Gregory who said, 'Do not be anxious about what you have, but about what you are.'

"All my blessings, dear children. May your life be sanctified with exemplary offspring, vitality of being and endless happy days together."

And then he rose and walked around the desk, placing his gnarled hands on both heads in beautiful benediction.

Episode:

On Saturday morning, Maggie woke with a fever. So unlike me, she thought, I'm never ill. Also, all of her joints ached and her forehead was warm and damp. 'It's but the excitement of tomorrow. No one need know about it at all.' In every part of that day, however, she sensed an illness that she did not understand.

Mrs. Wallace and her lady friends at the church, offered to take charge of the entire refreshment presentation for the reception of bride and groom following the ceremony. Agnes fervently prayed for a sunny day. They would use the large, side garden, between church and rectory for the lovely outdoor affair. This month of June saw it filled with a multitude of fragrant, beautiful roses that Father Sinclair devoutly tended, offering the perfect background.

The ladies planned to serve fresh, fruit-iced-creams, strawberry tarts, shortbread and butteries, fruit punch and a wedding cake, lovingly prepared by Agnes herself. Their best linen tablecloths would cover the smooth planks set on wooden trestles, which were always used for such church events. Obliging, clear weather was their only genuine concern.

The Halifax Chronicle, distributed each Wednesday, held the announcement of Maggie's impending marriage to Captain John Dix, along with an open invitation for friends to attend.

Mrs. Wallace guessed that there would be at least fifty guests, Maggie, being well known at Dalhousie University, would anticipate some of her professors, their wives, as well as fellow students attending. Then, there were the friends that John had made down at the docks. She imagined several of them would be there. Also, she must count her own neighbors on Fairmont Street. Agnes bustled about believing herself to be the grandmother she had always wished to be, her petite, round body, visible and obvious everywhere at once, merrily doing it all.

Maggie spent Saturday afternoon packing...and as she did so, her exhilaration ran wild. She wrote some thoughts in her journal, before placing it lovingly with her other journals between her sweaters in the steamer trunk.

In only two days, she would be striking out for the unknown with her husband. Her impressions of the United States were vague, and her curiosity of the town of New Bedford was particularly apprehensive. What would the small house on Union Street, which John owned and had described to her, be like? And to think, a home of her own, what a joy that would be. But then, she alternately worried about her housekeeping and cooking skills. She never had the chance to make actual meals since she left Mum Laura on Skye. There, she had taken over all of the cooking when Laura was obliged to help Bruce with the planting, and at harvest time, but now those days seemed so very long ago. What did she remember?

She had nearly completed packing the trunk, this time more judiciously regarding her choice of books, since she could leave most of them with Jane to keep for her, so she packed only her very favorites. Her wardrobe had increased measurably since those early days in Glasgow, and she was hard pressed to fit everything in.

A knock on the door of her room alerted her that it was not Jane, who would have merely walked in. Maggie opened it to find a smiling Agnes Wallace holding a large, prettily wrapped package in her arms.

"Just a few more things for you to pack, darlin', before you have no space."

She entered, moving a sweater from the cushioned chair to sit squarely amid the cases, clothing, books and trunk.

"Well, open this now, Maggie, for it is for you to take along."

The older, kindly, Agnes seemed very eager for her to see its contents.

Gleefully, Maggie tore through the wrap and lifted the box lid.

There, lovingly placed in tissue, was a complete lingerie trousseau, handmade, and exquisitely crafted. She wondered where this remarkable woman had found the time to fashion the beautiful contents, considering her busy schedule. She fingered the pieces, remarking over each and every one. There were three camisoles, all lace trimmed, three long slips of cotton batiste, and most stunning of all, two nightdresses and a full wrap to match them, all trimmed in elegant embroidery.

Maggie exclaimed over everything, and as she did so, the caring woman found this appreciation was all the reward that she needed.

"I only finished the last stitches early this morning before the entire house stirred. I am sorry that I could not bring it sooner. Do you think you will find room?"

Maggie's eyes were moist as she placed both her arms about the aging lady, as she said: "If it means tossing out my books and blouses, of course, these I shall treasure, always."

"If you'll just be thinking of me from time to time, when you put on one of these, and perchance write a letter, that is, about your new life, darlin'. That will make me especially happy. I will miss you so very much about this house, my sweet Maggie."

Episode:

Finally, it was Sunday, three o'clock, and with the sun's rays pouring into the beautiful little church through breathtaking stained glass, while casting mellow colors on a faultless scene, the guests waited expectantly for the service to begin. Charming garlands of greens with flowers among them, looped perfectly pew to pew, yet nothing seemed overdone in the entire setting. Maggie entered the vestibule, and waited calmly until she heard the music to signal her walk down the aisle toward the sanctuary. Father Sinclair stood before the altar awaiting her arrival, and there was John, straight and tall, so handsome in his new attire. All eyes first turned to Jane, and then to Maggie as they came down the aisle, singly. Jane had chosen a gown of emerald green, the color that always complemented her auburn hair. The only other color was the wide sash she had fashioned of the same McBain tartan of her late husband. This fell in long streamers down the back of her skirt.

Both mother and daughter held simple bouquets of greens with white heather.

As Maggie walked down the aisle towards him, John looked as though he might burst. His face shone and he beamed with such joy it had to be seen by all there. She looked exquisite, pure, youthful, blissful, yet above all, obviously, confident of herself.

The service came from The Common Book of Prayer and did not seem lengthy. Vows were spoken, the plain gold band placed on Maggie's finger, the Lord's Prayer recited by all attending, and a short prayer for the married couple was said by the pastor.

Maggie tried to keep every word in her memory, so that she might play it back at will. She knew now that she had never wished for anything as much. This was the day, above all others, which she was to treasure forever. John's heart was pounding so loudly, she could hear it precisely when the priest said:

'Those whom God hath joined
together, let no man put asunder.'

And so it was accomplished, forever and forever, repeated Maggie in her mind, for now she was his wife and she knew absolute ecstasy. She turned her face up to John in that moment; so that he might bend down to kiss her lips, tenderly.

For many years, following the wedding and reception of John and Maggie Dix, on warm, sunny days in June when all seemed perfection, the guests of that blending in Halifax would recall that other flawless day: that day when it seemed the entire universe was smiling on the ecstatic pair; with the fragrance of the roses, the exquisite food, the refined atmosphere, but most of all, the vibrations of *pure love,* communicated between this bride and her groom were totally unforgettable.

Episode:

Once more, in her young lifetime, a ship's horn was blasting as Maggie leaned hard against the solid rail. John stood very close to her side while they waved a fond farewell to Jane and Agnes, standing together at dockside. Matey and Martha Drummond had come down as well to bid this last good-bye to the young couple who waved in return as long as the sight of land remained. Then, they turned to give attention to the vessel that they would be aboard for the two-day trip to New Bedford.

Maggie was quick to blink aside her tears at the parting to take pleasure in exploring the ship with John. This was the start of a new life, these were to be special moments and she determined to savor every second of them with her husband.

John explained in detail just how everything worked on the vessel. Maggie was awed with his knowledge of this craft when he had spent his days only aboard whaling ships. He explained that his interests in ships extended to all sea-going vessels, and that he made it his leisure pursuit to study them with much appreciation. As he spoke in these animated terms, she found herself half listening to all of his details, for she was even more convinced that here, he was in his definitive realm. He was a man of the waves, and she must be content with that, at least for as long as it was his choice of profession.

Their cabin being cozy, the seas calm, the weather balmy, and with such exemplary company, this honeymoon trip would pass all too quickly for each of them.

Episode:

New Bedford astounded Maggie. She marveled at the activity, of how so many vessels, barrels, masts, riggings, wharves and men, could be all jammed in together here, and how they made any sense of it all. She had never seen such unrestrained bustle and all at one time. It *was* a world of men. There was not a woman in sight, and unexpectedly, it seemed a bit threatening to her. However, when she looked beyond the docks and into the town with its four church spires plainly visible, it gave her the reassurance that beyond these wharves, there stood a community of women, and one she would now join.

Buzzards Bay provided a superbly protected, tight location, and she became keenly aware of the reason for its sheltered existence and of this beehive of movement. Finally, they disembarked, to stand on the rough wharf, awaiting delivery of their luggage and trunk.

After they set foot on land, John led her to a wooden bench where she could wait, while he located a man to help take their things to 93 Union Street. Immediately, suddenly, a huge wave of warmth and flushing came over her such as she had never experienced, and it left her weak. While she waited, a trembling and a palpitation began to accompany this feeling. She was alone, unsure of what was happening to her. But, by the time John returned, some ten minutes later with a porter along with his horse and cart, the incident had passed, and she began feeling quite herself once again. It must be the strangeness of being on land once more, and the anticipation of viewing my own home for the first time, she determined, so she quickly dismissed it, jumping up merrily to follow the men.

93 Union Street was a one-story building of white clapboard, with painted light-blue shutters. It stood on a grassy plot, the white picket fence bordering the yard of the four-room building giving it a neat, inviting effect. Since John had not described it to her, she was pleasantly surprised. Two rose bushes, one, on either side of the front entrance added another pleasant touch. Three low steps led into a small hallway. From this, Maggie eagerly explored the square parlor, sparsely furnished, sparser than she had ever experienced. It held only a horsehair sofa, one overstuffed chair of dark-green brocade, and a square, dark wood table, set exactly in the middle of the room, and on it, a single tall white candle in a silver candlestick, aside a small scrimshaw box. There was a sturdily built fireplace and hearth of dark, red brick in the white-walled room with a small flat writing desk set between the doorway and a tall window, facing the road. The only bright addition to the room was an oblong, Oriental style carpet, placed in front of the sofa. The floors were of wide, dark stained wood.

Above the mantle, a painting of a rather stern looking man in a long, black frock coat, full white cravat, tan vest with a row of shiny buttons in close marching order down his chest, gave a look of family to the room. Viewing his chestnut-brown, hair and hazel-brown eyes, plus that same straight nose, she found herself looking at a likeness of John's father, certainly. John was busy helping the porter in bringing the luggage around to the rear door off the kitchen, and with that completed, he joined her, taking pleasure in showing the remainder of the small house to his bride.

He took her hand and they entered the dining room, directly across from the parlor, comprising only a heavy oak table and four chairs, and a sideboard holding dishes. The open shelves above this piece were empty of display. Another tall window facing the road let in ample sunbeams streaming across the same dark floor. A large delftware tureen set in the middle of the dining table was the only ornament in the room.

They entered the kitchen immediately behind the dining area, so that Maggie viewed the huge, black iron cook stove, a wood-box along its side, a dry sink, one large cabinet with a white porcelain working surface, and below it several drawers. Lastly, near the back door, there stood an ice cabinet for food storage. The room boasted no decoration at all, save two blue-checkered towels that hung off the dry sink. She tried to imagine herself making meals here, but that image was not easy to grasp just yet, for it looked daunting.

Finally they entered the bedroom, simply furnished with a double bed, two tall chests for clothing and a wardrobe. There was no evidence of any mirror or pictures, and certainly no frills. The one long window facing the rear of the house was draped in panels of a heavy rose fabric that could be closed against winter winds. The only colorful touch to the room was a hand-worked quilt of interlocking rings, the pattern in white, blue and rose covering their double bed. Maggie asked if this was the work of John's mother, and he assured her that it really was. A seaman's chest sat at the foot of the bed, plainly recognizable by its rope handles. Sadly, it reminded Maggie that this husband was only to be hers in this snug, small house for precious little time before he was again off to the sea.

John walked her out of the back door to proudly show her the stone walkway he had built on his last break from whaling, just before he met her. He said that he had planted tulips on either side of its entire length of the walk, and that his neighbor had told him that they were beautiful in the springtime, but he had yet to see them, being always at sea when they bloomed. She knew that he was very proud of this little home by his speech, and she said that it was a fine place for them to be together when he was at home. John said that he realized the furnishings were sparse. He had acquired most of the furniture when a house in town came up for sale, and the owners traveled westward.

However, he added, that most of the townspeople stayed on in New Bedford, for here were countless types of employment related to the sea, and most neighbors kept a fierce loyalty to this charming town.

"Darling, I know that a woman's touch is going to do a wonder inside here and especially with your talents. I did not need any more furnishings than I have here, for the least housekeeping to be done when I am at home, the better. I hope that you will be happy and content here while I am at sea. I have not spent three months in this house since I bought it, but it is my anchor on land, and a place that I looked forward to during my long months at sea."

He stood looking off somewhere into the distance, seemingly trying to make softer these things he said. John realized that it was to be a lonely habitat for her during these next months. Maggie's joy suddenly lessened, for when he hesitated here, so pitifully, she knew that it was very difficult to speak of being parted, and so soon after their marriage.

It took Maggie only the following day, while John was down at the docks for a meeting with the owners of the Gratitude, to unpack all of her clothing and to place her books on the desk, mantelpiece and on shelves in the parlor. The colors and smells of their bindings always gave her a special lift and a feeling of belonging here, somehow. Finding a lovely cut glass vase in the bottom of the kitchen cabinet, she set about placing yellow roses in it and put them on the square table in the middle of the parlor. She picked six more to float in the delft tureen in her dining room. And then she put a single rose on their bedroom bureau and three more in a water tumbler in her kitchen. True, now the bushes seemed a tad bare by her doorway, but the house took on a lived-in look with sweet fragrance in every room.

She was very pleased when she opened the wardrobe to find a full-length mirror on its inner door. Unpacking the trunk she found the fine soaps that had perfumed her lingerie on their voyage. These she placed on the nightstand next to a plain china water pitcher and basin. She unpacked the lovely hand-worked towels that Jane had given to her, along with sheets, pillowslips and tablecloths that the good women of Halifax had showered upon her. The pair of silver candlesticks from Matey and Martha as their wedding gift were placed on the mantelpiece beneath the unyielding eyes of John's father. She carefully set the dining room table with the delft china, found in the cabinet, and stood back. She had played house all morning, and was pleased with all of her handiwork. So much so that she boldly took up the market basket from the kitchen, closed her own front door, and walked the five blocks down to the shops to buy bread and fish for dinner. Holding her head high as she walked along, feeling very much a competent, married woman!

This day, being the 24th of June, Maggie and John had been married nearly one week, and in just one more, she, reflected, as she lit the fire in her cook stove to begin supper, John would be off to sea. Today he was supervising the storing of the first of the provisions for the voyage. He had promised, that tomorrow, Sunday, with no one about the docks, he would take her aboard for a full tour of the Gratitude. Her emotions were mixed all day. The wonderful excitement of being a wedded wife had suddenly given way to her vision of what these next month's might be like: John away at sea, and herself not knowing a soul in New Bedford, and then the constant worry for his safety. This all began a definite uneasiness inside of her.

She lit the candles on the mantel piece as the sun's rays started to fade, and a cool summer's eve set in. Whale men worked long hours at dockside, she thought, as well as at sea. This was but one other fact that she must become accustomed to. With the meal prepared, and warming on the rear of the stove, she decided to walk up the street, to see if John might be on his way home. She had just reached the corner of the neat little road, when she made out his large form swiftly walking towards her. Upon seeing her, he began to run, and this brought back that day in Halifax, when he had come to her from the sea. The thought that she would sit quietly at this address and wait for her sailor was born of that moment, and the beginnings of a plan began hatching in her clever Scot brain.

Episode:

The Gratitude was far different aboard than Maggie had imagined; for one thing, it had more room to move about. The captain's quarters were small and compact, true, but they were so tidy, everything one needed seemed to fit exactly into place. The bed swung on gimbals to counteract the roll of the ship and was of three-quarter size. John had a fine desk, a chair, and a small, built in couch. The head, or toilet, was in a separate small room adjoining the cabin, and was used exclusively by him. Small windowpanes in the aft portion of the cabin let in ample light to make the room quite cheerful, or so it seemed on this lovely, warm day at dockside. Maggie saw the first and second mate's cabins, situated close to Johns' as well as the foc'sle in the most forward part of the ship, where the remainder of the crew was quartered. The main cabin, where the officers took their meals, was situated just forward of the captain's cabin. Maggie marveled most at the galley for its trimness. From these small confines were served three meals daily to thirty men for months and sometimes years.

The Gratitude was 108 feet in length and her beam was one-fourth of that, or 26 feet with a depth of 18 feet. She had a working crew of three officers and twenty-seven able men.

Finally, after seeing every inch of her, John and Maggie sat on the main hatch cover in the center of the ship, thoroughly enjoying mid-day sunshine, while he explained the workings of the vessel to her.

"The whale is caught by a crew of six men in one of the five whale boats after they are lowered into the water. These boats hang from her sides on davits, off rails, two on the starboard and three on the port side. Each of these boats weighs 1,000 pounds, but in the water can hold another 1,000 pounds of gear, plus the weight of the six men. This smaller craft is superbly nimble, twenty-eight feet long and six feet wide. It is double ended, so it can reverse easily. All are planked with rot resistant cedar only one-half inch thick.

"Five men take their places at the oars, which are sixteen feet long, and propel the boat at a speed of five knots. The mate in the stern can shift this craft quickly with the turn of the twenty-foot steering oar. Tubs hold the whale line in coils near the centerboard. This line passes through a loggerhead at the stern, and then is strung through a chock at the bow. The line pays out as the whale attempts escape."

John stopped a moment to place his arm about Maggie, turning her to him, looking into her eyes, and determining if he was making this clear. He pointed to each location as he spoke. Maggie thought that she could distinguish clearly just what happened when a whale was sighted, and believed that there must be a rush of exhilaration for everyone on board when this occurred. Now, John was talking again, and she was his fervent listener.

"Once a whale is caught, he is hoisted upside the ship to the cutting-in stage, these are planks lowered near the waterline for the men to work upon, for each man uses a twenty-foot cutting spade. The spades, when not in use, are carried in racks on deck, see, over there," and he motioned to the area. "After the carcass is cut into pieces, huge iron kettles, each with the capacity of 250 gallons, are uncovered on deck and the trying-out process begins. Kindling is set under the kettles and the blubber is boiled, and all the while, water is poured into the 'duck-pen', a brick trough on the deck under the try-works to protect the deck from the intense heat of the fires. For the next fifty hours, or so, depending on the whale's size, men work in shifts, amid smoke, flames, and the stench of the oil, to flense, slice and boil the whale's thick blubber into 1,500-2,000 gallons of the finest oil we know of. We take ivory from the whale's great teeth, and also Spermaceti, a second, smaller quantity of better-quality oil. This brings an even greater price, as it is mainly sold to the candle makers of Massachusetts and elsewhere, and is also used by producers of perfumes. All oil is poured into barrels and stowed below."

Maggie sometimes winced during this last vivid description. She could almost feel the slicing and smell the stench of oil, but she did not let her inward feelings be seen by John. This was his world and to understand it was now her place in his life. She reached for his hand, nonetheless, as he continued: "This ship is fully equipped to sail as far as the Pacific Ocean for a cruise of two years or more. However, the owners of this vessel own two others, the Princess Jan, and the Laura J. Those sail the Pacific course, while the owners prefer to keep the Gratitude on the east coast of America, hunting the humpback, the fin, the sperm and the right. We travel as far as the Labrador Sea, to the north, and we venture as far south as the Gulf of Mexico. If we are fortunate, we can sometimes bring in a full cargo in only six to eight months, and since we have fewer miles to travel, the owners are satisfied when we have just a bit more than one-half of the ship's hold filled, for it gives them working capital.

Maggie's lovely hazel eyes went from John's eager face to the white scrubbed boards of the deck beneath her feet, and then, looking away, she held them tightly closed.

Had she really planned for this? Now, as the parting loomed only one week away, she was unsure that she could cope with this prospect of being without him.

Observing this sudden shift in disposition, John tried to change the subject. "I must show you the treasures that some of the natives gave to me when I was a boy in the Falkland Islands. We were after the fin in 1871. The fin is so fast, Maggie, it is a real challenge. I was just sixteen then and manning an oar in the whaleboat for the first time. On that sail, we also skirted Africa, where we found it grand for the humpback. I have sailed along both coasts of South America and I've been around the Cape three times coming and three times going, and that is some adventure, I'll tell you!"

Maggie was sure that she could hear stories of times at sea for a lifetime from John once she got him talking, but right now, her head was whirling with a scheme that she had no idea of how to bring forward.

On the following day, Monday, John was again overseeing the loading of stores aboard his vessel. Once she had set her house in order, she, a bit out of character, put on a bonnet in order to make a call on the wife of another captain. John had mentioned during supper last evening that the Laura J. had just docked on Saturday after spending twenty-three months in the Pacific. Mary Lewis, wife of the captain had accompanied her husband on the voyage, and Mary had spoken to John at dockside to congratulate him on his marriage and to ask if his bride could call on her one morning and soon so that they might become acquainted.

As Maggie approached the twelve-room home that John had described, she marveled at its splendor. Sea captains must make a very fine wage indeed to afford such a structure. Here, three of the Lewis children lived with their widowed aunt and their grandmother while Mary and Henry Lewis ploughed the seas. This enabled the children to attend school in New Bedford. Captain Henry and his wife had just returned from this journey with a new son, born one year previous on shipboard off the Gilbert Islands, all to the joy of sister, brothers, aunt, and grandmother who greeted him.

When John had unfolded this story, it came as a sudden revelation and surprise to Maggie. She had never heard of captains' wives accompanying their husbands on these sea voyages. It was a distinct American phenomenon, he said. Some of the crew objected strenuously to the practice, John alleged, but mostly among one another. They saw a woman aboard as a bad omen or ill luck in their superstitious fancies, but the captain had the final and undisputed say on his own vessel. John had remarked that it must be a very boring life for any woman, for unlike the men who had daily work to do, the ladies had nothing but free time to fill. Cook did not permit a woman into his galley and usually made that clear early on; this was a violation of his special domain. The more Maggie listened, the more she became resolute about visiting Mary Lewis promptly this day and hearing more.

Mrs. Lewis hastened into her living room, extending her hand, when she heard Maggie had come to call. She was a middle-aged, plain woman, her black hair pulled tight around her head and netted in a large bun at the back of her neck. She wore no ornament on her high-neck dress, yet she greeted Maggie with a beautiful open, happy face. It occurred to Maggie that her image of dress was due to some religious persuasion, probably Quaker. She had read that many of the captains and owners were very strict in their puritanical appearances, and she at once contrasted this with her own and her mum's easy manner of dress and beliefs. This sweet woman was probably the same age as her own mother, but looked much older and it was then she began to wonder how much the life at sea had accounted for the disparity.

After chatting pleasantly about John and their marriage in Nova Scotia, her own new home, and the sea journey to arrive here, Mary offered tea and the two settled into friendly conversation. By careful probing, Maggie learned all she need to know about this idea that was running furiously through her auburn head. Yes, true, Mary related, at times the crew did object openly to a female on board, especially when some ill befell them, yet they tolerated her presence for the most part, and she felt that some sailors secretly enjoyed a woman's place on the vessel, although they would never admit it. She said that she could understand that to some men, her presence was only a reminder of home, making them all the lonelier.

Mary went on to tell her many stories of her visits to exotic islands, or long beautiful days on the ocean, of sudden storms and their terrors, of the excitement of the whale hunt, and of the gamming, as she called it, or the meetings their ship had with a like vessel at sea. Then, they shared news from home, sometimes letters, and if she was lucky, she enthused, there might be a wife aboard like herself, and in this case, they would implore their husbands to tarry a bit longer for a good 'gam.'

Mary touched only briefly on how she missed her children, who remained at home, but spoke enthusiastically of how her two oldest boys would soon be joining their father to work aboard his ship. Had she not accompanied her husband, Henry, they would be forced to be apart for two years. She sighed. Then she spoke of Helen Cooper in this regard, a neighbor, living just down the hill. Helen did not accompany her husband and had been with him for only seven months in the past twelve years for she chose to stay at home and never go to sea, or perhaps *he* preferred it this way! Mary was not sure which, and here she smiled, knowingly.

Maggie sat there nodding with slender understanding, yet this woman made a great deal of sense. She seemed both eloquent and intelligent. Maggie did not mention her own disturbing thoughts about the voyage on which John was about to embark but thanked her hostess, most effusively, for being so kind and sharing her morning with another captain's wife.

Episode:

Now, in the full midday sun, the streets were alive with the townsfolk of New Bedford, a city of scarcely over 20,000 people, but whose harbor had boasted 400 whaling vessels in 1850, accounting for one-half the fleet of the entire world. That was the heyday, and when John's father must have sailed, she supposed. Whaling now was not as packed with activity as it once had been. The demand for whale oil was decreasing, and one day, Maggie expected, it might be a vanished occupation. She was just passing the N.B. Cordage Company where thousands of miles of whale line, so essential to the industry, were twisted. John had told her only yesterday, as they passed this way after their inspection of the Gratitude, that the rope made in this long shed, several city blocks long was composed of fifty-one hemp yarns, each of which could withstand a pull of 112 pounds, yet together, measured only two inches in circumference. He revealed a solemn face after saying those words, testifying to the mighty power of the whale. That sentence had frightened, and yet intrigued her, she recalled.

Today, these streets about the cordage company were crowded with workers, probably on their lunch break, and horse drawn wagons were busily hauling away huge quantities of rope to dockside for the whaleboats. In it all was an air of excitement, flurry and energy that Maggie knew her own father must have once felt. Could this be why she held this urge to tell John that *she* planned to *go along* with him to sea?

She had but five days to make ready. Her first and most important action had to be to tell her husband of her plans. Tonight, after the grand dinner she would prepare, and with him all relaxed and content, yes, then she would use all the wiles, all of the charm that she possessed to convince him that she was *not to* be left behind.

Episode:

Aboard the Gratitude

Remaining below deck in the captain's cabin until they were well out to sea and sailing effortlessly, seemed certainly the best way to begin this voyage. Maggie could hear the clamor of the crew handling lines, putting up sail and accomplishing the countless tasks to maneuver the Gratitude out of New Bedford harbor and on into the open sea in search of the mighty whale. It was only after John put his head into the cabin doorway, to see if she was comfortable and feeling no seasickness, that Maggie felt that she might venture out on deck. Once more, she experienced no ill effects by being aboard ship, even one of this smaller size, as compared to the one that brought her across the Atlantic Ocean.

And she wondered once more if she were truly following her father's calling in the way his daughter seemed to take to the sea.

By this time, most of the mates and crew knew that the captain's bride was sailing with them, for they had observed the loading of feminine gear on the last day prior to sailing, and the word spread quickly.

The Gratitude, being a 'plum pudding ship,' that is, one that only sails the Atlantic, had never been fitted out with thought of a woman aboard. So it was that the crew counted on as fact, never suspecting it might happen. John fully realized that a number of his men never having sailed with a lady aboard could be displeased, and he resolved to summarily quell any grumbling, should it occur.

Once under sail, Maggie saw no advantage by staying in the cabin, omens or no. She supposed that the sooner the crew saw that she brought no evil with her, the easier the trip would be for everyone. It was John who was swift to show her the vessel under full sail, and to then introduce her to his first mate.

Caleb Shields was a man of about John's age, with twinkling blue eyes and a patch of carrot-colored hair. He was slimmer and shorter than her husband and appeared likeable. She could not discern the least bit of animosity on his part for her being aboard; on the contrary, he remarked that this would be a very special passage, due to a 'lady's' presence. John explained that Caleb was himself born on a whaler in the middle of the Pacific, thus he knew much of whaling wives for his mother had been one of them.

Owen Poole, however, was quite another matter. The small, swarthy-skinned second mate, with his black piercing eyes made Maggie feel as though they might drill a blade straight through her and enjoy doing so. He was, possibly five years John's senior and had no smile for her when introduced, but only a sneer that she easily detected. Openly surly, he immediately excused himself by curtly saying he was required on the fore deck for men needing his direction. John was quick to beg Maggie's forgiveness for his shortness with her, for Owen, he said, at his best, was never a friendly sort, and now he felt that he had a reason to show his moodiness. He did, however, do his work with precision, demanding only the best of the men; he was a tireless worker and one of the finest harpooners in the fleet. John said this last bit with satisfaction, that is to say, any seaman would certainly attest to Owens's ability with the harpoon.

Maggie shrugged it all aside. Each man on board ship came from his own solitary place, and each one could not be faulted for his reaction to the other. She would not let this small matter bother her, she assured John. Her supreme joy in being aboard for the next eight months was the pleasure of her husband's company, this being all she could wish for made for perfect contentment.

She took the first full day at sea to put her clothes and belongings in order. John had traveled the seas so long alone he had become accustomed to using every nook and cranny of the cabin. She devised making her large steamer trunk, placed square in the middle of the cabin, a sometimes table set for two, covering it in the day with a proper cloth. She kept inside of it, most of her books and clothing that she did not use daily, such as extra skirts, blouses, and the boy-size oilskins that she had purchased at the mercantile just before their departure, these to be used in any foul weather.

She crammed her under-garments and soaps into the three small drawers built into one wall, while John kept most of his things in the sea chest that fit neatly beneath his desk, the large drawer underneath their three quarter bunk already held blankets and bedding.

Mary Lewis had told her of how she traveled with her portable foot-peddled sewing machine and her potted geraniums, while some of her friends took along a small parlor organ to play for services or to amuse them on the long days at sea. Maggie did feel satisfied that she was neither that domesticated nor musical, for she would have been hard put to find space for such items. She did think to pack her tin whistle, the one that Bruce had taught her to pipe when a child on Skye. Moreover, she made up her own medical kit after hearing Mary's tales of accidents and illnesses, even though she knew that the first mate kept a complete one ever ready in his cabin.

So the days began at sun up and found Maggie busily engaged writing in her journal. She had remained faithful to the notebook that Laura had secreted in her bag on that day of her train ride across the highlands. Every page had been filled by the time she moved from Glasgow to Edinburgh, and there she began another. The one in hand, started aboard the Gratitude, would be the fourth in the series which she intended to fill, year upon year. She realized now how very useful they were in reading back her thoughts, her adventures and her dreams.

Up on the sunny deck, a sweater thrown around her shoulders, as this craft headed north, she began writing again. They had finally picked up the warm current running in the North Atlantic and were taking advantage of its movement by making excellent time during these days under full sail. Stopping her busy pencil for the moment, she decided to read over the last few days of writing, to see if it made the sense that she intended. She had noted that several other whaling ships were seen for the first few days, all heading north in search of the Sperm and the Right. Maggie, stopping to look out over the waters, could only see endless, endless, endless seas. They made her feel that she was barely just beginning to understand these men who were giving their lives to them.

Here, aboard ship, the least variation of the normal was greeted with comment, much as is the pure delight of children. For, from a school of dolphins off the port bow, a pickup in strong wind in the forward sail, or even the diversion of a plum cobbler as a treat for the evening meal, they all brought forth the pleasure of celebration. These events were eagerly whispered about from one sailor to the next. Yes, Maggie observed, the ordinary on land, became the exceptional at sea. Most all of the sailors were unschooled, but by no means unlearned. They all could read the signs of the elements.

July 4.

It is with hesitation that I begin this account of life aboard a whaler. I do believe this might be a useful report for later days, yet it is with humility that I begin, not understanding all the various workings of this ship as yet, or least of all the various jobs of crewmembers. These I am determined to learn, however.

On this vessel, The Gratitude, on this fourth day of July, 1887: beside myself, wife of the master of the ship; John Foote Dix, master; Caleb Shields, first mate; Owen Poole, second mate; and twenty seven crew, one of which is cook; one cooper; four harpooners and the remainder, various crew members. All of these I will meet over the next days.

We are a whaling vessel out of New Bedford upon the sea for about eight months' time depending on our catch, the weather and our provisions. We will be sailing on the Atlantic Ocean, Baffin Bay, the Davis Straits, and other bodies of water to their north.

John has been part of the crew of a whaling ship for seventeen years, beginning at the age of fifteen, as cabin boy, deck hand, and advancing steadily to head flenser, second mate, first mate, and now on his fifth voyage, captain of this vessel. He remains one of the youngest masters on the east coast of America.

I feel most snug and secure as I write, and I look upon this journal as one recreation and enjoyment of this voyage. I am fully aware that this venture will not be easy at times, yet I see it as rich in knowledge and the passageway of a lifetime.

July 5,

I stopped abruptly in my writing of yesterday, when John called me to the rail to see a wondrous sight. In the distance, what looked to be a beautiful white cloud seemingly headed straight for us. It sat right on the horizon and I strained to make out the shape of what it might be. John knew, even at that distance, it was the Barnaby K, out of New London, and I finally made out the foresails and her trim bow. Both crews gave salutes as we passed the other with shouts of good cheer going back and forth between the captains for I found that they were good friends.

William Carlson, the master of the Barnaby, had sailed with John in 1876, when he was first flenser, and they had been through some dour weather and rough seas together. Master Carlson had not yet heard of our marriage, and as John shouted the news, he pointed to me standing beside him and was grinning like a child with a new toy. Captain Carlson waved both of his arms uproariously. He is not yet a married man. The weather, being too brisk for an anchor and a bit of gamming, compelled both to sail on, hoping to meet again on a calmer day. The Barnaby K. had been at sea for three months and carries 450 filled barrels. This captain knew the elements with more exactness than a hundred professors of science, and also knew more about human nature than the sociologist. John has described him just so. Most captains come to sea as young boys, and seem destined to remain here for most of their lives.

John is calling for me and so I must finish this later.
He has spotted dolphins off the starboard bow and believes I might enjoy viewing them . . .

Often, Maggie dwelt with the thought that these men with so much free time, of how they could profitably use it to enjoy the great books of the world. That would be if only they had the advantage of being able to read. But what a pity, hardly a man among them, below the rank of mate, could read at all. True, on occasion, there was an educated man among those quartered in the foc'sle, one lost soul seeking either adventure or escape from the trials of his life on land. These *misfits,* as the captains spoke of them, kept to themselves, did read a good amount, and wrote or 'scribbled a bit,' as they sullenly called it. These men usually left the sea after one or two voyages, ready to take up life on shore once more, unlike the other 'weathered seamen.'

Maggie clearly saw how all of the crew yearned, with a cavernous ache, for the dear ones somewhere at home. This longing, she felt, was the one factor that both united and motivated them. Their caring needs were sometimes imprinted into intricate carvings of scrimshaw to which they devoted long hours, working their loneliness into a sperm whale's tooth or the creation of decorative and useful gifts from that beautiful ivory. It meant a vision of home and family to them, but at present these images were only perceived in their mind's eye.

During the weeks of the sail, Maggie and John came to know the other very well. She found him to be the extremely caring, loving man she had first recognized, ever concerned of her feelings and comfort. They sat in their cabin, or if weather permitted, on deck for long hours, mainly following the evening meal, talking of their childhood and sharing their dreams of the future as the vessel moved effortlessly over the silent, dark sea.

The Gratitude had been away from port for three and one-half weeks. With not a whale sighted thus far, John was not the least discouraged. He told Maggie, that an early start of the catch meant a light catch to the crew, making her know that a little superstition was afoot even here . . . She *was not* the only member of this sail, who believed in signs! With the weather this fair and life so good, it seemed to her, that this sail could go on forever.

Maggie took great delight in sitting on the wooden lounge chair which was placed on deck for her, exclusively. She spent most days gazing at the glorious waves, and then writing copiously of her observations, chiefly in her journal. She wrote poetry as well, but kept these strictly to herself.

She also wrote long letters to Mum Jane and to Mrs. Wallace in Halifax, to Laura, Bruce and the girls on Skye, E. Ferguson in Edinburgh, Marion in Baddeck, Molly Grant in

Glasgow, and dear Dr. Bell, who was now residing, for a time at least, in America carrying on his work with the deaf. She had no idea of when these might be sent as they would have to be given to a ship sailing for home, but it gave her pleasure, relating her happiness to family and to friends. She hoped that the Gratitude would meet another vessel soon, but she felt no urgency. All was sublime; life took on a slower pace here than she had ever known, and with John so near, she wanted for nothing.

The men in the foc'sle had finally become accustomed to a woman on board she felt. A few of them, as they passed, mumbled a garbled, "mornin' mum," however she did wish that they would sight the whale shortly or she might be blamed for some ill luck. It was nearing August and cooler winds and waters becoming the rule each day as they entered the Labrador Sea. Amazing sunrises and sunsets were spectacular here and Maggie missed very few. Despite so much free time, she continued her custom of rising early and taking her scones and tea, or biscuits, as they called them on board, in the main cabin, or occasionally, if the wind was not too brisk, on deck. The cook of the ship was Portuguese. Maggie easily made friends with him, and contrary to what Mary Lewis had told her, this cook was not averse to letting her show him how to make oat scones, as all of the ingredients were available for them. This was Laura's recipe, a simple flour-oat biscuit with little shortening. He delighted in making them every morning, not only for Maggie, but also to the pleasure of the entire crew. And along with the plum and the apple butters in the larder, her mornings could not be more agreeable.

Roger, or so they all called the cook, Maggie being sure this was not his given name, was a merry sort, using his ingenuity on most days to create a meal that the men could enjoy for his own satisfaction as well as for theirs. Except for the oatcakes, Maggie steered clear of his galley, following the sage advice of Mary, given to her earlier in New Bedford.

So then life moved peacefully until the evening when she unintentionally overheard Owen Poole voice a curt remark about her unwanted presence to a fellow crewmember. He had a cutting, sharp tongue, and even though it came *from his* type, it hurt. Maggie never dealt with backbiting well, anyway. She certainly was not about to mention this to John. The remark was to the effect that the entire crew would far better off if their captain put his wife on the next passing vessel headed for port and then they could get down to the business of catching whales. She was a jinx, and of that he was sure!

Maggie had remained coolly indifferent to this second mate, thus far, but now she intended to treat him frostily.

During mid-morning of that next day as she sat on deck in her white, high-necked sweater, knitted for her by Laura, with a woolen shawl about her lower body to shield out the brisk winds, she heard the loud cry for the first time, the cry that was to become to her ears, all too common. From the uppermost crosstrees, loud and clear, 'Thar she blows' and again even louder, 'Thar she blows.' This sighting, however, proved to be but a false alarm, as this whale dove deep, not to be sighted again.

The next day found Maggie seated at John's desk while he strode the deck. Here she could look directly above to view the ship's compass, a two-sided instrument, which could be read by the helmsman on the deck above and the person at the desk below. Ingenious, she thought, and marked its reading in her journal as she began a page. She entered the main cabin for her breakfast soon after, and upon seeing her; Owen Poole made his hasty exit, though he had not finished his meal. It sorely disturbed her to find this sort of animosity towards her person and she felt it unjust, for her only transgression was being a woman and that infuriated her sense of fairness.

On this day, they had reached the whaling grounds, the aim of their sail. Now, the ship moved about encircling a ten-mile radius, with light sail by day, furled topsails and back mainsails, and then dropping sails by night. Lookouts climbed to their precarious perches in the crosstrees, one hundred feet above the endless rolling sea, steadying them only by holding to the horizontal hoops that enclosed them on the platform. This was wearisome work, and the foremast crew shared the duty in two-hour shifts. It always left Maggie breathless to watch their ascent. It was Caleb, the first mate, who told Maggie what to expect when they did spot a whale.

"It will, in all probability, be a humpback or a sperm that we sight first. The sperm usually sends up twelve feet of spray of condensed moisture, which hangs in the air for about three seconds. This spray can be seen for about six miles. Cautious lookouts wait for a second spurt before calling out, 'Thar she blows', or sometimes only 'Thar blows.' They also call out 'She breeches' if the whale thrusts its head high above the water's surface and again if the breeching whale falls back to the sea, he shouts, 'She white waters.'"

Caleb's eyes were alight with the adventure of the hunt, as he described how every man of the crew springs into action as the call comes, each knowing exactly his position in the chase. Maggie found the description fascinating. She had no idea that it was truly a 'chase.'

They sat in the main cabin lingering over their second cup of tea as John came in to join them. He had heard only the tail end of their conversation, but added: "I've not yet tried to describe the stimulation of the boats being lowered and of the chase itself to you, as I felt that you must see it to believe it, but soon enough now you will have that chance. My senses tell me we are not far from a whale, or perhaps a school of them. The time is right and we are in a fine spot. Caleb here, can tell you many tales if he cares to though, Maggie, for he has seen some real strange incidents on the 'other side,' that is the term we use for the Pacific. Caleb has spent more years there than he has here in the Atlantic with me. What is it Caleb, four trips around the horn, besides the one that carried you home as a toddler?"

Caleb nodded, as he offered a self-conscious, boyish smile, and John continued: "He can tell you tales of the Sandwich Islands, Galapagos, Rorotonga, Tahiti and the Great Loo Choo!" beamed John with pride in his freckled first-mate.

Her captain had been very accurate, for it was only on the next morning, as Maggie was dressing, that the shout rang out so shrill and bold through the thin morning air that it startled her. Exactly as Caleb had described, 'Thar she blows' and again with only a moment's interval, 'Thar she blows.' Maggie hurried into her boots, and pulling on her wide neck sweater, rushed up on deck afraid that she might miss some moments of her first whale hunt. Two boats, loaded with men, were already being lowered from the davits into the cold waters. Maggie saw six men in each, with Caleb commanding one and dark Owen Poole, the other. She could not imagine how they had accomplished this so quickly. Maggie looked out into the direction to which the lookout still pointed. There, just barely, could she make out a huge dark shape against the horizon, but clearly a geyser of whetted air shot high against the blue skies to a forward angle of about forty-five degrees and arched into the ocean. John was beside her now.

"She's a sperm all right," he remarked, using his spyglass just acquired from the main cabin. "I think she may rightly be ready to go down for a dive. We'll have to wait 'till she surfaces and hope she comes up true."

Maggie knew this whale could dive and come up in an altogether separate area from where it first was spotted, and the whaleboats must not be too close when she made ready. Thus, the twelve men in boats took an 'easy' oar, to watch for any sign. The ship and the boats were about a mile from the beast, when exactly to John's pronouncement, the sperm, having filled her lungs with air, dove sharply and was quickly lost from sight. This was where the captain must make the right decision, reasoned Maggie. The whale could reappear within thirty minutes or so, in the same area, or might swim for ten miles from them before surfacing for air again.

John told her that he chose to think that this whale was feeding from the way the petrels were circling overhead and dipping into the waters to pluck fragments of her leavings. He chose to keep the two boats in the water and close to the ship so that he might send them out speedily when the whale reappeared. He took out the gold watch that he wore on a chain across his vest, and waited patiently with the crew, ever scanning the horizon for a shape she noted so that you could hear a pin drop; every man was so completely still. Then suddenly, the shrill voice rang out once more: 'Thar she blows,' and this time it was on the starboard side of the Gratitude, only about a quarter-mile distant. Again, they all saw the unmistakable spout. Without any hesitation, both boats made for the shape, first with the long oars skimming the calm ocean smoothly, then as they drew closer, the mates ordered the oars shipped and the paddles brought out for a quieter slip through the waters.

The whale had spouted once again, just as one boat reached its side. Each man was alert and ready. Maggie could feel the tension build until the harpooner let go with a lunge so powerful, she could not believe one man might move his arm with such force and precision. The huge beast rose from the waves, with a shudder that seemed to convulse its entire form, to come crashing down on the sea, forcing huge walls of water with it.

The men in the crafts moved instantly to be well out of the whale's path when it 'white watered,' with the harpoon still fixed securely into the whale in a vital spot the men paid out the line keeping out of harm's way. In only a few more moments, the great mammal gave an audible, eerie gasp and rolled onto its side. It lay quiet in the water, a dark pool of red blood, staining the sea for a quarter of a mile around it.

The entire effect on Maggie McBain Dix was extraordinary. The excitement of the scene left her flushed and breathless, but the inner revulsion made her ill and nauseous. No one seemed to notice her reaction as every man had all he could do with the job at hand. It became a somewhat frenzied effort now, with each man carrying out his prescribed action.

Maggie slipped silently into her cabin as all the hard work began, finding that she must lie down on the bed to compose herself, she was that shaken. She kept asking herself, if it were merely the sight of such a mammoth beast, caught and killed in such a manner, or the danger that she perceived to the men she had come to know well that made her feel so weak. She wondered if future catches would become easier to handle, or if she would forever feel as she did now . . . Then all went black . . . Somewhere above her she could hear John calling to her and she tried hard to understand the words. He seemed tunnels of miles away as he kept repeating her name over and over again. It was when she saw his blurred, worried face bending over her own that she realized that she had fainted, yes fainted, for the first time in her life!

It was over the evening meal, which John insisted she eat, that Maggie began to feel embarrassed and self-conscious before the crew. John assured her that *no one* other than he knew of her fainting, but she felt that all of the men were abuzz with her weakness. Maybe she had been wrong to sail aboard a whaler. Perhaps she was not made of such sturdy stock, as those other captains' wives. Perhaps she did not have the inner vitality that she thought she had.

Caleb and John were the only others in the warm, main cabin, as they ate their cod in silence. Finally, Caleb broke the quiet with a comment on the size of the sperm, which was now secured to the side of the ship with strong lines.

"She's forty-five foot, if she's one, John, a real great start to our catch. I'll wager we sight one or two more on the 'morrow, if we keep the northern shoreline course. We'll have to keep the try-works going full speed this trip, if I'm any judge of the signs."

Maggie listened as the two friends made the schedule for the next day's crew in flensing and for the try-works while she tried desperately to finish her potatoes and cod, then she offered some feeble excuse so she might hasten to the cabin. When John finally came to bed, after all the extra duties of this day were accomplished, Maggie pretended to be asleep, while feeling quite guilty in doing so, for this was the first time since marriage that she acted divisive, but the trauma of this day hung heavily on her mind.

As Maggie woke on the day following the first catch, sun was streaming in through the port opposite her bed. She sensed it must be very late, never having slept until the sun was this high. She was sure that John had been especially quiet so as not to waken her, and she was touched to see the tray with its teapot, cup and scones on the stool placed alongside the bed, his charming offering.

Once dressed and on deck in the crisp, clean air, she was amazed at all of the activity. Every man was hard at work at his allotted task. The flensing stage was set up on the side of the ship, and two men were cutting huge chunks of the whale's flesh, which in turn, was hoisted in buckets to other waiting hands above, and then into iron kettles, their roaring fires belching out a stench that her nostrils were to identify with revulsion many times in the coming months.

The flesh was boiled, or 'tried-out,' as they called it until it became the oil that was stored in some of the hundreds of barrels aboard for the purpose. Earlier the cooper had formed metal hoops about the barrels to secure them, and when the oil was cool and poured into them, they were sent below deck to the hold.

Maggie was standing next to the main cabin, endeavoring to stay out of the men's way, watching the entire process in wonderment, even though it had been described to her in detail.

When Caleb came up behind her, he spoke softly: "It *is* a strange sight for the newcomer, I am sure, Maggie." Caleb had noted her strained, sensitive features as she stared intently at the process; he went on: "I can still remember the day when I, as a boy of ten, saw my first whale tried-out. It does take a bit of getting used to. The men here take it all in a day's work, and in fact, are never so cheerful and alive, as when they are seeing the results of the catch entering the hold. It brings them one day closer to the end of the voyage, to home and to their share of the profit."

She turned to him, realizing that he was attempting to be very kind. He could sense her distaste for the scene, and was endeavoring to make her perceive it as commonplace.

Yet she knew she was one, who would never discern the logic of a catch, no matter how many she might witness. The beast had been so unaware, so vulnerable. This trying-out day was to be but another day that burned into Maggie's soul.

Standing there, it seemed to her that the captain had the most difficult job aboard the whaler, not only the responsibility of the crew, but the overseeing of the dozen separate tasks it took to put the whale to the product. John was active everywhere, and Maggie saw little of him this day.

It was very late in the evening, when John finally came into their cabin for sleep. Unlike the night before, she was up waiting for him and wished to talk. She had so many questions about the feelings she had been holding during this day, and his opinions mattered.

"What did you think of the catch, then Maggie, my girl?"

John seemed so weary, as he sat on the foot of the bunk and pulled off his boots, but he radiated an air of accomplishment and he seemed pleased with himself.

"I can truly say, John, that I have never witnessed anything to match it. Your entire operation works so smoothly and the men are enormously intent."

Maggie did not wish to deflate his pride in this endeavor and found she was skirting an inner sadness that she had wished to speak of, now fearing that it would take his spirit down. I have no right, she thought, gazing at him, to impose my morals, or intrude in the life this man has chosen for himself. I am a visitor here, and I wanted to come along. Perhaps I judge my own reaction too hurriedly.

And so she only said, "It gets so busy these days on deck; I believe that I will begin that afghan I have planned to make for us beginning tomorrow, John. We will certainly need it soon, with the weather becoming even colder. Somehow, all that activity on deck makes me wish to stay below, out of the way, at least until the try-works is finished."

"As you wish my darlin' and then lying down and patting her place beside his, urging her to come to bed, he added, "Oh, I am glad that you wanted to come sailing with me."

With that said he, completely fatigued, placed his arm about Maggie's waist and was in a deep sleep before she could say another word. Maggie lay awake next to this lovable, rough man for several hours, simply accepting this day. Finally, the roll of the ship and his nearness lulled her into peaceful sleep.

The try works complete, today found Maggie sitting on deck, dreaming of huge, fresh tomatoes and crisp cucumbers from Mrs. Wallace's garden. She faced the sea, but thought of her last home in Nova Scotia, with a fondness. All the putting up of the first whale was over at present, and she was in a contented, near dreamlike reverie. She envisioned a strawberry tart, exactly the kind her aging friend had become famous for in the Halifax Ladies Auxiliary. Plump, handpicked berries, oozing their red juice, all ripe and lovely, served with the thickest clotted cream. Agnes's tarts certainly rivaled any of Molly Grant's delicacies at the tearoom.

Roger saw Maggie's far-away look, as he tossed the parings of the supper potatoes overboard.

Trying to be sociable, he commented on the beautiful, sunny day, just as Maggie came out of her daydream to the firm reality of fish and potatoes for yet another meal.

"A penny for your thoughts," Roger laughed, and Maggie found that she must bend the truth a bit, lest she injure his culinary ego. He actually did a competent job with what he had on hand. No sailor ever went hungry, although at times, it did tend to be monotonous.

"Just remembering Halifax and some nice people there, some I love dearly, Roger. What about your home? Where is your family?"

Cook had become so easy to talk to, that is, ever since the scone lesson. He seemed grateful that she never over-stepped her place to try to take over his domain in the galley. Secretly, he was glad that there was a woman on board. He shared none of the crew's superstition, but considered her to be a good omen.

"My home and my family are in New Bedford. I came to America from Portugal when I was sixteen. I worked in hotel kitchens in Lisbon before that. I was born in a small village north of Lisbon, and lived there with mother, father, three brothers and a sister. We were very poor. My father was a fisherman, until he lost a leg in an accident. I saw no future there, so when a sailing ship docked to buy supplies, they recruited men to work. It was an American ship, so two of my brothers signed on with me, and we left Portugal that spring. I began to work on whalers out of New Bedford. That is nearly twenty years ago when I became a cook, and my brothers, crewmen. They are both aboard a whaler on the 'other side' right now. I've not seen them for two years."

He was gazing out to sea now himself, and Maggie was surprised at his long speech. These were the most words she had heard from anyone on board, except perhaps for Caleb, and she recognized that Roger was eager to share his thoughts of family with someone who would listen.

"I worked very hard in America for three years. I learned the language, and when my brothers and I saved enough, we were able to send for mama, papa, and young Manuel and Maria. We all live in one large house there and they are happy. I married a girl from Boston and we have four little ones. Someday, when I save enough money, I will leave the sea and build an inn and a restaurant there in New Bedford for other families like ours. Then after my day's work, I will sit in the sun and take pleasure in my large family."

Roger was the one who seemed lost in a daydream now, as his hands still held the huge pan from the parings, and his eyes were set on the horizon.

Maggie was filled with more understanding for these sailors and their dreams than she could have guessed months before, and this all from one undemanding question about his family. He turned and headed for the galley, but not before he nodded his head and smiled at her civility.

"Thank you," he said, "for this good talk. Ma'am, I better get that fish started before I have the crew a' hollering!"

Maggie looked after him, dumbfounded. *He* had done all the talking, she, the listening, but perhaps that is exactly what these lonely men need, a good listener.

Episode:

In the weeks that followed the first whale catch, there was a succession of kills. Only a few days later, two more sperms were sighted and caught. The crew barely finished storing the barrels, when two humpback whales were seen, late on an afternoon, in bone-chilling weather. John judged it too late to try to take them with nighttime coming on, but to set anchor, hoping they would still be in the vicinity with morning light. And sure enough, as she was rousing herself from a night's sleep, she heard that shrill cry once more, and the two humpbacks were in view when she moved topsides.

The beauty of their shapes, as they seemed to frolic between her and the horizon, would never cease to delight her, but the knowledge that they were about to be hunted and killed, gave her a stabbing sense of depression. She had not conveyed this response to another person and her thought was that perhaps keeping it all within her made it the more difficult to deal with, yet she vowed that she would speak of her sadness of the 'kills' to no one.

After the boats were lowered, she watched the hunt, but only until they were in striking distance of the animals, then she turned her back and entered the main cabin. She picked up a book and tried to read; however, all the commotion on deck made that impossible. It was only when Caleb came dashing into the cabin for the spyglass, that she realized John was not topsides. "Where is my husband?" asked Maggie, looking into Caleb's open, excited face.

"Why, he's out on the chase."

At this, Maggie rushed to the rail. In that moment, a bitter current of air started from the north, and with the sea rising by the minute, snowflakes began to fall. One moment, it had seemed a fine cold day, and in the next, all was altered. Caleb was at her side, intently searching through the arctic waves to catch a glimpse of the two small boats on the wild sea.

"Why did John go out this time, Caleb?" Maggie needed an answer for some sort of reassurance.

"John always takes one of the boats, when the sea is stirred," Caleb answered promptly, not taking his eyes from the water. "He leaves either Owen or I on board; he says it is his responsibility. I thought you knew that he was out there. They will be fine, Maggie, don't you fret. Our captain and the men have been in harder blows than this."

However, she noted the urgency with which he kept scanning the horizon for the boats and the whales. She closely watched the sea as she stood next to him, feeling frozen to the spot, snow covering her hair, and a wind that would not stop.

If she were this cold and stiff, how could those twelve men out there in the huge waves, wet and frigid, manage to do the work intended? Although she had begun to abhor the industry, she could not but admire the courage of these men who risked their lives each time they stepped into a whaleboat.

It seemed hours that the two stood at the rail, watching for any signs of a boat. Their vision was impaired by the now ponderous waves and the ceaseless howl of the wind. Maggie was afraid, really afraid, for the first time in her life. Her mind could not help but return to the journal that Jane had read to her two years earlier, describing the day when her father was lost at sea. Her thoughts were so far away, she barely heard Caleb at her elbow, urging her into the main cabin for warmth. He was saying that her presence here would not make the chase move along any faster and his captain would most certainly have his hide if she should take a cold. Inside of the cabin, although she felt warmer beside the iron stove going full blast, she did not know what to do. Did all wives feel this way about their man at sea, or were those really the wise ones, women unaware of these immediate dangers, by being safe at home?

Maggie could not estimate the length of time that had passed since the boats had gone out in pursuit of the humpbacks. Caleb had finally come into the cabin to warm himself, and to see if she was all right, but only for a few moments, and then she could see him through the port, standing straight against the rail, ever searching for a sign.

Roger came in to bring her a cup of his hot bean soup, and she thanked him for thinking of her, but drank very little of it. Her stomach felt unsettled, and she wished the incessant roar of the wind would cease. At one point, with no one about, she clasped her hands over her ears in an effort to seal it out.

Finally, she saw one lookout, Davey Leeds, come down from his post, and another, Jim Eddy, climb the 100 feet of bending mast to take his place. With the sea this savage, lookouts changed watches every hour, in place of every two. Even at that. Davey, who had just left the hoops, looked as frozen as a winter turnip. His nose and ears were bright red, yet his face, the color of ashes. He headed immediately for the galley to get a mug of hot coffee.

Jimmy must have just reached the high platform, when his cry was heard, dimly at first, against the howl of wind, but, yes, louder now. Maggie was sure she heard the words, 'whaleboat on the starboard,' and again 'one whaleboat heading in.' Her heart leapt in her throat, John, John, please let it be John, and the guilt of another boat still out in the dark did not affect her. Let it be John, she kept breathing, as she rushed out on deck, to make this shape out only dimly, for with twilight gone, it was difficult to distinguish anything in the tossing, twisting waves.

This craft seemed to lose as much sea as it gained, no, perhaps it was drawing nearer, inch-by-inch. She could make out only the shapes of the men and she counted, one, two, three, four, five, six. Yes, there were six, but she could not make out their identities. Caleb had all hands ready to get lines to the boat as soon as it was within reach. The constant bobbing made one think that it surely would be swamped with every crest, and Maggie began saying all the prayers that she knew. Caleb, again permitted her to stand next to him, as he could see her alarm, and he hoped that she did not know what he already did, for this was the whaleboat commanded by Owen Poole, and would not be bringing her captain on board, not yet! Caleb spoke to her now; he had to as they raised Owen's boat of men. It was John's boat that was still out there in the cold.

The darkness closed in completely, but the wind never stopped its shrill wail; the bitter cold was intense. Maggie sat wide-eyed, curled into a corner of the lounge on one side of the cabin. She could think of only one thing, John and five other men were out in this icy, tossing sea in an open boat, without benefit of food or shelter. It was near midnight now, with a full six hours until daylight before a search might be sent out to find them.

The crew had been most kind to her. She knew this in a sort of hazy sense, making her unable to acknowledge their attempts of consolation. She did remember Caleb trying to tell her of the time on the Pacific, when one of their boats was out for two days and nights in a storm, only to be found safe and sound on the third day when that storm abated. He begged her to go to her cabin for some sleep so that she might be on lookout with them during the first rays of dawn, but she could only think of her man on that sea, of how helpless she had become and how she *must* stay topsides.

Poole said little when his crew finally secured the boat that he commanded. He spoke no word at all to Maggie, but only to Caleb. As soon as they had reached the two whales, John's boat got a harpoon off into the larger of the two, but not in a vital spot, and it looked to Owen, that they were off on 'a sleigh ride,' or so all whalers called it. This whale had strength enough to pull that boat and all of its crew on a scary, wild ride.

Unless they severed the line to him, they were destined to follow wherever the beast chose. Most times, the crew would ride this out, to either tire the whale until they could finish it off, or with the possibility of inflicting another more deadly wound. In any case, they had not seen John's boat since that time, and they had all they could do, to fight their way back, through the wild seas to the Gratitude. All of his men were exhausted and were bedded down so they might be ready for the next busy morning. His story only filled her with more terror than she already possessed. She was incapable of any sleep.

Roger came into the cabin, somewhere in the middle of the night, placing more fuel in the stove to keep Maggie warm. He looked so sympathetic; Maggie could not help but reassure him that *she* was certain all would be well. He insisted that she drink the hot tea he had just prepared, and he sat with her speaking of other topics, trying to pass the hours. What a kind person, thought Maggie. She must tell John how very good he had been to her, when her captain was safe on board again. She would not lose her conviction that he was all right.

With the first light showing on the horizon, Caleb was right there at the rail taking his own watch on deck. As she joined him, the first encouraging thing she noticed was that the sea and wind had calmed to only heavy breezes. The worst of the storm was over.

They were traveling now in the Davis Strait, not far from the barren coast of Greenland. Maggie had plotted this course in her journal just as John had taught her to do only yesterday. She wished, at least for this day, that they were sailing near a warmer, less hostile shore.

With sunrise, and through each passing hour, as they stood watch together, she and Caleb could note a distinct change in the sea. A warming began, and then finally the winds died to a mere light breeze. "The only problem with such light winds is that we cannot put up sail for any search," declared Maggie, in a distraught tone.

Caleb quickly offered that the rule for this circumstance was to stay the course that their captain had set; that is, the mother ship should remain relatively at rest and let the lost boat find *it*. He intended to circle in arcs of only three miles even if they found wind. His duty was to send out one or more whaleboats, and with oar power, search the surrounding vicinity.

Crews were eager and waiting to begin, and contrary to what Maggie had expected, Owen Poole was the first and most ready of all. Finally, it was determined that two whaleboats were to be sent out, Caleb at the helm of one and Poole in charge of the other. The Gratitude was placed in the hands of the ship's cooper, Henry Hawks. He was told to 'lay to;' and keep the coffee hot, for all in the three boats would be ready for that warming beverage when they returned.

Maggie began to appreciate the loyalty of these men, one to another. They placed such trust in each of their fellows, for their very lives depended on them and the small petty woes of every day disappeared in the true desire to locate their shipmates.

She watched the boats until they were out of sight. Each took a different direction, while Maggie went into her own cabin to put on fresh clothes and fix her hair. She did not want John to see her in such a rumpled, unkempt fashion. Back on deck, within fifteen minutes time, and the weather had changed once more. The sun now broke through full, and the sea was a sheet of glass. It actually seemed temperate to her skin, and she marveled at these ever-changing, mysterious waters. She had some hint this day of why her husband found them so fascinating.

There was a small crew aboard the vessel now. With the eighteen men off in boats, only twelve remained, plus Maggie. The young, agile lookouts were vigilant at their posts to spot anything which looked like a whaleboat, and cook suppressed his nervousness by beginning to prepare a substantial lunch for all the returning crew.

There was never a discouraging word of 'what if,' to be heard from anyone, but it was duties as usual and all effort to the reunion.

Mr. Hawks placed a comfortable chair on the now sunny port deck, for Maggie to do her waiting. She tried again to take up a book and then the afghan, but it was no use. Her eyes continually scanned the horizon, and it was she, simultaneous with the boy's call from above, who spotted the small craft, just on the rim of the horizon. How long would it be until she could make out the occupants? With these calm waters, this boat seemed to fairly fly across the surface. It was plain that the men were rowing hard. Then, what sounded like music to her ears, she heard John's deep voice, calling out her name, and all of the anxiety was over.

It was a tired, but happy group of men that climbed out of that boat. All were laughing and quick to tell their story. All was not flawless, however, for as John took Maggie into his arms, she saw the strips of white cloth tied all about his left forearm, and the caked, dried blood that showed beneath.

"What has happened to you? Let me take a look at this." She began at once to remove the crude bandage.

"It's nothing, Maggie, my love, just a scratch," and gently removing her small hands from this arm said, "We'll have Caleb take a look, as soon as he decides we are not out there on the ocean. Come on now, share a big breakfast with me."

It was only a short half-hour and all the boats were safe in their davits once more. John had shot off two flares from the Gratitude, and both search parties saw them and returned.

"You see why the vessel is named so, my darling. We have a wonderful record aboard this old ship. All hands safe again, and no one the worse for it, but I haven't told you the best of it yet. In the storm, after the old humpback took us on that wild sleigh ride, we finally got off a fine shot at her and she's out there now, about ten miles east, all secured with a buoy and marked for towing. I think that I'll send Caleb after her, though. I feel like I need a little nap!"

Episode:

The Gratitude was nearly one-half full of capacity of oil and the calendar spelled only October. The bark now spent its days in great circles in the Davis Straits, or in the south end of Baffin Bay, taking an average of a whale every ten days or so, a remarkable record said Caleb to Owen Poole loudly one day as the two passed on deck so that and Maggie overheard them. She wondered if Caleb, in his impish way, was trying to bedevil Owen a bit, by his back-handed remark, alluding that even with a woman's curse aboard, they were doing better this trip than on any that either of them had yet sailed. She smiled to herself and wished she had a look at Poole's face.

"Of course," he retorted, "the voyage is not yet over, Mr. Shields." It was just like him Maggie fumed, always with the sour last words.

It was about this time, that Maggie felt the fevers and flushes, which she had experienced both on the day prior to her wedding and on her arrival in Massachusetts. On those days, she had been under the strain of excitement, and she chalked it up to that, but now the ill feelings were coming with more regularity, and she really was under no stress. Her joints all ached, especially in the early mornings, and she attributed this to the damp, salt air. Her private diagnoses made it nonetheless painful, however. She determined not to mention this to John. He certainly had enough to keep his mind occupied. One mainsail had been torn to shreds in a dreadful blow, and with only one spare aboard, and a poor one at that, John was busily engineering several of the crew in sewing a new main from some old canvas stored below deck.

Supplies were holding out well, but the meals were boring. She tried to imagine the voyages of several years and the task of storing food for such a stretch of time. She did remember, though, that usually in the Pacific, they could replenish some foods from the tropical islands and wasn't that a warm, pleasant thought.

John made a remarkable recovery from the gash in his arm. It seemed to give him no trouble in his duties, but she was sure it pained him a great deal. It had left a dreadful, jagged scar. He made light of it and was back in the whaleboats only one week after it happened. She was getting used to his being lowered into the sea, in search of the leviathan, but she always made sure she was at the rail, to bid him a safe trip, and to give him a kiss for luck.

It was on one of these evenings, when Maggie was feeling especially feverish and ill, but did not wish John to suspect, so after their dinner, she took down a favorite book and tried to read. Her eyes became strained, the print on the page was unclear, and she was developing a headache, so she passed the volume over to John, who sat whittling on a piece of hardwood. He did many lovely carvings for her, and these she was storing in her chest for keepsakes.

"Would you mind reading a few pages to me, darling?" Maggie asked in her happy voice, trying not to show her pain. "My eyes seem to be salt-sore tonight and I would love to hear *your* voice read some of my favorite verses."

At first, John continued to look at the piece of wood in his hand, as though he had not heard, then, when Maggie handed the book to him, he looked up and set the carving aside. He stood and opened the book to the marked page, and his face reddened in a manner that Maggie had never seen before. He cleared his throat, put the open book on the desk, turned and faced her:

"I knew this moment would come one day, Maggie." He stared down at the cabin floor, as if to find the right words, "I wanted to tell you long ago, first, when we were courting, then, as soon as we married, but the time never seemed just right. I was afraid at first, afraid that you would not marry me if you knew, and then once you had, that you would be so embarrassed."

Now looking into her lovely green eyes, he spoke the words that were so very distressing for him: "Maggie, *I cannot* read . . . *I never actually learned to read!* She gazed at him with large, incredulous eyes.

"But the reports, the charts . . . why, being a captain you *have to read* . . . I see . . . you are only worried that your reading won't sound right to my ear. You never have a chance to read aloud."

Maggie sat on the small wicker chair, looking up into John's now tormented face. She knew that she was doing a clumsy job of trying to explain away this terrible secret he had been straining under for so many years.

"That's it, isn't it dear, you have not read anything but those papers essential to your work, and you are afraid that I will be critical?"

John faced her squarely, and she felt this to be the first real crisis in their marriage. How could he make her understand? For the first time, Maggie saw John's great brown eyes redden, as though tears might brim over.

He picked up the book once more, and leaning in, closer to her, gripped her arm, probably tighter than he knew. He opened it at random and again sat, staring at the characters on the page, while his eyes *did* well with water.

"Listen to me, Maggie Dix, listen, I do not know what one single word says on this page. My skull cannot sort them out in any manner. I tell you, I have, by no means, learned to read!"

He heavily lowered his head sitting down dejectedly in his own chair with his face bent low, staring at the cabin floor. Maggie moved quickly now, she stood, then knelt beside her wonderful, intelligent, creative husband, and took his great head in her arms.

"Oh, my poor darling, what an extreme weight you have had to carry all these years," then added, thinking logically, "and what a magnificent job you have done! You have been lacking this important tool, and you have risen to become captain of your own ship. Oh, John, you are truly remarkable, remarkable." She repeated the words over and over again, for they came straight from her heart.

They sat there in silence, she kneeling, her small arms trying to encompass this great man who she had promised to follow to the ends of the earth, while his head lay heavy on her bosom. The wheels in her brain fairly whirled. A remedy, yes, why it was so simple, here she was, the consummate teacher, and now she had a pupil. She could fill all of her time now with method and plan for his learning. Yes, they could, in this little cabin, triumph over the secret he hid from the world, and do it together!

Even on the next day, as Maggie sat in the cabin, with papers and books scattered all about her, did she marvel at the will and the fortitude of her man. He must have worked so painstakingly, compensating for the actuality of not being able to read. He had finally explained last evening, as they lay in their berth together, locked in each other's arms when all was dark, save the pale moonlight coming through the port, of the multitude of tricks he had devised to learn and to locate all of the charts and maps he required. Of how he had carefully, when he was mate to his own captain, memorized so many important symbols. It was difficult to explain, even to him; of how he had play acted the entire difficult procedures in order to fool the most trusting officer. For, because he knew the sea from such a young age, he found he was believed by them without doubt. Yet, each time a superior had been in his presence, he was certain that he would be found out and he always lived with that constant fear.

John admitted that when he fell in love with her, he threw caution to the winds, relying on their passion to get him through this deception. But in these weeks aboard the ship, that deliberate, empty, awful feeling of deceit returned to his life again, however he could never tell her, he was that ashamed. Now, he was accordingly relieved; she would never know the peace he felt after his confession. He said that this was the only secret that he had kept from anyone in his lifetime, and as long as he did his job well, he felt it had not mattered; yet with her, there was a sinful feeling of holding back the truth, and now he could sleep easy once again.

Maggie had not presented the idea of teaching him to read on that night. She was wise enough to know; he had been through enough traumatic experience for one day, but that did not diminish her will to right this terrible injustice that had befallen her handsome, clever husband.

The books she had packed for the voyage were few, only some of her favorites: two poetry anthologies, her copy of Lockhart, one of Milton, some works of Sir Walter Scott and a novel by the new author, Stevenson. No books that she could use for John as a primary text. She therefore, must invent her own textbook, especially for him. She tried to remember some of the first lessons which she had taught on Skye. If she began with the alphabet, and worked into the most simple sentences, just as she had done with her pupils, it should work for John. She could not affront his sensibilities, however, with childlike words like cat, dog, house and the like; no, she would have to use basic words that had meaning for him, words of the sea. Finally she devised a set of stories, using every letter of the alphabet and which were structured relating to the deep so that the instruction might be interesting. This took her several days but she wanted to have her lesson plans in good order before she presented anything to him.

On the very next evening after her plan was accomplished, in the quiet of their cabin, huddled over the whale oil lamp, he surprisingly resisted little. It was a picture of honest concentration, the devoted wife/teacher, and the willing amicable pupil, now both determined, each in their own proud manner, to defeat this inexplicable intrusion within their absolute happiness.

Only a second week into their studies, and Maggie had a hint of the root problem in his reading aptitude. Something very similar had been experienced in a pupil named James Buchanan, one of the twins on Skye. He was then a fifth grader, and had the peculiar perplexity of reversing his letters, both when he tried to write and when he read. He also had trouble telling time, yet in most other ways, he seemed the brightest and most willing of all her students. She had consulted the limited texts offered to her at that time, and found similar cases noted. She read that persons with this problem were usually of higher than average intelligence and deficient only in this one channel. It could be corrected with exacting care and once mastered; it did not seem to affect additional learning.

She reasoned this must have been John's dilemma in the few years that he attended school, ending in the fifth grade; no teacher recognized it, nor took the trouble to find out why he could not put his letters together and make words of them, thus he was merely passed through, until he had to drop out of school when his father died.

How many others are there in this world, she wondered, who suffer from this perceived shame, through no fault of their own, to feel the consequences of this travesty for the remainder of their lives?

But, her chief concern must be for John, and only him. Merely after their first week of lessons, she was beginning to see a new self-confidence emerge to her enormous elation.

This secret that they shared was unexpectedly bringing the two of them even closer. She noted that when he passed her on the deck during the daytime hours, as she knit or read, a glance stirred between the two and a private knowing look would be shared. It was as though they alone, were privileged to this special confidence, closing out the remainder of the world.

It took two months, yet when the gate was unlocked, it was incredible how rapidly John progressed. They spent three hours every evening reading and rereading the stories that Maggie had contrived, and he would willingly spend at least that many more, pouring over the other books that Maggie brought on the voyage or any other reading matter which he could lay his hands on. He exhausted his charts too, discovering new delights in them each day. He found old journals in the high cabin bookcase that former masters of the Gratitude had written, and he struggled to read every word of them. He asked Maggie about books written about sailing or adventures at sea, and if they might buy these when they returned to port. It seemed to Maggie that an entire new world was given to him as a beautiful gift with his ability to read, and she experienced a pure sense of thankfulness. It was she who had been the one to open that closed door. She thought that she had been fulfilled when she became John's wife, but now, the total man had come into full being, and his appeal was irresistible.

With the approach of mid-October, the ship and crew entered into their fourth month at sea. On those long nights in the cozy cabin, John and Maggie continued the practice of sharing their innermost thoughts just before retiring. This night, Maggie sat brushing out her warm brown curls until they glistened in the lamplight, while she shared with John the story of the little summer of St. Luke, that mild spell of weather, which usually comes about in the middle of October. She told him that October 18th was called St. Luke's Day and it was the day when she was born. It would always have special meaning for her.

"Since this is my birth date, my mum reminds me each year, and did so in all of my early life, that he is my patron saint, and because of that, I began to take a special interest in the evangelist. Did you know that St. Luke was a great physician, as well as the author of the third gospel and the Acts of the Apostles? He was an educated non-Jew, who converted to Jesus, without becoming a Jew. Born somewhere in Syria, probably Antioch, he was a cultured, well-educated scientist, and perhaps a fine painter as well. He became Paul's co-worker. The fact that the mild spell of weather never fails to fall on my birthday has always intrigued me.

I have heard that some people in America call this their 'Indian Summer,' a time when they are granted this mild spell to bring in the last of the summer crops. It is a lovely respite just before the start of a bleak winter. So far in my lifetime, I have enjoyed beautiful weather on my birthday for as long as I have memory. But what about these Davis Straits, John; do you think they qualify for a breather from our icy wind in celebration of good St. Luke?"

John was listening intently to his charming wife, watching her slender arms brush the shiny, heavy hair through each stroke.

"We will see, won't we, darlin'? I know that your birthday is but four days off. I wish that we were on shore so that I could give you a proper gift and a fine party. But we will celebrate it here and together, oh' my darlin', almost nineteen and so lovely and *my* Maggie." He rose to his feet then, and towering over her, caressed the auburn curls with his huge, rough hands.

On the very next morning, Roger and John had their heads close together at the doorway to the galley. Maggie saw them there but pretended not to notice, in case they were planning something on her account. She knew that Roger had few supplies to work any surprise so she expected little.

Her afghan was near completion and she was proud of her handiwork. It was blue and white, soft and warm, and would make the next several months more comfortable for sleeping, for the nights were growing longer and so much colder. However, this day was dawning fair and she took her tea topsides, facing the sun. They had not spotted a whale for five days, and were circling in the humpback grounds in huge arcs. Only two days before, they had a good 'gam' with the bark, Heroes, out of Nantucket. It was a pleasant time, the two captains chatting about their catch, the weather, and most important, about news from home. The vessel, Heroes, was at the beginning of her sail, and brought them news of the deaths of Ulysses S. Grant in America, and the writer Victor Hugo in France. It also brought her a newspaper and the mail that Maggie read greedily. It seemed, by the news of the press, that Grover Cleveland was establishing himself nicely in the White House, after being inaugurated earlier this year, and information of an operetta staged in London by a pair of authors named Gilbert and Sullivan, called The Mikado was a delight to music fans. What a treat, smiled Maggie, is a tabloid when one is separated from the world for so many months. She read and reread it with a needed hunger.

Unfortunately, Captain Smyth of the Heroes had no wife aboard, but Maggie enjoyed his company greatly. He was a jovial man and she knew the visit was good for John as he shared stories of this passage and of former ones with another captain. He stayed long enough to play a game of cribbage with John and at times the two were seized with some riotous laughter. Captain Smyth was heartened to learn of the enormous supply of oil which the Gratitude had taken in less than four months, and he said this was to be a fine season for the Atlantic fleet, perhaps much like the 'old' days, for he was a man of fifty-eight years and had experienced the heyday of whaling.

All through this month, Maggie wished that she had packed more books, not only for herself, for she had read through all of those aboard for the fourth and fifth time, but for John, who now could not get enough of reading. The Boston Chronicle that Captain Smyth had given to them was entirely read by John, and to her amazement, there were few words that he did not read and understand effortlessly. He seemed now secure in his skill, and she delighted once again in her remarkable partner.

Episode:

"I have a question for you tonight, my girl." John had settled back into his comfortable captain's chair with his arms resting on its curved circle of polished wood, his feet stretched out long before him, a look of contentment circling his broad face. Maggie sat on her usual small wicker chair, which was closer to the cabin floor by nearly a foot, busily engaged in edging the warm coverlet to which she had devoted so many hours. She had not expected any intense inquiry this night, and it was unusual for John to preface his words. They always spent some moments of companionship, after their evening meal, before beginning their studies. Perhaps this is something to do with my birthday tomorrow, Maggie thought, as she had noted John engaged in some unusual secretive errands during the past few days.

John began again, gazing into her face as she sat beside him working so diligently. He waited until she finished the few stitches to complete her work to its corner and when she finally looked up into at him, he said, "Maggie, you certainly have more insight into matters of the heart than I do. You have studied ancient philosophers and the great minds of our time. Here is the question that I have been pondering for many days:

When a man's heart is as full as this one is of mine with a love so overflowing for another person, how can it be contained?"

Watching her perplexed face, he knew he was not making himself clear, so he began once more.

"What I am trying to say, darlin', is this: when does this love I feel for you reach its conclusion? Does it have an end, just like all other things on earth? I am trying to understand how I can, with every passing day, every hour in fact, how do I constantly find these things about you that make me love you more and more? Glory knows that I own great capacities! I've been told that I eat more than the average man, and I work harder too. I am strong because I have been given this large frame, but here is my dilemma, do I . . . , can I, *love more*? Now that I am reading, I find people in domestic circumstances who have a life which takes on a tiresome pattern, really a familiar, ordinary place in their lives without passion. It is a familiar sort of place, akin to so many other's . . . Maggie, my feelings cannot be bottled so, for I believe that these persons become so accustomed to their companion and that they grow numb to the beautiful state of matrimony.

And they are certainly fools! It is as if their mate becomes as comfy as an 'old shoe,' and they give no thought to her at all. Could it happen that our love take this deadly course? I think not! I know that this could *never* be the case for me!"

John paused here to see if he was making his point clear, and seeing Maggie all warm and glowing, he continued: "Darling Maggie, with every new day, my love for you grows by such amounts that I cannot judge just how I can contain it, and extending that to the remainder of our lives, I cannot forecast the outcome for I am *consumed* with love."

He stopped, at last, and Maggie sat there astounded by his beautiful speech. John and she had good discussions about the world and life, but he generally spoke in short utterances. She could see, by this sincere attitude that he meant all he said, and she was nothing but flattered. It was wonderful to be loved with such fervor. How could she answer him?

"Dear John, in everything there are degrees of intensity; otherwise, we would all be made identical, doing the same work daily and thinking the same thoughts. This is what is so wonderful about our universe, my dear, for each one of us is unique, making us dissimilar from any other, I do believe that in the entire world, there are only a few matches, or melding of two souls so close to perfection that even the fairies, beasties, and yes, even God, smiles down on these who find this unimaginable truth. There have been records of such loves in history, John, yet they are few and far between. I like also, to believe that *ours is* such an extraordinary love, one that is perhaps beyond compare on this entire planet."

She sat quietly, hands clasped about her knees, as was usual when she was speaking earnestly. Maggie had laid aside her afghan, sensing the seriousness of her husband's words. Now, she wondered if she was making sense to him.

"I am not as educated as you might think, dear. With each passing day, I only know the extent of all the knowledge that I *wish* I knew. I look at life as one great learning experience, but I am drifting far from your question. Maybe it is near sacrilege to believe that out of all the persons in the world, our love is something set apart, more perfect, more sacred, and somehow even incomparable with others. How can we two be so fortunate? Do other couples feel this way and not show or speak of it, but perhaps only to each other?"

John examined her face with total understanding.

"Could it be, Maggie, that our love *is* without equal, and that no two people on earth have ever felt this oneness that we are privileged to? It makes one have a true belief in the God that enabled me to find you out of all other women. There are no words that truly can ever express the feelings that I have for you, Maggie. It will take the remainder of my life to show you how much I love you."

Maggie blushed after this last declaration. She had never dreamed of being loved with such fervor. His speech was probably the finest birthday gift that she could imagine. Not even in their first days of marriage had John spoken so. She wondered if the exposure that he now had through the world of books could be making him more aware of all life about them. He clearly was thinking with deeper conviction than he held previously. Maggie scrapped all thought of studies for this one evening, at least and moved into his arms.

Episode:

St Luke's Day dawned with a sunrise that would rival any on Skye. The day was breathtaking, and Maggie began to think that this evidence of magic, which she had fallen under as a child, was presently very much all about her. As she sat on deck, sipping her tea, she scarcely heard Caleb come up behind her and with a flourish, present a package wrapped in a scrap of calico. How lovely to be remembered on one's special day out here in the middle of Baffin Bay on a whaling ship. She lost no time unwrapping the small bundle to find a sperm whale's tooth, carefully worked with her name, sea birds and flowers all carved there to perfection.

"This is a gift that I shall always treasure, Caleb." And looking over all the intricate workings, she thought of the many hours that it had taken this good friend to complete it.

"So then, John has told people of my birth date, has he now?"

"No, in fact he did not willingly tell me of it. I asked him at least a month ago when your birthday might be, for I was working on this then and I wanted an excuse to give you a present."

Caleb's bright blue eyes twinkled when he spoke, and even now in the late fall, his freckles stood out dark and as numerous as in the summertime. She thought of how fortunate her husband was to have this fun loving, enthusiastic sailor as his first in command. It made the trip easier and it certainly gave her less anxiety.

"Thank you, Sir Caleb; I'll keep this safe in the bottom of our trunk until I can place it on my own mantelpiece."

This proved to be only the first of other surprises ahead on that day. At the midday lunch, Roger managed to somehow come up with several large, rich biscuit-type cakes which he split in two and filled with delicious raspberry jam. The likes of such a confection had not been seen earlier on this trip, and Maggie judged that these preserves had been set-aside for a special occasion. What a delight in the eating and how thoughtful he was. He not only made one for the cabin, but three for the foc'sle', thus the entire crew profited from their captain's wife reaching nineteen.

Much later, in the warmth of their own cabin, with only the gentle rock of the waves to take notice, John gave to Maggie the only gift that he could. He picked up the book which she had asked him to read to her so many weeks before, and read that page to perfection. This truly was her most cherished gift.

Maggie noted an eloquence that John now possessed, one that was not evident before he could read fluently. He seemed more aware now of the subtlest changes in the sea as she saw him taking out his notebook to jot these evidences down. She wondered at this phenomenon, and thought it might make an interesting study, the correlation of a man's concern for the world about him with his ability to read. She might pursue this reasoning when back on land with more texts available to her.

At present, the ship moved forward in the wintry, blustery days of November, Maggie now spent long hours with her journal. On occasion, Baffin Island could be viewed off the port bow, and although, it was a silent, wooded scene, this evidence imparted a queer feeling in her, to view land, and yet be a portion of the sea for such a long period of time. The crew was committed to the routine work of cleaning the ship, repairing sails and mending lines until another whale was sighted, then the industry began all over again. As the weather grew even colder, they all expected ample encounters, all conditions being just right for the 'beasts' to appear.

Maggie always cringed when the sailors used the term 'beast.' To her, it conjured up a vision of some terrible enemy of man. She supposed that she too, should look on these creatures of the deep with loathing, for due to the hunting of them hadn't she lost her own father, but she could never find it in her heart to hate them. Fear them, yes, because she saw the gigantic power they possessed, but *she* felt no hostility. The men who made them prey were the aggressors, not the mammal. In her most secret heart, she wished John was not engaged in this world of the hunt. She must be slow to express this however, for he was the man, and he must determine his particular chosen occupation. Besides, what else did he know but the sea?

John was so eager for Maggie to sit in her chair this evening that he literally picked her up and placed her there, just after they had closed their door to the outer world. She, weighing but one hundred and eighteen pounds to his two hundred and forty, made this task quite effortless. "I have found a piece that I want to read to you, Maggie, my girl." He had the custom of addressing her so, when he was excited about something, or when he was very serious.

"I came across a volume of poems by a Robert Burns, when I was rummaging high up in the old captain's locker amid some dusty, aged books and papers this morning. I found this so interesting that I sat here and read for a time while Caleb was on watch. I found one poem that suits you and me, darlin', so much so, that I could not wait to share it with you tonight."

He sat at his desk and opened the flat, gray volume, and then finding the page, he read,

"My Highland Lassie, O

But fickle Fortune frowns on me
When I maun' cross the raging sea;
But while my crimson currents flow
I'll love my Highland lassie, O
She has my heart, she has my hand,
My secret troth and honor's band;
'Till the mortal stroke shall law me low,
I'm thine, my Highland lassie, O."

'Now, whatever do you think of that, darlin'? It's as though it was written just for us. Have you ever heard of this fellow, Robert Burns? It says in this book, that he's lived in Scotland."

Maggie found it difficult to answer. Of course, Burns had been read to her from cradle on, and she could recite nearly every poem that he wrote from memory, but she could not take away John's pleasure of discovery and how it energized him, so she sat there mute and thrilled that he took elation in poetic words, their meaning, and that he wished to share them with her.

Finally, she looked up and spoke: "Yes, John, I do believe that I have heard of him. Come now, read more of them to me."

"I would like you to read them to me Maggie, would you?" and he handed her the thin volume. She leafed through it for a moment.

"Here is a chorus of one that I believe I remember:
My hearts' in the Highlands,
my heart is not here,
My hearts' in the Highlands

a-chasing the deer,
A-chasing the wild deer
and following the roe.
My hearts in the Highlands
wherever I go!"

"Oh my, but that was lovely! It sounds as though you know it very well. And about that sentiment, do you get huge longings for Scotland?"

She sat there very still after his question. She had not spent any great time pining for her homeland, but it was very true, a part of her heart would always be somewhere up there in the wild, dark, stony crags and the mists of the hills would never be far from her thought.

Another week, another whale, but still Maggie could not get used to the sight. She tended to make herself busy in her cabin during the flensing, and appeared on deck only to see the boats off, especially if John was in one of them. This day, it was two Beluga whales caught. These were pure white and small by comparison to the Humpback, only eighteen feet in length and weighing about one ton each. She had glimpsed them as she went into the main cabin for dinner, but the sight of the two tied to the ship's side, waiting flensing, did something to her appetite.

Was she taking this all too seriously? Why did she have such sympathy for the whale? Why didn't she feel the same for all the fish in the ocean? Was there something different about these creatures? How she wished she could resolve this conflict within her, but the constant search and catch cycle that she was bound to be witness to, this slaughter, had to last for a few months more.

Only last evening, John and she talked about the probable length of this voyage. If the good catch continued as it had, John felt that they would be headed for New Bedford about the beginning of February. He said that he must be very vigilant in watching the sign of weather from here on, for it was easy to be caught in the ice flows during the winter months. He had to read the currents and continue in lee of land for the greater share of the time, moving out into the open bay only on warmer days.

Maggie had asked, last evening, if there was to be any celebration aboard the Gratitude at Christmas time as it was only a week distant. John offered that although he never allowed the men to drink any spirits aboard his vessel, he did yield a bit during the holiday season, for it was at this time of the year when the men felt their strong longing for home and family the keenest. They needed a little merry making. For this reason, he kept some port and some good Jamaica rum on board which he could ration as he saw fit.

During the small preparation for the holiday, John finally told Maggie the story of Owen Poole, his second mate, who was so belligerent and sullen toward Maggie and to others on the crew, as well. It was because of Owen, that John had to be most careful about the liquor on board, and why he guarded it in his own quarters. Maggie was amazed one evening, when John pushed aside her heavy trunk, to expose a hatch beneath the carpet on which the trunk stood. She watched as he opened the hatch door, neatly crafted of floorboards, to reveal a supply of casks and bottles that she had previously not known existed.

"Owen was a very different man just a half dozen years ago than the one he appears to be now, Maggie. He then was the man who looked to have everything. He, as the first mate on the bark, Savannah, out of New Bedford, was quite near being called up for captain's papers when he came home from a most successful trip of two years in the Pacific. He returned to a fine share of that voyage, and almost immediately, met a beautiful girl named Alice, who was daughter of the Savannah's owner. She was just eighteen, and so lovely that her beauty was the talk of the town. She had long golden curls, powder blue eyes and the form of an angel.

"I witnessed the two falling in love almost at once, and Owen went to Alice's father, Mr. Evers, to ask for her hand in marriage, but Evers was a stubborn man who had decided his daughter should have no part of seamen. He wanted Alice to marry a prominent, wealthy lawyer, one he had chosen for her. She was miserable at the thought, for she had fallen in genuine love and ran away with Owen to someplace where the two were married.

"They returned to New Bedford, and settled into a fine little home that Owen purchased with his share, but after only a month's time, Alice's father forcibly brought Alice to his own home, where she was kept a literal captive. Evers forbade her to even see Owen, thinking, I suppose, that she would come to her senses to see things his way. Evers managed, with his money and influence, to have the marriage annulled, and Owen, seeing he could do nothing against her parents, took an additional sail of a year's time with another owner, signing on again as first mate. He vowed that with the money from another share, he could hire a lawyer to fight for what was truly his. He loved her so dearly, Maggie, maybe nearly the way in which I love you."

John looked at Maggie's face and seeing it so intent and sad, went quickly on to finish his tale.

"We were shipmates aboard that vessel, Freedom, and I was second mate to Owen. He confided this story to me on that long year at sea as each day he longed so desperately to return to New Bedford. He received only one letter from Alice on that lengthy, agonizing trip. It came about seven months after we went to sea. She said she had paid a maid to get this letter to a vessel about to sail and hoped against hope that he would receive it. She wanted him to know that he was to become a father in a few months. Expressing her undying love for him, she said that she knew they would somehow be together when he returned, even if they had to leave Massachusetts and whaling. Her parents could not deny Owen the right to his own child, but alas, it was never to be.

"When we arrived home, almost a year to the day of our departure, Owen made straight for the Evers' home, only to find Alice's mother there to tell him that because of him, they had lost their only child, Alice. It seems that in all of her loneliness and heartbreak, Alice became disconsolate during the last months before giving birth to a premature son. She lived only one short week following his birth. Hearing this, Owen became enraged, like no person that I have ever encountered. In frenzy, like a madman, he demanded to see his son, who by that time had been legally adopted by the Evers, but they would not permit it. Owen finally did speak secretly, with the maid who had helped Alice, and she told him his son was a beautiful, healthy child, and she had helped Alice baptize the tiny one, to name him Owen after his father."

John took another deep breath, and seeing the tears all welled in the eyes of his wife, wondered if he should have told this sad story to her at all.

"Oh John, what a dreadful heartbreak to bear, it is such a calamity for this poor, poor man. Such a tale of cruelty against two lovers, more bitter than I have ever heard, oh, John, the hopeless man." And Maggie put her head into her hands in sorrow.

"I have had to tell you what sadness occurred in Owen's life, so you might understand this care that I must take with the spirits aboard." John gestured to the bottles he had liberated from their hiding place.

"Owen Poole was a broken man from that day on. He saw no reason to go on living, and so set out to destroy his life with drink. He became known in every tavern on the waterfront as a sodden drunk, a tippler of the worst sort. He stopped caring for his appearance, his eating habits, and actually tried to kill himself with liquor.

"I was gone over a year on another whaler after those bitter days. It was then, that I was made captain, and I found only a shell of the man when I returned. It was our Caleb who finally worked the miracle. He took Owen into his own rooms on the waterfront and nursed him back to relative health. I know Caleb took much abuse from Owen, and it is only his good heart that could work the marvel for I know it took great resolve to turn him around.

"And it was Caleb who convinced me to take Owen on my last voyage and on this one as my second mate. I fear that he will never be the man we once knew, but Caleb managed to get him off the spirits and that was the first great step. This is the reason that I must monitor these bottles so that Owen Poole will not have his first drink, and that is for certain!"

Fortunately, for all of their sake's, the small holiday festivities went off without a hitch. Although all of the other seamen reveled in the spirits that their captain brought out for fellowship, Owen Poole seemed to take no notice, as he remained in his cabin for most of the merriment. Maggie could not help but have very different feelings now for this man whose life was dealt such an unfortunate blow. It had taught her a good lesson, she believed. She must never censor any person's visible exterior too quickly, neither in the way they behaved or spoke to her, for there might be underlying causes accounting for those actions. She must never set herself up as judge, never again!

The holiday, itself, was enjoyable. John ordered that no work be done aboard the vessel for that day, and Maggie convinced Roger to let her help concoct a plum pudding of sorts, enough for the entire crew, and a sweet sauce to pour over it. She was positive it was not what they could have produced with the proper ingredients, but the men were most pleased to eat it, and some of them poured a share of spirits over their portion and lit it, to the laughter of all.

Maggie saw small instruments come out from hiding places, such as she had not heard on the entire sail: a small Concertina, a tiny fiddle and some sort of horn were produced, so she joined in the fun by playing her tin whistle for the crew to everyone's amazement, including her husband's. It was a good time, a united time, and they all went to their quarters feeling the satisfying warmth in sharing the holiday with friends.

Episode:

In these last months of the voyage with the weather so bitter, Maggie could be on deck very little, and so she resolved to set out a course for herself of self-improvement. There was no more that she could teach John, as far as reading was concerned, that is, he could now read anything that she could, and his comprehension was flawless.

Maggie felt the need, however, to fill these long days with a useful task, one that would involve her completely, so as to make the time pass easily. By day, she took over John's desk, confirming her commitment to paper and pen.

The small world of a ship was like an island afloat, each person carrying out his role that supported the whole, each essential to the other, and yet each a unique entity, every man his own psychopath. She had been toying with the idea for many months, now it must come to fruition. It was the writer she determined to become.

First, she resolved to make what study she could of the whales they had caught. In this, she had John's help, for he had seen enough of their behavior in the past fifteen years, to tell her nearly all she need know, while Caleb filled in the remainder of her query.

She had not come across any books in her studies on land on this topic, and she wondered how many might have been written. If there were such books, perhaps her observations, as a wife on a whaler, could add to those accounts.

Second, she thought it might be interesting to write of the crew on the ship from her perspective as a wife aboard, if for no other reason, than to read it back to herself in later years as a remembrance. She decided not to use the real names of these men, but to characterize them, allowing the reader to see them from her perspective. She began with Owen Poole, of course, a logical choice, since his sad story was so much on her mind. Then, she wrote of Roger, and his life in Portugal, as well as at sea. By now, they had enjoyed so many long talks; she felt that she knew his entire family, intimately. Caleb Shields was the third, and after him, she asked John each evening to tell her the story of every man of this crew that he had knowledge of as she took notes. Each day she would write a story filled with the facts that he told to her, and within a month's time, her efforts were becoming most pleasing. Not only was she finding productive use of her time, but she was coming to know each of these 'misfits,' as society called them, as distinct individuals with a poignant story of their own.

As the days progressed, Maggie looked forward to each new day, for as the whale oil and baleen were being processed on deck and then stored in the hold, January slipped by. John had finally lengthened his estimate of their voyage, but he concluded that by mid-March, the Gratitude must be heading for port and home.

Today, Maggie wondered if in some future time, she might miss these leisurely days spent in her cozy cabin. One conviction was abundantly clear, as it had not been in July, which was, the honest understanding of why each of these men had taken to the sea for their life's work. John had been a great help in opening her eyes to recognize the entire man, not only what appeared on the surface.

John was playing it safe, said Caleb to Maggie on the last day of January, for there was room in the hold for more than a month's catch at least, but every sailor among them including his captain, realized the danger of being caught in the ice. Out in the strait, where the currents kept a good flow, there was less chance of it, true, but no whaler could ever forget that terrible disaster of the Arctic whalers in 1871. Then the entire fleet of whale ships was lost to Alaska's icy cape. The ice closed in and destroyed all but seven of a forty-ship fleet.

John was too canny to let this happen. "He is a truly fine captain," so with this, Caleb ended his lesson for Maggie on this day.

Episode:

The first week of February came and went without a sighting. Maggie shivered when she thought of those boys in the crosstrees. Every hour they climbed, secured themselves to the hoops, and then scanned the sea constantly for the sign of whales. Now, in this bitter weather, they were nearly frozen each time they returned to deck, and all for what seemed to Maggie, a meager fraction of the split from this long, bitter expedition.

John had explained to her that owners received one-third of the haul, the ship itself, received one-third for repair and refitting, and then the remaining one-third was divided among the entire crew, according to his standing, or job aboard. Of this last third, the captain received one-third of it, or as John figured, on this trip, perhaps about $2,000 dollars, with the lookouts receiving about $200 dollars each, but out of this amount was taken the money for their purchases in the ship's 'slop' chest, a container of odd clothing brought along for the crew, to replace clothing that wore to rags on the voyage. In all, one of these seventeen or eighteen-year old lookouts, could expect to take home about $125-$150 dollars for this freezing, aching life at sea for eight months of their time. She shivered again when she considered it.

With the storms becoming suddenly severe, John decided to change course, and to seek slightly calmer waters. Thus, he sailed southward to the lower end of the Labrador Sea, just north of Newfoundland, near the mouth of the St. Lawrence River. This had been in recent years a good spot to hunt the Right whale and secondly, the Humpback. Both of these, being baleen type, supplied great quantities of oil and baleen. This might complete the catch well and much easier than continuing to search for the Sperm.

Every grateful sailor noted the difference in weather as the Gratitude hugged the Newfoundland shoreline. The sun was shining brightly on the first day that they traversed these waters, and the winds died to a breeze.

They had just completed their first wide arc of the morning, when the now familiar call rang out, 'Thar she blows.' It was little Jimmy in the crosstrees, who pointed to a spout off the bow, only a half-mile distant. The tall plume of mist from the whale looked twenty feet high, and Owen Poole was quick to gather his crew into a whaleboat on the starboard side. Maggie was quite familiar with that call now and it did not shock her as once it had.

John said that he would take the other boat and left Caleb in command. Maggie gave him a kiss and no argument; it was not her place to decide who should go and who should stay, though, so close to the end of the voyage, she wished he would stay aboard. These giants still gave her some dread whenever a boat was lowered into the sea.

She stood on deck this day, and watched as the whale seemed completely unaware of the two boats heading towards it, but just as she saw them slipping ever so quietly toward the whale, in only that instant, another whale surfaced very close to the Gratitude, cutting John's boat off from sight, momentarily. In the swells around this second whale, so close to the ship, she saw it rise slowly like a floating black island. She had never witnessed a living giant this close, and it was another Humpback, immense, incredible, and preposterous. Her eyes glued to its tremendous form. Caleb immediately ordered another boat eased into the water on the port side, so as not to disturb this whale, as he again put Mr. Hawks, the cooper, in charge of the vessel, taking this third crew guardedly around the ship, himself, to try for the catch.

She watched as the Humpback slowly dropped its colossal head to send a roll of sea awash across its back as it came out of the sea by some two to three feet. After a blow of breath from his spout-hole, Maggie got her first glimpse of the two far boats closing in on the other whale.

Within what only seemed minutes, Caleb and crew had maneuvered their craft between the ship and the second Humpback, already close enough to take aim. Still, this whale was unaware of the boat's existence, its small eyes set in the sides of its broad head, unable to see forward or aft of an arc of 125 degrees on each side. It just remained there, filling its lungs with air, as the harpooner laid his paddle on the floorboards and stood in the prow, the iron in his hand, a six-foot shaft attached to a 30-inch harpoon iron, with a line attached to the far end. The needle, a sharp, steel barb on a pivot, was designed to toggle open so it would not pull out of the whale's flesh. Maggie was mesmerized, glued to her spot at the rail, unable to make a sound or to move away from the scene.

As the harpooner lifted the iron, he placed his knee into the 'clumsy cleat,' or knee brace, cut into the plank across the boat's bow. The whale was now a moving target, for it continued to proceed ahead at about three knots, Maggie judged, with its great back rising and falling with the waves. The harpooner lifted the iron with both hands and struck straight down into the thick blubber, then grasping the second harpoon, struck again clear to its socket and tossed out some ninety feet of line. All hands took oars and the whaleboat backed off briskly, away from the bewildered behemoth, which crashed his huge flukes causing walls of water to rise about him.

Horrifying as the scene unfolded, Maggie felt like stone, compelled to watch this drama.

Caleb now took over with a tricky maneuver, most definitely, for two persons had to quickly change places in the rocking boat. A false move now would turn them all into the rolling sea. The mate paid out the harpoon line, coiled amidships, for the whale was beginning to dive in pain, as the sharp barbs seared his flesh. The line that passed, first over the snubbing post, or loggerhead, at the stern, and then forward over a roller guarded by a chock pin at the bow, pulled taut as the whale increased speed trying somehow to rid itself of this terrible hurt. The wood of the loggerhead was smoking from the friction of the line running over it, and the close oarsman dipped water on it to keep it from catching fire.

At last the whale was tiring, yet he surfaced once more, nearly catching the entire boat with his long fluke. Then he turned sharply and dove again towing the whaleboat behind. Experienced, Caleb quickly had to place his sharp lance into the gigantic beast, who had now taken the entire first tub of line about 1000 feet, as it finally began to show signs of slowing. Immediately, all the oarsmen grasped the line in their two hands and with all of their strength began pulling the boat *toward* the humpback on the other end.

Every man of the crew that remained on the ship, along with Maggie, watched the spectacle unfold before him, alert to do anything he might do, but actually helpless to assist until the whale ended its attempt to escape.

The whale line had to be carefully coiled again; all the while they advanced, for if the whale should choose to dive again they must be ready. As the target came closer, Caleb was intent on the area that he must hit, a space of about three foot square where was clustered the vital life of the Humpback, the arteries near the heart and the lungs. A miss at these close quarters, could mean disaster for the entire crew, thus all depended on Caleb.

His thrust was swift and clean, and immediately penetrated the mark, causing the whale's lungs to be flooded with blood and cutting off the heart's blood supply. The boat backed off as the mate called out, 'stern all,' and the whale surfaced, spouting a pinkish mist in the air. "His chimney's afire," rang the call of the oarsman, and the death was mercifully brief. Red blood staining the sea, the giant rolled over on its great side within six or seven minutes.

Maggie stood there aghast. She had never experienced such a horrific tragedy so near her person. In one way she was indebted to the supremacy above, in that, she had now seen deadliness. It caused her spirit to nearly compress, and yet she could not show her distaste, not now before the crew. However, it was a sight that she would long remember, perhaps for a lifetime and maybe attempt to seek a remedy for it in some small way in the future.

It was only after the occurrence was ended and with the relief of these men safe, that Maggie and the crew turned their attention to the other two whaleboats, but they were now out of sight. After securing this whale to a floating device and marker, and taking the men back on board, the Gratitude set out to find their comrades.

With the sun so low in the leaden winter sky, Maggie was apprehensive. The ship was sailing in huge circles, but could not locate the two whaleboats.

As they neared the place where this search began, the sight of the dead, floating Humpback was very evident. Caleb determined to use the last remaining moments of light to have his men secure this colossus to the buoy with chain to get ahead of the next day's employment. As the men proceeded in the task, the thought of spending another night not knowing of her husband's fate was beginning to terrify Maggie, who now felt no longer a young girl on a great adventure, but very much a woman with her captain in danger once more.

The period of foreboding ended quickly with the sharp call from the crosstrees, "Light off the port bow," and soon they all saw lights moving steadily for them, two oil lamps in separate boats, making their way to the welcoming ship. Caleb was the first to see why they moved at such a slow pace through the dark water. Each craft was hauling behind it, the carcass of a huge whale. Undeniably, they had made their catch!

Everyone was in good spirits as they helped the crews aboard, until it became evident in the shadowy beam of light that one man had to be carried. Owen Poole was unconscious and as they took him to his cabin. John looked very grave, as serious as Maggie could ever remember. She learned later, from an oarsman on Owens' boat, that as Owen was preparing to throw his second lance into the whale that they had all but secured, he was hit by one huge fluke and as he fell backward, he hit his head sharply on the edge of the coiling bucket and cut it deeply. Now he lay motionless as John sat beside him.

It was Caleb, who washed and bandaged his head, but Owen gave no notice of feeling or hearing anything. They continued to call out his name, but he remained in a cavernous sleep. John told Maggie, out of any other person's hearing, of how he had seen a cabin boy in just this same manner when the boy slipped during a storm and hit his head on an iron cleat on the deck. This had happened many years before, when John was a harpooner. That sad time, he revealed, the youngster never roused from the spell-like sleep, but passed away within a week's time of the accident to be buried at sea. John vowed that he would sit with Owen day and night, for as long as it took, talking to him, until he awoke from this terrible state. Knowing how insignificant Owen Poole valued his own life, since his loss of Alice, Maggie was concerned that he might have no will to fight for it.

The flensing of this huge catch began at dawn on the next morning and would continue, day and night, until the three great whales were processed. John estimated this might take weeks of constant work. It was a sober, hard-working crew on these long, hard days. Although each man had his own sentiment about the surly, dark Poole, he remained a part of the team, and each man anxiously waited to hear of his recovery.

John was true to his word. He ordered his meals brought into Owens's cabin, and he continued to talk and to read to him, day in and day out. He left the completion of the whales' processing to Caleb, and only on a few occasions did they reverse roles, so that John might check the men's progress. Maggie felt helpless. She sat, most days, with the two of them, tucked into the corner of the small cabin, reading, sewing and praying. On the few occasions, when John's voice gave out, she took over the reading out loud, and thought enigmatically of the irony of her, the person who Owen Poole despised most, sitting beside him now.

It was the fourth day after the accident, when, as he lay there still and pale that Maggie was alone with him while John went off to relieve Caleb who badly needed a rest. Maggie was reading aloud, softly, from her book of poetry. The poem was a love sonnet, one of Elizabeth Barrett Browning's, and as she paused at a stanza, she saw the faintest flutter of eyelids from her charge. Her heart leapt. Should she call John? No, she dared not leave Owen. She cleared her throat and read on, louder. Yes, another movement of his eyes, and then as she watched, transfixed, a hand rose weakly to his knee, and she read on, her voice quivering with emotion, but afraid to stop for fear that she would break this spell. Slowly, Owen opened his eyes, and for only a second, she was positive, he smiled a small smile, and then seemed to fall to sleep once more.

When Caleb looked in at Owen, after the movements that she witnessed, he seemed sure that the deeper sleep was altered, for this sleep was one of normalcy and the injured man moved about from time to time changing position. Besides, Caleb believed that now his breathing was deeper and more regular. He predicted Owen would wake soon, as if from a single night's sleep, with no recollection of his time unconscious. It all proved true. Only three anxious hours had elapsed, when Owen woke to complete disbelief that he had lost four days and nights of his life. He was helped into a chair, to sip the broth Roger had kept warm on his range, and in every way, Owen was on a recovery road.

Only a day later, curiously, John and Caleb both remarked that Owen seemed a different person than he had been only a week before. He was compliant and had lost his callous spitefulness. This frightful experience had somehow worked a personality change, truly a miracle!

Finally, alone that evening, John told Maggie that this was the Owen that he had known as a boy, and he only hoped the change was permanent, for the man's sake, as well as for all on board. Maggie wondered secretly, if her presence might still evoke the darker side of Poole, thus she vowed to keep out of his sight for the remainder of the voyage if that was possible.

The weather held and with the crew's spirits rekindled by their second mate's recovery, they had all three whales processed and in barrels in just over twelve days' time.

"That will be all of it then," observed John as the last of the barrels, brim full of oil, were bound and lashed topsides as the hold was entirely full. Never had John viewed such a catch. He shook his head in near disbelief as he surveyed the lot, only late February with no possibility of hauling an ounce more. He ventured to Caleb, that this might be a record catch for the number of days at sea. They must look into the record books when they reached port. They lost no time in hoisting full sail for the happy trek homeward.

The clean-up work, requiring the vessel to be made 'ship-shape' would be accomplished as they headed southward along the coast. Depending on favorable winds, that could take anywhere from ten days to two weeks, for now they were laden with a heavy cargo.

Captain Dix was most particular about the condition of the ship once whaling was at an end. Every component of the vessel, including each brick of the furnace in the try-works, was scrubbed with a lye solution. The purged caldrons were then set upside down over the boiler and lashed tight. The cooling tank and all of the tools used in the rendering-out process were scrubbed until a face could be reflected in the metal surface. The blubber room was washed not once, but three and four times to remove any trace of the greasy residue and the infected odor that had totally permeated the entire voyage. Once all this was accomplished, John had teams of men go over every inch of the Gratitude, rubbing down decks, cleaning each chain, cleat and rail to a like-new condition. John prided himself in taking a ship immaculate and orderly into port. Maggie was impressed as she viewed the ship, for on just one day out of New Bedford it looked as neat as it had when she stepped aboard, eight months before.

Maggie was experiencing confusing feelings on this last day before reaching port. She sat in her usual place on deck, no book or knitting in hand. The weather was pleasant, not too cool for her as she had dressed in her high neck, ivory sweater once more. The ship was as clean as the proverbial whistle, and the crew was all-joyous to be so close to reaching their homes.

Her mind kept going over every one of the past months and what they had meant for her: The honeymoon at sea was glorious, heaven, she thought, yet the fear she had recognized on this voyage for her husband was dreadful, unspeakable, and nothing she would ever wish to experience again. The delight of being with John for twenty-four hours of every day was a fact she would treasure forever, but the thought of him making a sea trip without her was now, preposterous. The catching of the whales had been extremely enlightening, but the fact that her entire being abhorred the ritual was ingrained so deeply in her psyche that she would loathe to be any part of it in the future. Yes, the future, what did it hold? She could not be content with his career of continually roaming the sea, and yet what did he know but that? He had worked to the top of this profession, was esteemed by his crew and the owners, but did that matter if she and he were to be parted, even for a week? She was trying to grasp the entire dilemma on this last day at sea, but somehow, nothing could replace her internal disquiet.

Episode:

New Bedford – 1888

Daily living in a house with a roof overhead and no swirling waters below, was viewed with separate divergence by the newlyweds as individuals, but as a couple, their obvious bliss could not be hidden. Maggie was happy to settle into a routine of quiet domesticity in her neat little house and garden. John, however, was off to the docks as soon as the few needed repairs were accomplished on his white clapboard cottage.

John found the owners jubilant with the Gratitude's grand haul and surprisingly they were busy fitting out yet another vessel to add to their fleet. Unlike most owners at this time, who were getting out of whaling, so sure that they had seen its best days, Riddle and James shrewdly managed this small fleet, securing a substantial fortune for each of them and were content to see their enterprise expand, for the next few years, at least. John received a princely share of the last voyage, and a hefty bonus as well. After this passage, a good deal of refitting had to be done to the Gratitude, so it appeared that Maggie and he were destined to enjoy life in New Bedford for some time. Invitations were prompt in coming. The grand, magnificent captain and his insightful, beautiful young wife were much sought after for dinner parties and like gatherings. Maggie, anxious to make new friends, attended, while John protested that it was not his style to take pleasure in such affairs, but sometimes he and Maggie were the last to leave a gathering. Once the hosts began talking of the sea, John happily recounted such exciting tales that his eager listeners begged him to stay on and on.

Lovely weeks flew by as late springtime approached. John and Maggie planted a good sized vegetable garden, reminding her greatly of Skye and Scotland. With each seed that she planted, she thought of those days with Bruce, first when she was only five, herself parting the rich brown furrows as John did for her now. Maggie took great pleasure in showing her husband a few of the skills in which she excelled, this planting being one.

They did not neglect their reading; in fact, with all the books she obtained due to the letters she was incessantly writing, John had at his fingertips nearly everything published about the sea and ships, as well as periodicals. He read voraciously, sitting at their dining table, his head held in his hands beneath the oil lamp until late in the evening. It was as though he must make up for all those years he was deprived. Maggie looked up from her own book with real tenderness when she viewed his great form so intent, bent over and held captive by these volumes.

It was sometime in that spring, that Maggie took upon herself an act, not really in character with her nature. She was never one to meddle in other people's lives, only quick to remedy anything amiss in her own. However, at a luncheon given by her now good friend, Mary Lewis, the captain's wife so instrumental in her decision to go off a-whaling, she was introduced to the stiff and proud Cora Evers, grandmother and guardian to little Owen Poole, son of the Gratitude's second mate. Mary had arranged that the young children of the ladies in attendance be invited for companionship to her own children. Young Owen, or now the renamed Harman was a frail boy, His name change, done early on, was given to him because it was his grandfather Evers name. Harman was to be there at the event as one six-year old guest.

Realizing that this haughty Mrs. Evers had no idea that Maggie knew the child's real story, she had skillfully worked her way into Cora's graces with the sole idea of befriending tiny Harman. Maggie actually had no developed plan beyond this first meeting, as she explained to John later, but as the *fates* would have it, she was able to convince Cora Evers, that as a teacher, she would be pleased to have little Harman come to her home on several afternoons to try to release his reclusive mannerisms by the use of primary teaching. He was an extremely shy child and seemed lost, even in the company of other children. While Cora Evers was skeptical at first, Maggie used her glib tongue, and at last convinced her of the lessons. It was plain that Mrs. Evers cared deeply for the boy, but smothered him with such affection; no one else had a place in his little life.

It was not merely chance that brought Owen Poole to choose this very afternoon, while Maggie was working with Harman, to stop by to inspect his captain's, or as Maggie put it, 'farmer John's garden.' The two old friends sat in the sunshine on the bench, just outside the kitchen door, passing the time of day. Neither she nor John felt like conspirators, but merely concerned comrades, who could no longer endure the wretched injustice of it all. Maggie had made it clear to Mrs. Evers that she needed at least three hours with the boy to make any headway, so that the trio in this backyard had no fear of being found out.

What a glorious afternoon they all spent together. Owen gave no hint of his true identity, but played the part of a jolly uncle or friend to the boy who seemed to take to him immediately. Harman rode high on Owens's broad shoulders about the yard, and then Owen patiently taught him to catch a ball and finally sitting quietly, watched Harman with Maggie as she read to him aloud from her favorite children's storybook.

The newlyweds had never seen any man look as grateful, when at last it was time to leave this happy first meeting between father and son. One of the most poignant memories of her entire lifetime was to be this one of Owen, who only months before, openly showed his hatred for her, now taking leave of her home by grasping her hand, looking into her eyes, and saying: "You have given my life back to me, dear Maggie."

Episode:

The custom of a Sunday stroll down to the harbor to see the ships at anchor and smell the good salt air was firmly established by summertime. This was a grand day in mid-June very close to the first anniversary of John and Maggie's memorable wedding day. Everything in the world for them seemed so exactly right. On this day they both had specific plans on their minds to discuss with the other. They sat at last on the sea grass surrounding the lighthouse, a good walk from the town, and situated on a gentle, sloping piece of ground where the view of New Bedford and the glassy sea was unparalleled. Four church spires stood out clearly in Sunday serenity, and the view from this peaceful hillside with its rolling grassy soil slanting to the waterfront of rocking vessels at anchor was a dream-like setting. It was John, first to break the serene silence. Stretching out his full form on the mossy slope, he looked seven feet tall to Maggie's miniature form beside him. Gesturing to the harbor, he began haltingly, telling her of his meeting with Mr. Riddle on just the day before to hear a sobering fact: The Gratitude was now only days away from being ready for the sea. Maggie had expected this speech was near and thought that she had rehearsed her response completely, but suddenly against his disclosure, all her fine words went pale and insignificant.

"We haven't spoken of exactly what we will do now, Maggie. These wonderful days with you in our little home have been so perfect, yet I knew that one day I would have to get back to work, and I just learned that this next voyage will sadly be of a longer duration than my last." Seeing her face pained, he hurried on: "It came as a huge surprise to me, too."

He lay there waiting for her to speak, unable to broach the subject of her coming along with him once again, for this they *had* been able to discuss, on the long spring nights in the quiet of their bedroom, Maggie's true feelings about the killing of the whale. She had even expressed to him, that she believed that one day; man would look back on all of it with a genuine repugnance. However, she was quick to concede that the practice was still valid for the present, as it was in the natural sequence of man's survival. He understood her words, spoken so, as not to invalidate his profession. He also recognized her gentle soul, so affirmative in that she would not wound his sensitivity.

One night, she had told him that the last thing she would do was to demean his work at sea, yet she knew that she could never again be witness to those large mammals being slaughtered. And within her, silently, she knew that she dreaded any separation from this man that she loved so dearly, and that there *had* to be a different solution.

"John, have you ever thought of a life away from whaling and the sea?" There, she had said it, deciding to take the plunge and hurry on, not waiting for a response. Maggie sat on the grass, her arms about her knees, in that position that he had grown so accustomed to when she was very serious. She looked straight into his surprised eyes.

"I am not speaking of this without a great deal of thought; in fact, I have rehearsed this speech a thousand times in my head. We two have such a beautiful relationship, my dearest, and with only one life to live, I cannot bear the thought of these separations that we must endure for the sake of your work. There has to be something else that could be equally rewarding for you as a man, and to give us our lifetime without being parted".

Maggie stopped here, seeing John wanted to speak: "Maggie, my love, it is not the work that I am wedded to, it is you, my darling girl. But this is the only thing that I have ever done or known. I would not be doing my proper duty to you as a husband to be at loose ends, searching for employment away from the sea, and where would that be? Can you tell me?"

Now John's head was lowered to his chest, as though the problem was impossible to solve and he had no plan to offer.

"Your sister, Anita, has been begging us, by her letters, to come to Philadelphia for a visit, John. You have said, so many times, of how very much you would like to see her. Could we afford to take a few months and perhaps see if you might find some kind of work that might be satisfying to you there?"

John sat up and faced Maggie, sensing this was a momentous decision in their lives:

"Well, we are in the best cash situation that I have ever enjoyed, even after our recent three months of leisure. Our needs are small, and I have put the entire bonus, as well as my share of the last voyage into the Seamen's Bank here in New Bedford. No, darling, it is not the immediate need for money which concerns me, but understand, should I choose to leave the sea, it is not easy to return. The owners are a critical lot. They are prudent and possessive, and they give no quarter to those who withdraw from their employ. I would be cutting off the limb that holds the fruit, so to speak, if you can see what I mean, Maggie? I am already thirty-three years old, and should be firm in my trade."

These very doubts were the reason why Maggie had been reluctant to speak to him about any change in his lifestyle, and she could plainly offer no guarantee or even positive ideas of employment, but she had to try one more approach.

"John, I care little for any grand worldly possessions, but when I think of a life where we are apart for more days than we are together it frightens me. I wish to be a portion of your life every day I have breath, especially now after I have tasted the joy of these months together."

"Would you consider me taking just one more trip then, Maggie? Perhaps in that interval, I could think through the possibilities of doing something else besides the sea."

John was desperately playing for time and she saw it clearly. It must be a frightening prospect to leave all one has known and to strike out for the uncertain. Yet, something in Maggie's intuition kept telling her that this was the precise time to make the new start.

"I truly think another voyage would solve nothing, dearest." She tried to be very soft now and not push the controversy. "I want this to be the best outcome for both of us."

Then looking out at the gulls relentlessly sweeping over the moving sea. She added: "I do believe that I could not bear you being at sea on the day when *our first-born* comes into this world. Is that a selfish sentiment on my part?"

Maggie was blushing now, and not looking directly at John. She had not wished to use this fact that she was to bear his child in the coming December as any part of her plea, but it had simply rushed from her lips in a torrent of happiness. She turned her gaze to him now, as he sat immobile, trying to comprehend the words, and then, slowly as they connected in clarity:

"Our own, *our baby*, Oh, my darlin' is there *no end* to the magnificent things that *you* can do!"

Episode:

Once John had made the decision, there was no stopping him. He met with Riddle and James, promptly at eight on Monday morning, resigning his position as captain, naming Caleb Shields as his likely successor. The owners were shocked and disappointed, but quick to honor his suggestion. John then set about selling his house and surprisingly, when he told Caleb of putting it on the block, Caleb jumped at the chance to buy it. He said that he was very tired of coming back to the boarding house on the docks and with a captain's share. He smilingly ventured that he might even take on a wife if he could find one like Maggie, and he winked in his delight at the wonderful possibility.

John then wrote to his sister, Anita, in Philadelphia, responding to her plea that they come there for a lengthy visit, all the while telling friends, sister, employers and anyone who would listen that he was about to become a father, while his exuberance escaped not one other soul.

Maggie had no idea of the joy and excitement that her news would create. Surely no other woman in the world had ever been pregnant, by the way her adoring husband reacted. Everything was positive for him now, certain this was the right course to take, and with no trouble his finding something much better than whaling to support his little family. John was suddenly the jovial optimist. Maggie found him laughing with Owen on her return from market, and she could not remember John's face as wreathed in smiles. Truly, she thought, the fairies and beasties were certainly to be trusted today for her woman's intuition.

Episode:

So this was Philadelphia. They could not believe the lofty, opulent dwellings seen all along the route. These were large homes, fenced in, complete with carriage houses, spectacular gardens and in every respect, like nothing they had ever envisioned. Curiously, this trip, for Maggie, could only be likened to the magic carriage ride that she had experienced in the Royal Gardens of Edinburgh with her friend for the serene feelings she was enjoying, but now that excursion seemed centuries ago.

The grandeur of the Hansom cabs that stood with their drivers at the Haverford Station, awaiting the arrival of travelers, was fascinating, to say the least. The ride about the unusual winding roads, finally to stop before the sumptuous Endicott estate was nothing but enjoyable. This home, with its ten rooms, stable, carriage house and bubbling brook, running the entire perimeter, at once gave Maggie a slight 'poor relation' perception. She secretly hoped it did not have this same affect on her husband. Although John knew that Anita had married into a prominent and well-to-do Philadelphia family, he certainly had no idea of the wealth that he now recognized. His sister had never alluded to all this affluence.

But, here was Anita, running at full speed to meet them, down the winding path, her arms full of the glory of the September mums that she had been cutting from her magnificent garden. Her huge picture hat with its ribbons fairly trailing near the ground behind her in her eagerness to embrace the brother she had not seen for so many years and to greet his very young bride.

Maggie was relieved as she saw this tall, graceful Anita, with her open grin on a face sprinkled with freckles. Her long, soft curling hair was haphazardly flying in the cool breeze. No sedate matron here as she had imagined when she viewed the huge dormers and fenced in austerity of this property. She was quickly taken into Anita's freckled long arms, and held there so lovingly, she sensed this lissome sister of her husband was of as fine a disposition as he, and was to become a true companion and a friend. The fates were alive with every one of them, at this moment.

During all of that first splendid afternoon, as the siblings sat and talked of all the years of happenings since their last meeting, Maggie felt the contented supporter, sitting, listening and feeling the real love between the two. It gave her the vision of the wonderful parents that they must have shared.

Anita could be easily perceived as a free spirit, whose happening into the lap of luxury had in no way affected her open, easy life style. This elated older sister, took such delight in showing Maggie and John the room that she had prepared for them, you would think her a child with a new toy. The home was comprised of three distinct stories with a wide porch surrounding the lower portion. The narrower third floor held a large, airy bedroom and a lovely, bright sitting room complete with fireplace. From this vantage point, one could view the adjacent forest, the hills and the charming little brook at the back of the property rushing over small, brown boulders. It was a pleasant apartment, which Anita convinced them was theirs for as long as they might stay. She delighted in the fact of the anticipated new member to the family, and said that she was thrilled that she was to become an aunt. After much pleading, she did elicit a promise from both of them; they would live right here, at least until after the birth of their baby in December.

During the trip to Haverford, John told Maggie of the hope that his sister and Kenneth Endicott held these many years, that of raising a family of their own, but sadly Anita, now nearing thirty-seven, was becoming regretfully reconciled to a childless home.

Maggie had seen a gardener, a male servant and a cook, about the home on their arrival; however, she noted that Anita had carried some of the smaller valises to the third story herself, not bothering to call for the hired help. Anita seemed to accomplish her independence as a matter of course and she sensed that the servants were familiar with this trait. As she helped Maggie unpack, she sent her brother out to walk the grounds, so the women could chat and become comfy with each other.

Dinner that first evening, around the huge, polished wood table set with fresh flowers, fragrant and distributed also all about the spacious rooms, was delightful. Kenneth proved as unassuming and natural as his wife, thought Maggie, studying the two interact over the delicious roast duckling and crisp fall vegetables. Anita was not the sort who could have married a man who put on airs or was snobbish. They laughed and enjoyed each other. Maggie reflected on her own pregnancy with a hint of guilt, in that she should be so fortunate to be so blessed in this little over one year of marriage, and these two pleasant people should have to wait so very long for the child they might never have.

Ironic, wasn't it? "This fate on the far side of the mountain, where the sun is so late to shine!" It was Mum Laura's description of just such a circumstance and she would have described it so, for a fact!

Tucked snug in the huge bedroom, so unlike any she had ever known, Maggie could not have waxed more enthusiastic about her feelings for John's lovely sister. Softly, with a sigh of confirmation, he agreed totally as they settled into the warm comfort of falling asleep in Haverford.

Foggy vapor, starting in a mist rose from the little stream. Maggie viewed all this in the early morn, before the house awoke. It looked nearly like the brook on Skye that she had crossed a thousand times when she went to fetch the sheep from pasture for Bruce. All was quiet as she stood in her nightclothes looking out through the leaded glass casement, pushed open now to greet the new day. The scene below gave her an eerie, ethereal feeling as she half expected to see the green fairy dog, belly low, dragging through the haze. She surmised the train trip and the excitement of meeting John's sister had lulled her into cavernous dreams. She was having trouble staying in bed these days after five in the morning. Her body was in physical change, and she guessed her routine would never be as before. Yet, she was completely content, for she dearly loved this early time of day with the world dawning to birds and animals quietly waking. She could feel nature's spirit surround her body in a fresh delicate softness that she felt at no other time. She recalled the coolness that she loved. The thin air of the highlands had conditioned her to this sharpness of emotion. Crisp air seemed as much a part of her as much as the hand that opened this glass, letting in the misty, moist daybreak.

Episode:

Anita lost no time in showing her guests her adopted city. While Kenneth spent his days as a maritime lawyer in the downtown section of Philadelphia, she took a week of days to let them view the appealing town with its Lemon Hill Tower, Fairmount Reservoir, horse drawn trolley cars, and the enormous bastions of learning. There was a special respect for science and medicine in this city. It was called Quakertown, a city of clubs and fine residences, serene in contentment, conformity and conversation. Five miles of continuous wharves on the Delaware River and the four miles along the Schuylkill, where vast imports arrived daily were exciting to John. Here, West Indian molasses, tropical fruit, wool from England, glassware from Germany and coffee from Rotterdam, all combined to captivate one's imagination. Once he learned his way about the metropolis, John parted from the girls early each day to wander for hours among these shops and ships, a never-ending diversion for a man of the sea.

The women visited the Academy of Fine Arts, the new row houses in north Philadelphia, saw the Italian street markets with their welcoming aromas, the Jewish merchants in the south of the city, and visited friends of Anita's in Germantown and on Chestnut Hill.

John reported, on that evening that the shops along Front Street on the Delaware had little of the salty atmosphere of New Bedford, but more of what he thought a European marketplace might be, and he found it all truly fascinating.

That week was a great learning experience for Maggie. She had not dreamed of the advances taking place in the world, and it gave her fresh hope, confirming her resolve once more; there certainly must be a place in it for her strong, intelligent husband.

When just over one week had passed, the pair, nearly worn out from the fatiguing sight-seeing, really looked forward to spending a quiet Sunday at home with the Endicotts.

Once more, Maggie was up very early seeking a cup of tea as she ventured into the large kitchen. Ellen O'Leary stood there putting her white starched apron over her head to begin Sunday breakfast and then lighting the fire in the massive cook stove. Maggie had met the talented cook earlier that week, but this was her first chance to converse with her. The darling, small woman reminded her so much of Agnes Wallace back in Halifax with her roundness of figure and apple cheeks, that she at once took a fancy to her.

Ellen would have none of permitting Maggie to fix her own tea, but scurried about taking down teapot, putting on the teakettle, setting out a china cup and saucer, and all in the twinkling of an eye while humming snatches of an Irish folk song, as she bustled about. Ellen was very jolly at six in the morning and Maggie had always found this an admirable trait. As she sat there watching her, sipping the hot sweet tea, she was once again in the Grant Tearoom with her convivial friend, Molly, mixing up the butteries. When Maggie offered to help with the filling of the saltcellars that she saw set out, Ellen refused. It seemed to her, that her condition as mother expectant had not a little to do with such kind consideration.

Ellen O'Leary was as Irish as the songs she sang, and it did not take long for Maggie to encourage the blarney flowing from her lips.

She loved her employer, that was certainly plain enough. Every biscuit she made, every cobbler turned out, had the stamp of love baked into it. Here, she found a position and a home with the Endicotts, and she was not about to lose them. Her own large family had been nearly wiped out by the potato famine in Ireland in 1848, when she was just seventeen. She had left her home that year for America with only an aged aunt, an aunt who felt she could do nothing less for the girl, than to bring her here to America. But as soon as they arrived, she promptly died, leaving Ellen knowing no one, and without any skill for employment. She told Maggie of how she had worked in the coffee houses of Philadelphia where she earned barely enough to pay for lodging and food, but ever so slowly, she watched the cooks that she worked under and studied food preparation in her room at night from any books she could obtain. Finally she had worked her way to cook in a fine restaurant in the city's heart and it was here that Anita discovered her. That had been seventeen years before, and she now felt very much a part of this home and family.

No, she answered to Maggie's question, she had never indulged herself in the thought of marriage. She had just never taken the time. Sitting now at the heavy worktable, richly laden with the breakfast ingredients, she smilingly offered: "There are those who are meant to be ladies and gentlemen, who marry and the like, and those who are meant to serve them. This I learned in Ireland." She rose, turned, and had her back to Maggie, tending to the fire in her cook stove. Maggie could not see her sweet, honest broad face, but she knew that Ellen meant just that.

It was in the second week of their visit, when John began to be restless and decided he had enough of viewing the city. He set out to find some 'good, hard, honest work to put his muscle to,' as he explained to Kenneth, who cordially offered an introduction to his law partners and perhaps find something in their firm for him. But burly, independent John politely drew the line at that and thanked him, saying an office was not his 'cup of tea.' No, he had seen a placard in the window of the harbor master's office on Front Street, during his solitary exploring, asking for help, and he guessed that he would find out what it was all about.

John came home that evening to tell Maggie of some really fine people that he had met. Mr. Wiggins had, without hesitation, offered him employment as an assistant on one of the tugs, which guided the ocean liners into berths in the harbor. The pay would be minimal, but it was a start, and he was to begin the next day, which seemed to please him greatly. She knew he was destined for better things, yet this *was* a beginning, for he was to be on the water and what he knew best for the present.

It was Maggie too, who despite her condition, longed for some useful pursuit of effort after this single week of leisure. Anita understood completely, for she was engaged in many philanthropic endeavors herself; she was presently coordinator of women in their fight for their own art classes at The Academy of Fine Arts.

Studying there privately, she had become rather a fine artist, herself, using her great love of flowers to create wonderfully realistic still-life, so fine that Kenneth proudly hung many of these in their home. When Maggie and she visited the Academy, she was slow to mention her painting of a bowl of anemones, prominently displayed in the foyer, one which Maggie had admired. It was only after the director pointed the fact out to Maggie, that, blushing, Anita in high spirits, proudly admitted it was her own.

Anita's other interests included the University Hospital, where she chaired all sorts of fundraisers for the indigent persons of the city. Her own childhood days in New Bedford, growing up without a father and being poor, were not soon forgotten. She had become one of their most generous benefactors. Kenneth sometimes joked, that half of all he earned was given to heal the sick and feed the poor, but Maggie could tell by his good nature that he dearly loved his wife for all of her generous works.

While trying to find the right activity for Maggie to occupy a portion of her days, Anita came upon a request to view the new Lutheran Orphanage on Beacon Street, and invited her to come along. They both agreed that the architect had done a marvelous job. Aesthetically, it seemed more like a spacious mansion than an institution. Maggie was impressed by the loving care taken to create this homelike atmosphere.

The orphanage had opened to forty-three children, between the ages of six months and twelve years and was funded in part by the Lutheran Church, with the remainder of the money from contributions and city funds. It boasted high ceilings, an airy kitchen, neat dormitory style bedrooms each for eight children, and three separate nurseries to each accommodate four babies under two years of age. There were two lovely front parlors, where the children could study or play, and it gave a homey feeling throughout. The children, who were over six years of age, where allowed to attend the public school, and this fact, being a new concept for orphans, impressed Maggie greatly.

The children here were all neat and well cared for. They seemed adequately nourished, and in all aspects it seemed that the directors were proud of their accomplishments.

Yet, how very sad it was, thought Maggie, to be without any mother or father to care for you. What turmoil a child must go through with such a burden. She felt a huge empathy for each of them, especially the smaller ones, who had no understanding of the why of it all. If she could do anything to fill the awful, empty place that each of these lonely children must experience, she determined that she would do so. The home was now looking for teachers or at least interested women to help with the children.

That evening, as Maggie told John of her day, she absolutely glowed. He listened intently, as she said that she had found a splendid direction for her time in these months before the birth of her own child. It would be so fulfilling to give her knowledge and understanding to these little ones. It was her plan to volunteer at the orphanage for three days of the week to teach the children less than six years of age. These little ones had time heavy on their hands without adult direction. It certainly would not be difficult or heavy work, and she assured her husband that there was nothing that she would enjoy more. Anita had already agreed to transport her to the home on her way to her own meetings, and to pick her up in the carriage at day's end.

In all of her persuasive dialogue, John had just sat back thinking of how exquisite she looked when she was energized by a concern so close to her heart. He could do no less than give his wholehearted approval.

"Oh, but the children are so beautiful, John. I will wake each morning so thrilled to be among them."

Maggie had believed for many years that the education of children should begin *long* before they entered public school at age six. She knew instinctively that the development of the whole person must begin very early, and finally, she had the opportunity to try out her long-studied concepts.

The director of the home, a Mrs. Henrietta Miller, was a kind-hearted, though solid disciplinarian, who ruled the house with firm love. She was of German extraction and believed rigorously in a strict body of rules; however, when approached with the idea of Maggie teaching the two to six year-old children, she seemed delighted. She gave free rein with her ideas of open classes for them. The children were as eager as their young teacher. The class consisted of eight little ones, ages, three, four and five. They clustered about Maggie from the time she entered the parlor now selected for lessons, all anxious to see what the armful of packages contained that Maggie brought with her each day. The trustees were cooperative in furnishing two long, low tables and chairs so that the little ones could sit or stand to accomplish the various lessons Maggie devised. She had prepared all types of fabrics in different textures and patterns, had cut out shapes of both numerals and the alphabet, devised puzzles in the familiar shapes of animals, fruits and vegetables. She brought clay for them to form, and yarn balls of bright colors to instruct every aspect of what she felt they could absorb.

She was delighted each day with the attention these children embraced in carefully following all the orderly tasks she set before them. They had such desire to do well, that it confirmed her belief that she was making a difference in their lives. Maggie took notes about the reactions of each child to the special materials and to each other as well as to her. It seemed their appetite for learning was insatiable.

It was after Maggie had been working with the little people for two weeks, when Mrs. Miller asked if she might allow the trustees to look in on them one afternoon. She seemed pleased with the orphans' exemplary behavior and the precision with which they accomplished their lessons. She was confident in the manner of pure joy she saw in the little ones as they were allowed to attend these lessons, and she told the adults that she wished she could persuade Maggie to come to them daily in place of only three days, as the children benefited so, yet she knew this might be asking unreasonably of her time.

Maggie was truly pleased. Every day, after being with the children, she would talk of little else with Anita, Kenneth, and John. She even 'bent' Ellen O'Leary's ear, over a late afternoon cup of tea. On the days that she was at home, she worked industriously on the materials for the children or would spend hours with her journals about her diverse observations.

October was upon them all with momentum, as the occupants of the Endicott home were each busily engaged in their particular activity. The move here had been wise then, both John and Maggie, agreed. He said that he missed the whaling very little, although he did know that he had some reservations on leaving New Bedford, he was now enjoying the stimulation of new sights, and he was continually amazed at the varied, good people he met on the Delaware River. Of course, there was no question on how Maggie had taken to this new life, for she could not have been more content.

John did offer on this evening that there was only one disturbing matter which concerned him. The two sat in their sitting room, high above in his sister's home, and Maggie was quick to have him tell her about it. He said that in the last two days, there appeared new faces about the docks, stirring up the workers there, telling them the pay they received was unfair by being too little and their hours too long.

These persons were trying to create unrest and discontent among all the men, and he had witnessed a fistfight over the matter, only that day. He was concerned for Mr. Wiggins and the foreman, for they seemed to him, fair and honest people, who cared for the workmen. He hoped that this would not escalate into a wharf war, such as he had seen when he was a boy. If it did, he was hard put to choose sides, for he liked both his fellow workers and the men who had given him employment.

Was life never free from worry? Young Maggie thought of this, beneath the warm covers of that same long night. She reflected over the raising of her own unborn in these troublesome times as she lay awake in the darkness beside her good husband. In her heart, she knew that it fell on the two of them to teach their own children the basic precepts early in life so that they would grow to be fine people. There was, certainly, much responsibility in raising another human being!

These were the four principles that she aimed to instill. She counted them over and over, on these sleepless nights and she would soon ask John if he felt the same as she did about them.

If she could encourage only four qualities in her children, she felt, they in turn, could avoid the petty jealousy and gossip that she found men and women fall into, and she might avoid unhappiness in their lives. One was the respect for all life; the second was to take wonder in all natural beauty in the world about them; the third was to be fiercely honest in all things; and the fourth was to honor and obey their parents. If she could inspire these in her child, or her children, should she be so blessed, then her existence would be exceptional and fulfilling.

Until this time, she had never truly appreciated her own mother, Jane, or Mum Laura for all of the lovely values they had given to her. This realization was now consummate as she thought of the raising of her own children.

Regardless of John's concern, she looked forward to her planning and belief in the future. She was joyful with each new day's incredible happiness. Maggie felt a beautiful acceptance in her person these days, John caring for her as he did, Anita and Kenneth, a real family to share their joy, and a child soon to be born. What more could any person ask of life?

John had alerted his sister to the date of Maggie's birthday as it was fast approaching. This time, he was in a position to buy his bride a truly proper gift. Each evening, after work, he took time to search the shops trying to find exactly the right present for her, but with no success. It had to be an object, precisely exceptional to match her beauty and tell of his love for her. Finally, on the very eve of the date, he came upon a very small shop, nearly hidden away on a short side-street not far from the docks. The sole proprietor was a tiny wizened man, almost elf-like in appearance. He sat perched on a high stool, preoccupied in his work as John entered, so that he failed to even look up. A single piece of silver jewelry, displayed on a velvet blue cushion, was what had suddenly caught John's eye as he had all but passed by the miniature display glass. Overjoyed to notice it, he gazed at the intricate piece of silver, so cunningly, skillfully crafted into the most beautiful Scottish thistle brooch that he had ever seen.

The small man seemed delighted that his work had been admired as he inquired for whom it was meant. John proudly told him that it was to be a gift for his wife's twentieth birthday and the gnome-like figure set to work busily engraving her initials, *M.M.D.* on the flat back surface of the stunning flower of Scotland. And then, as an afterthought, something induced John to ask him if he could possibly add the tiny script, *'The Little Summer of St. Luke'* to the piece. The man did so with exquisite precision, and then set it into a purple box, lined with the same color of blue velvet as the pillow it had rested upon in the window. He accepted the quoted sum of twenty dollars gratefully as John gladly gave it, although it easily represented his full pay for two weeks' work at dockside. Thanking him, John took off into the evening dusk, box in hand in his absolute delight.

Episode:

Ellen O'Leary was in her glory. She loved nothing more than a party. Anita trusted her judgment as to the menu as she planned this small dinner party for Maggie's birthday celebration. She invited only two other couples besides the four of them: Kenneth's law partner, Walter and his wife, Helen, and the noted fine artist, Chapman, who had just returned from France with his wife, Hermione. These were companionable, animated persons whom Anita felt Maggie might enjoy.

As John fixed his gaze on his wife, sitting on the brocade bench at the triple mirrored dressing table in their bedroom brushing out her curls before placing them in a loose lavender ribbon at the base of her neck, he marveled at the wonderful events that had happened since his meeting with this girl/woman, now so much a part of his world, for he could imagine of no world without her.

"I'm nearly ready, John, are we late?" Maggie turned to him wondering this, as she sensed his unusual impatience.

John explained that his eagerness was not to descend to the parlors below, for they had ample time, but his excitement was the desire to present his gift to her before the party began. He rose from the overstuffed chair on which he sat, thoroughly enjoying the ritual of her making ready. It always gave him pleasure when he could watch her so.

"I have a little something here I would like you to wear to the party tonight, my darling," and he pulled the charming small box from his pocket, and handed it to her. "I hope it is to your liking, my dear. Happy Birthday!"

Maggie was visibly touched, even before she attempted to open the gift, her color deepened and her eyes grew moist. How very thoughtful was this man she had married. Then with an audible gasp she lifted the cover to view the delicate, artistic pin. There was no doubt in his mind that he had chosen the keepsake that Maggie would forever treasure.

With a genuine flourish, he pinned it to the lavender frock as she kissed his cheek so close to her own. They made their way downstairs to the lovely party, but this could only be small added enjoyment to John's tender and loving presentation.

Two weeks following the purchase of the thistle brooch, a most curious occurrence came about, one that even in his later years, John could not let his mind dwell on for very long. Anita was so taken with the quality and uniqueness of the beautiful brooch of silver that she asked if John would take her to the same shop, so that she might buy a gift for a valued friend.

John was absolutely sure that he knew exactly where the shop stood; in fact, he drove the carriage directly to the spot, but although the shops about it were just as he remembered, a cordage shop on one side and a tinker on the other, the tiny store with the miniature glass window had vanished completely. The merchants, whom he questioned on both sides, and equally those across the street, swore it was never there at all. While John drove Anita down every street for miles all about this dock area, there was no indication of the small store.

Anita, thinking her brother had merely forgotten where he shopped in this bustling Philadelphia, dismissed the matter easily, but for many nights, John relived and pondered the facts, but only to a certain point, for he was confident, if he delved into the matter too deeply, he was certain to believe in the 'little people, the fairies and beasties' to the same degree as his darling wife.

Episode:

Days at the orphanage were delightful and untroubled for Maggie. Each of the eight children in her charge was a joy for her. That did not mean, however, she did not single out one child who captivated her heart completely.

Edith with the golden-locks was a beauty at just three years old. Her open sweetness and intelligence found their way into Maggie's core from the very first day. The sensitivity she had for one so young and her remarkable vocabulary, that no one could explain, set her apart. She was able to memorize long poems and recite them with ease to the wonder of her elders, and to such an extent that Maggie guessed her to be near genius. The manner in which she could comprehend the most difficult puzzles, some even more easily than the five year old children, astounded Maggie.

Although it was not in her job description to inquire into any of the children's backgrounds, Maggie asked a favor of Mrs. Miller, that is, if she would make an exception in Edith's case. This was because Maggie found her of special interest for study. The findings were remarkable, Edith's young mother had died in childbirth, and her grief stricken father had taken his own life soon after, not able to bear his own life without her. He was not wealthy, but had acquired enough funds for Edith to be cared for, yet with neither father nor mother, or any relatives to whom she might go, she became a ward of the state. Maggie noted in her journal, that curiously without either parent for influence, here was a child who excelled in all she tried, and she hoped that one day she might pursue the why of it all.

Episode

"Carrots and more carrots," voiced Ellen O'Leary, loudly, as she set another plate of these beside the horizontal expectant mother. Maggie was now confined to the long green velvet couch in the smaller of the two front parlors of the Endicott home. Dr. Sessions had prescribed complete bed rest for at least four days. This occurred when Anita had called him after Maggie experienced a fainting spell on their way home from the orphanage on Monday afternoon. Today was Wednesday and Ellen bustled about and into the room each hour with her offering of just the right ingredient that she felt most lacking in Maggie's diet.

"Mark my word, young lady, your body needs the orange vegetables. They are very important at this stage." And so saying, she proceeded to plump the three pillows beneath Maggie's head and back and stand there at attention until the plate of carrots was clean, not that Maggie minded. This concern and attention was comforting, even though she might never look at pumpkin, sweet potato, squash, and carrots, especially, in the months ahead.

She had felt in excellent health all during the pleasant day of her little classes, but just after stepping into the carriage for their ride home this day, her head began to swim and she could not stop her yawning, then suddenly she found herself being plucked from the leather seats and helped into this parlor where she was being pampered and indulged by all of the household. Kind Dr. Sessions did not want her to walk the winding stairway to their third floor nest until he was sure she was perfectly well, thus the entire house seemed to keep Maggie at their watchful center here in this parlor.

John was beside himself with worry. Even though Maggie had cautioned Anita to minimize the incident to her brother, there was no way of avoiding his obvious anxiety. He had hovered over her all that evening until Anita finally convinced him that *he* would be a case for the good doctor if he did not leave her to get some sleep, and that he should go off to bed. By Wednesday, he, seeing Maggie in great spirits and looking as vibrant and comely as ever, resigned her to the capable and firm hands of Miss O'Leary, as he went off to work.

The only concern that Maggie suffered were the children. She was positive there was no need to be disturbed with her condition and she said so to Anita all that day. She felt that the little ones would be confused and disappointed when she did not appear at the orphanage. It was a wakeup call in a way for Maggie, as she realized that she must soon find a replacement for herself before her baby arrived. She had hoped to spend at least one more month with the wee sweethearts.

Finally, after a good deal of Maggie's distress, Anita agreed to replace her, but only until she felt ready to return. Anita had so many misgivings: how would she know how to act around them, and what would she say? She was no teacher, she declared to Maggie who would hear none of it. They carefully went over all the materials that she had planned for the week, until Anita seemed to feel comfortable. Now, it was this inexperienced thirty-seven year-old who left the home in an energized, hopeful fashion on the late gorgeous October morn.

The woman who came to dinner that evening was one whom John, Kenneth nor Maggie, had never witnessed before. *All* Anita could talk of was the children. It was as though an entire piece of her personality had been buried, hidden, and now suddenly burst forth. Her warm, brown eyes danced as she moved her hands expressively, telling of her extreme pleasure with this day.

Maggie, who had been allowed to sit at the dining table for the hour of the meal, could only smile knowingly into her pumpkin soup. Here they were again she thought, the gnomes at work, causing the magic of fate to be played out once again. She knew now exactly why she was taken ill for these days; it was so plain to her; it all had happened so that Anita could experience those beautiful, happy children.

It was only then, in a logical sequence of events, that Anita's heart was completely taken by little Edith too, and consequently this happy occurrence prompted her to arrange for the little blonde darling, to be allowed to spend the Thanksgiving holiday weekend in the Endicott home. It was also agreed that Anita would take over Maggie's work with the children until a permanent teacher could be found. The trustees, upon seeing the great progress of the pre-school age youngsters and the attention that it had created at like institutions in other cities, now voted to hire a salaried teacher for their institute, beginning in the New Year.

Episode:

Thanksgiving Day had never been so festive. In all the years that Ellen O'Leary prepared the huge feasts for friends and family, never had the joy been this great, for now, all were keenly aware of the lively three- year-old under their roof.

Anita decorated the holiday table with the delight of a schoolgirl, singing as she did so. She divulged to Maggie, that she hoped Kenneth would fall in love with the precocious child as quickly and as hopelessly as she had.

"Are we too old to be contemplating adoption?" came Anita's straightforward query to Maggie, closing the door of their guest bedroom after reading the little beauty to sleep as the long and wonderful holiday of thanks came to a close.

"Of course, you are not too old. Why, look at you, you seem like a girl yourself with that blush on your cheeks and your beaming face." Maggie had closely watched the two adult, prospective parents all afternoon: Kenneth playing hide and seek with Edith all about the first floor, and Edith, gleefully nymph-like, hiding herself behind Ellen's ample apron skirt just as the dinner was served to the laughter of them all. And throughout the tasteful dinner, Anita could not help but gaze at Edith with a look of yearning that nearly tore at Maggie's heartstrings. She seemed so consumed by love for the child, and then the two of them, Kenneth and Anita, putting the youngster to bed after hearing her prayers. It seemed a match made in heaven, itself.

Maggie continued to say her words of advice with no one else in hearing distance. "Anita, as long as you have asked for it, I would lose no time in making arrangements to bring Edith to live here permanently and forever. When something is this right, do not think about it twice or you might lose it. I am a firm believer in fate, but then you may have noticed that!"

It was the first week of December, right after the first snowfall of the season, when John arrived home in mid-morning with his head bandaged. Maggie, now in her last weeks of pregnancy, was not prepared for such a sight.

"I tell you, it's but a scratch. Doctor Taylor, down at the docks, just felt that I needed this to hold my head on, that is all."

John was laughing, standing tall, over his now plump wife, who was often relegated to the green sofa by Ellen in her concern for Maggie's rest during these last days. And it was Ellen who had let John in by her back kitchen door, and who sat Maggie down on the sofa first, lest the sight of her wounded husband shock her.

"It happened just as I got to the docks, this morning, Maggie. These outsiders, who I was telling you about some weeks ago, were there today in full force to bar the men from getting to the ships to unload. They told the men that they were there to stop the work entirely, until the men were given shorter hours and more pay. Then, when someone in the work crew tried to bypass them and get to the ships, some bricks were flying, and one just nicked me in the side of the head. Honestly, it is but a scratch. You, above anyone, should know what a thick head I have, now don't you, teacher?" And John winked and smiled broadly down at his shaken wife.

Yet, Maggie could see beneath John's bravado, there was a deep unease for his fellow workers. He was attempting to make light of the incident for her sake, but she knew him now, all too well.

"I hope you will stay away from this entire ruckus, for a time, John. I do have real need of you right now, you know."

And seeing the worry in his young wife's eyes, he sat down beside her and cradled her head in his arms.

During the long hours of that same night, Kenneth and his brother-in-law worked arduously, strategizing and drawing up documents which John could present to both the owners and the workers on the very next day on the Philadelphia docks. It was John's proposal and his initiative to move on this immediately, right when the crisis occurred, before it turned to tragedy. His years at sea had created his prompt reaction to danger. He knew the problem and the players; he had connection with a maritime lawyer, and he despised needless bloodshed; therefore, he felt it his responsibility to quell this dilemma, if he could.

Having worked with many types of men for so many years, he felt sure that he might pull off a settlement, keeping both management and worker satisfied. And so he embarked on his first real job of concession, a skill that in later years would be highly valued.

"You know that you have a very bright and generous man for your husband!"

It was Kenneth, sitting with Maggie in the parlor over a cup of tea, as early December shadows fell over the generally sunny, snow reflected room, who was celebrating John's special traits.

"Of course, I know." Maggie said, blushing, happily, "but tell me why you say it, anyway?"

Neither Anita nor John had arrived home from the orphanage or the docks and Kenneth was pleased to have this opportunity to speak with Maggie alone, mainly about John's recent masterful accomplishment on the waterfront.

"It is this conciliation he has accomplished, and so quickly. I have never seen a thing like it. Within only two days, he curbed the workers' fears, sat with the owners, receiving reasonable concessions on the workers' behalf, and the entire business did not miss a beat. There was no real shutdown, no bloodshed, and both parties went away happy as larks. Maggie, I do believe John has a real calling among men in making them listen to reason. Perhaps it does stem from his long relation with men of the sea and his understanding of what motivates them, but, honestly, you have one very interesting person there. Thank God for him."

Maggie sat, pulling in all of the compliments for her husband and storing the rhetoric in her brain and memory. She did know what a clever, combative energy John embraced, but now others were seeing it too, and that knowledge was immensely rewarding.

"I do know John has many talents and powers and that only few have seen the beginnings of his intelligence, and I thank you, Kenneth, for giving me *your* assessment of his gifts. The fact of his saving men and owners from injury and the help he accomplished for their families makes me very pleased indeed. I realize now that I was selfish to ask him not to deal with this problem, and I believe that I have learned a good lesson from that. John is his own man, and will always do what he believes to be right, no matter how I might try to influence him. I *will* attempt to keep my advice to myself from here on."

Ellen O'Leary entered the parlor just as Maggie finished her speech. She brought a fresh tea tray with slices of banana-walnut bread, still warm from the oven, one of Maggie's favorites.

"Oh, dear Ellen, you'll have me so that I'll never get into those frocks that I brought with me from Massachusetts. The temptations here are that great! One thing is sure, this baby will be addicted to some of the finest cooking and baking this side of the Atlantic and that's a fact!"

So saying, she reached for a fragrant, fruity slice of the bread to Ellen's obvious elation.

No sooner than she set the tray down, when in came brother and sister from their day's work, and the entire room was filled with good nature, laughter and comradeship. Maggie would enter this day into her journal to later think back upon it with a special tenderness.

Episode:

It had been Maggie's wish to deliver her first child in this home of her good relatives, and all was in readiness for the birth; however, it was not to be. Late in the second week of December, on a visit to Dr. Sessions, he advised that she should immediately be admitted to the new University Hospital, where he was a teaching obstetrician. Here, he explained to Maggie and John, she would most likely have to remain until the delivery, due to her severe condition called uremia, a malady, which should, undoubtedly, be corrected after the birth. But for now, it had to be monitored and treated by the medical staff on a daily basis.

Of course, Maggie was disappointed, and these long days in the hospital were difficult, for she missed her familiar surroundings and conversations with family, but most of all, she missed John. The visiting hours were very strict; she could see him in the solarium only for one hour of each afternoon and evening. A full week went by, and she pleaded with her doctor to let her move back home to wait. He sat at her bedside, speaking to her gravely, just as John came into the room for his afternoon visit.

"You will have to do as I say, young lady," and the doctor patted her arm kindly, but his admonition was firm.

"You will not have to wait too much longer," and as he cast an erudite glance at John, he exited the room, confident that her husband would convince her to remain.

The birth of Robert McBain Dix was one that the staff of the hospital would long remember. This wee slip of a girl, named Maggie, so petite, despite the outstanding mass that preceded her, was to hold the record for hours in labor that would stand for some forty years in the hospital's history. Robert was finally born on December 19th after a total thirty-two hours of real labor. Neither Dr. Sessions, John, nor the nurses, who changed duty every twelve of those hours, could not fathom the strength and courage of this wee Scottish lass who never complained or cried in the days that it took for her son to be born. Maggie merely repeated over and again, that maxim that her mum had told her: 'Anything worth doing was worth doing well,' and she vowed she would stay true to that, no matter what she endured. However, that bravery paid off handsomely when Robert, whom she named after her lost father, was born a beautiful, healthy, ten-pound child with dark hair and an angelic face, appearing more like a baby one-month old, than newly born.

John felt unhinged after the first twenty-four hours, and a complete shell of himself near the birth. But he was first at Maggie's bedside as soon as they would allow it, and he came bearing all the beautiful flowers his arms could carry from the hospital greenhouse. When he kissed his darling, he told her that she had given him the most wonderful gift on earth, and he could not believe it possible but he loved her more dearly than before. His Maggie smiled when she heard his words and those that said her son was very well, and she finally fell into a peaceful sleep that lasted, not for hours, but for an entire day!

It was usual that mother and newborn be confined to the hospital for a period of a week to ten days. However, with the Christmas holiday approaching and Maggie and the baby doing so well, Dr. Sessions cautiously permitted her and little Robert to be taken home on Christmas Eve in the hands of the proud, swaggering father, who, for all of his size and strength was but putty in the hands of this blanketed, ten-pound bundle.

And what a merry time it was. Anita and Ellen outdid themselves with the dazzling tree, garlands of decoration placed everywhere, and every imagined foodstuff available at market. The polished table groaned with roasts and fowl, vegetables and fruits, nuts, and desserts of all description, from plum puddings with hard sauce, to cakes, cookies and baked breads. This had been the only outlet poor Ellen had for all of her stored energy awaiting Maggie's arrival home with the precious babe. It seemed she had used every fretful moment working in her kitchen while she waited for news.

With their adoption papers in the hands of Kenneth's partner, the couple was granted the right to bring Edith to their home for her first family Christmas. About the tall, beautiful tree stood stacks of brightly wrapped gifts and shiny new toys, enough to delight the heart of any three-year old as well as the adults attending her.

Thomas, the carriage driver and gardener, added his gift for the new baby, early, in the form of a wooden cradle that he had skillfully crafted of cherry wood, cut from the Endicott property. It was an attractive and sturdily built crib, taking a place of honor in the corner of the main parlor so that guests might admire the sleeping cherub who reigned supreme, relatively close to the bedecked tree.

As Christmas evening came to an end, John and a tired yet buoyant Maggie found themselves once more in their little world atop the sleeping house. In the wonder of the bountiful day and at this moment, complete with their little family, they gloried over and again at the miracle that had taken place as each tiptoed to the cradle, now placed in their room, to peek at their sleeping son.

John voiced it first: "Will there ever be such a night as this, my darling? It is as if all the blessings of heaven are smiling down upon us, and I have no way to express my thanks to match the splendor of it."

She took a long time to respond, so long, John thought she had fallen asleep after her grand, but strenuous day.

"Every dream I've ever had, has been fulfilled with the birth of our son, John, and I promise you, I shall try to be the best mother possible to Robert, yet he will take none of this love that I hold for you."

She reached for his large, rough hand and took it in her own. "Oh, dearest, we are so blessed, so blessed." And with that she curled into the crook of his huge arm and fell asleep, content.

Episode:

Maggie let no great amount of time elapse before she asked Anita and Kenneth to become Godparents for Robert. Although she attended services only sporadically, she firmly believed in the rite of Holy Baptism in the Episcopal Church, and she contacted the priest at nearby St. Barnabas, just one week into the New Year.

So then, it was accomplished. The four adults and the infant Robert McBain Dix made their way to the font on the second Sunday of January, after the last lesson at morning service and before the entire congregation; Robert received the everlasting consecration of God's heavenly washing for a life dedicated to His service.

Once the little family was able to travel Maggie knew it was exactly the time to begin the founding of a permanent home, for as kind as the Endicotts were, and they did plead with them to stay, she determined to strike out now for her little family's future. In all of the contemplative time she recently experienced while in the hospital, many realities were clear, especially as to where her family must go. She believed she had come up with the ideal solution. Who was it, more than any other on earth that she wished to show their beautiful young son to? Of course, it was so logical that they would travel to Mum Jane.

Letters had moved between herself and her mother on a regular schedule, so much so, that the postman in Philadelphia was surprised if he did not see the familiar handwriting and postmark from Nova Scotia at least once per week. Just about the same time as John and Maggie had moved to Pennsylvania, Jane wrote a letter of such volume that it had to be sent in a large manila envelope for it held immense news. It told Maggie what she had already guessed: Mr. Angus Williams, now a permanent border at the Wallace home, was at present 'courting' her mother, as Jane shyly put it. His dealing of the 'selling of the malt,' or otherwise known as Scotch sales all about Canada and in North America was doing very well indeed. Jane seemed most happy with the idea of a beau in this part of her life and wanted to break this news straightforwardly to her daughter, thus the long, indulgent letter. Maggie could not have been more pleased. Her delightful mother had been alone for far too many years and the idea of a new life about to begin for her was to be a pleasurable occurrence and she wrote to tell her so.

Then, in her next letter, about the time of Robert's birth, came the news of Jane's marriage to Angus in a quiet ceremony right in Agnes Wallace's front parlor. The newlyweds were leaving for Chicago on the day following the ceremony where Angus would be setting up his headquarters for the entire North American import operation. The sales were doing extremely well and as soon as the couple was settled, Jane hoped that John, Maggie and little Robert would join them there and perhaps stay permanently in Chicago, or if not, then at least arrive for a very long visit. Jane was accordingly excited to be a grandmother and she could not wait until she held her grandson in her arms.

Maggie read her mother's letters over and over. The prospect of being near Jane again and the challenge of a vibrant city in the new leading center of America set her pulses racing. She conveyed all this to John in her most persuasive manner.

"The thing I am most concerned about is that there is no ocean there, Maggie, it is land-locked!" John was appealing to her understanding. He knew that if he lived somewhere on the seacoast, he was confident of finding some sort of work. These months in Philadelphia had proven that for although he did not see himself raising a family on the wages of a tug man, he now had no fear of providing a good living in any place connected to the sea. Could she understand?

Maggie did not say a word, but commenced to take the large atlas which she knew Anita kept in the desk drawer of the parlor to place it on top of the desk. Opening the book to the new State of Illinois, the eighteenth admitted to the union, she pointed to the city of Chicago and the *enormous* expanse of Lake Michigan, adjoining that city.

"Does this seem to be a small body of water, John? I imagine there is all manner of gainful enterprise on this gigantic lake, as well as on these rivers which spring from it. I believe *you* could adapt to any of this without difficulty." And like a prim teacher, she tapped her pencil stridently on the firm map, to impress her point.

"Now it is not evermore of which I am speaking. After we visit with Mum and show off our darling, we could come back here to find our special place in the sun, or even go back to Massachusetts if that is what you wish. But let us take a look at the opportunities that might just await us there in the new city of Chicago. We must *never* close our minds to *any* fine possibilities. I do love you so very much, my dear John. I only want our little family to be secure and joyful forever."

Maggie had been charismatic and eloquent, as usual, and left John positively *longing* to venture to Chicago as soon as she had finished her speech . . . and so they did . . . and so they did!

- The End -

POSTSCRIPT.

The journals now numbered a complete four. Perhaps you might enjoy reading the pages that Maggie wrote into the beginning of the fifth journal as she, John and little Robert traveled by train from Philadelphia to Chicago.

March 20, 1889.

Here we are, the three of us, on a train taking us into the unknown, nonetheless I have such positive feelings of this new adventure!

Once more, I am traveling to a place that I have never seen as I open this new journal to create a recollection of all that is happening and will happen in our new city of Chicago.

Before I begin today, I reread portions of my previous four journals. It seems that much has been accomplished in only three years. I am, beyond doubt, exceedingly glad that I have written these diaries for the pure pleasure they give.

This journey seems a tranquil respite, for here on the train I sit by the window, again looking at the scenery passing by, and thinking over my short, yet packed life until this moment.

John is holding our sleeping son and we are just underway, our bags packed into the space above us along with our two trunks safe in the baggage car. The weather out of doors is cool, yet the stove at the rear of this coach is fired and keeping us suitably warm. I chose to be near the middle of the coach, so as not to be too far, nor too near the heater, because of our sweet, little baby, Robert.

It was difficult to leave Anita, Kenneth and Edith, but they said that they would plan to come for a visit should we decide to make Chicago our permanent home. How very wonderful that will be.

When I began this account of one young girl of sixteen about to be reunited with the mother that she had not seen in three years and not lived with for twelve, I admit, I was a novice, a quiet, unwise beginner unaware with any part of this world. Yet, when I recall those happy days on Skye with my foster family; Laura, Bruce and the girls, I have such wholesome memories of growing up amid those lovely crags and cloudy hills where I was secure in my mystical beliefs. It was a safe and grand beginning of my life. Then, on that other train trip to Glasgow and to live in Edinburgh for a time in my sixteenth year was joy profound. I had mother, friends, and an occupation that I treasured. Molly Grant there in Glasgow will forever be a part of a grateful Maggie, as will my darling dead Mark, Doctor Bell, Edward Ferguson, little wordless Peter, Mr. Deal, and all of the grand persons and memories left behind there.

After I won the Dalhousie Prize and we, Mum Jane and I, were off to Nova Scotia, how adult I felt to be finally traveling to the new world across the ocean, and on to a university, my childhood dream. The year there, living in Agnes Wallace's boarding home was a revelation itself. The studies that I had merely imaged in my head took on such reality that there I truly 'fell in love' with learning.

And after that, on my eighteenth birthday, on those flat rocks, overlooking the ocean, I encountered the love of my life in an extraordinary piece of destiny, for faithfully The Little Summer of St. Luke once more worked its miracle in my life. Even now, I have difficulty believing the marvel of it, for it is the most exhilarating, amazing occurrence in all of my days and there will probably never be anything to match its wonder. For there was John, my dearest, John, here sitting beside me, this, compassionate, strong man that I've learned to love more dearly with each day and who is truly my rock and my life.

Then I must not forget lovely Marion who gladly listened to my dreams and my hope of seeing my sailor-captain once more after he sailed so far away in the sea.

Our beautiful marriage in Halifax with such wonderful people in attendance will always be as sacred to me as will our days on board The Gratitude in the freezing ocean; that experience has taught me so much. Though, I will never believe in the hunt for those fantastic creatures of the sea, it was an education itself and another experience that I would trade with no one. The closeness that it brought to our marriage, in that John and I were together every hour of the day and night is a wealth I will always carry. And the friends met there, dear Caleb, Owen, and all the wonderful men and boys of that ship taught me so many strong, personal traits, those I must keep all through this existence.

Philadelphia and my contentment there with the small children will ever have a piece of my heart. As will Anita, Kenneth and little Edith, but mostly giving birth of our son. Who can describe such ecstasy? It is impossible!

And here we are on our way to show off our child to his grandmother.

We are about to enter into an entire new life, a move to a city we know little of, but one that, if we are open to fresh possibilities and take heed of what the 'fates' have in store, we will find true happiness on our arrival, and in the years ahead, of that I am certain!

I do and always will look forward to each new day!

For now,
Maggie

My novel, ***The Dreamin' Tree*** is a sequel to this novel,
The Little Summer of St. Luke.

Please read it to enjoy the remainder of the story of Maggie, John and their growing family.

Doris Dix Caruso, Author

59164119R00140

Made in the USA
Charleston, SC
29 July 2016